Considering the Consequences

The Development Implications of Initiatives on Taxation, Anti-money Laundering and Combating the Financing of Terrorism

Considering the Consequences

The Development Implications of Initiatives on Taxation, Anti-money Laundering and Combating the Financing of Terrorism

JC Sharman and Percy S Mistry

Commonwealth Secretariat

Commonwealth Secretariat
Marlborough House
Pall Mall
London SW1Y 5HX
United Kingdom

Published by the Commonwealth Secretariat
Edited by Jane Lanigan
Designed by SJI Services
Cover design by Tattersall, Hammarling and Silk
Index by Indexing Specialists (UK) Ltd
Printed by Hobbs the Printer, Totton, Hampshire

Views and opinions expressed in this publication are the responsibility of the authors and should in no way be attributed to the institutions to which they are affiliated or to the Commonwealth Secretariat.

Wherever possible, the Commonwealth Secretariat uses paper sourced from sustainable forests or from sources that minimise a destructive impact on the environment.

Cover photo credit: GMB Akash/Panos Pictures

Copies of this publication may be obtained from

The Publications Section
Commonwealth Secretariat
Marlborough House
Pall Mall
London SW1Y 5HX
United Kingdom
Tel: +44 (0)20 7747 6534
Fax: +44 (0)20 7839 9081
E-mail: publications@commonwealth.int
Web: www.thecommonwealth.org/publications

A catalogue record for this publication is available from the British Library.

ISBN: 978-0-85092-874-7

Contents

Foreword

The study undertaken by JC Sharman and Percy S Mistry, with funding from the Commonwealth Secretariat and the FIRST (Financial Sector Reform and Strengthening) Initiative, seeks to provide the first assessment of the costs incurred from implementing the international standards on anti-money laundering and countering financing of terrorism (AML/CFT). The study provides a clear insight on the policies and procedures utilised in the compliance process and contrasts the associated costs with benefits.

Before reflecting on the implications of the findings, it is important to reiterate that the Commonwealth Secretariat and its member states remain committed to the global fight against money laundering and the financing of terrorism. This has been clearly demonstrated in communiqués issued by Commonwealth Heads of Government, as well as finance and law ministers. It is also reflected in the measures that members have put in place for the adoption of the standards and the support provided by the Secretariat to meet this goal. The Commonwealth Secretariat continues to allocate dedicated funding to train officials on both the standards and assessment methodology; and it has provided technical experts to assist with implementation strategies. Despite the support provided by this and other international organisations, it is clear that a significant shift in human and financial resources is needed to achieve effective compliance with the standards.

The Financial Action Task Force (FATF) rating and compliance process has serious bearings on the reputation of a country and affects the manner in which financial flows are transmitted. It is, therefore, salient that the approach adopted takes account of the specific social and economic constraints faced by different countries. While it is true that one cannot place a value on the gains to be derived from this international co-operation, it is also true that these gains can only be achieved at a cost that must be borne by individual states, and often to the detriment of other national priorities. This reiterates the need to assess the true costs of implementation, and to use this as a guide for other proposed strategies. Failure to do so will cause small developing countries to feel burdened and pressurised by the process.

The study has raised the question as to whether the benefits derived from the implementation of standards such as AML/CFT are accruing to countries in proportion to the costs being incurred. The findings indicate that there is need for further international assistance to help small developing countries put in place the necessary infrastructure for compliance. The findings also imply that the implementation of the AML/CFT standards needs to be customised at the national level, to ensure a more equitable sharing of the burden without producing further risks. The question has also been raised about advancing a more cost-effective subset of essential criteria without compromising the safety and soundness of the international financial system.

Indrajit Coomaraswamy
Director, Economic Affairs Division

List of Abbreviations

ADB	Asian Development Bank
AML	Anti-money laundering
AMLA	Anti-Money Laundering Authority (Barbados)
APG	Asian-Pacific Group on Money Laundering
BoM	Bank of Mauritius
BCBS	Basel Committee on Banking Supervision
BIBA	Barbados International Business Association
BIDC	Barbados Investment and Development Corporation
BIS	Bank for International Settlements
BSS	Barbados Statistical Service
CARIB	Caribbean Association of Regulators of International Business
CARICOM	Caribbean Community
CFATF	Caribbean Financial Action Task Force
CFT	Countering financing of terrorism
CSP	Corporate service provider (known as management company in Mauritius)
DTAT	Double tax avoidance treaty
ESAAMLG	Eastern and Southern African Anti-Money Laundering Group
ECAMLA	Economic Crime and Anti-Money Laundering Act (Mauritius)
ECO	Economic Crimes Office (Mauritius)
EIC	Exempt insurance company
EIHC	Exempt insurance holding company
EIMC	Exempt insurance management company
EU	European Union
EPZ	Export processing zone
FATF	Financial Action Task Force
FIRST	Financial Sector Reform & Strengthening
FIAMLA	Financial Intelligence and Anti-Money Laundering Act (Mauritius)

FIU	Financial Intelligence Unit (Barbados, Mauritius, Vanuatu)
FSC	Foreign sales corporation (Barbados)
FSC	Financial Services Commission (Mauritius)
FSF	Financial Stability Forum (G7)
FSSA	Financial System Stability Assessment
FSAP	Financial Sector Assessment Program
FTRA	Financial Transactions Reporting Act (Vanuatu)
GBC	Global business company (in Barbados: international business company, in Vanuatu: international company)
GDDS	General Data Dissemination System (of the IMF)
GDP	Gross Domestic Product
GNI	Gross National Income
HTC	Harmful Tax Competition
HNWI	High net-worth individual
ICAC	Independent Commission Against Corruption (Mauritius)
ICT	Information and communications technology
IAIS	International Association of Insurance Supervisors
IBC	International business company (in Vanuatu: international company, in Mauritius: global business company)
IFC	International financial centre
IFS	International financial services
IFI	International financial institution (World Bank, International Monetary Fund)
IFSA	International Financial Services Act 2002-5 (Barbados)
IMF	International Monetary Fund
IOSCO	International Organisation of Securities Commissions
ITIE	International tax information exchange
IT	Information technology
ITIO	International Trade and Investment Organisation
KYC/DD	Know-your-customer/due diligence
MC	Management company (corporate service provider in Barbados)

MBA	Mauritius Bankers Association
MOBAA	Mauritius Offshore Business Activities Authority
MOU	Memorandum of Understanding
MoF	Ministry of Finance (Mauritius)
NBFI	Non-bank financial institution
NCCT	Non-Cooperative Countries and Territories
OFC	Offshore financial centre (Mauritius)
OGBS	Offshore Group of Banking Supervisors
OSB	Offshore/international banks
OECD	Organisation for Economic Co-operation and Development
RIA	Regulatory impact assessment
RBV	Reserve Bank of Vanuatu
SEC	Securities and Exchange Commission (Mauritius)
SCC	Segregated cell company
SLO	State Law Office (Mauritius, Vanuatu)
SPV	Special purpose vehicle
SRL	Society with restricted liability
SEM	Stock Exchange of Mauritius
STR	Suspicious transaction report
TA	Technical assistance
TIEA	Tax Information Exchange Agreement
UK	United Kingdom
UNODC	United Nations Office for Drugs and Crime
US	United States of America
VAT	Value Added Tax
VFCA	Vanuatu Financial Centre Association
VFSC	Vanuatu Financial Services Commission
VIPA	Vanuatu Investment Promotion Authority
VMA	Vanuatu Maritime Authority
WTO	World Trade Organization

Summary

The project – *Considering the Consequences: the Developmental Implications of Initiatives on Taxation, Anti-money Laundering and Combating the Financing of Terrorism* – was commissioned by the Commonwealth Secretariat and financed by the Financial Sector Reform and Strengthening (FIRST) Initiative. Its objective was to assess the impact of recent multilateral regulatory initiatives on small Commonwealth international financial centres (IFCs). This final report draws together, distils and synthesises the results of three country studies, assessing the costs and benefits of these initiatives for Barbados, Mauritius and Vanuatu. The country studies are themselves based on survey data (quantitative and qualitative) compiled by local consultants in each jurisdiction in conjunction with the two lead consultants.

Although this report cannot be taken as definitive, given the need for further investigation of this issue, the authors find that recent multilateral regulatory initiatives have had a significant net negative impact on the three IFCs under consideration. That is, the costs involved in meeting the new standards have exceeded the identifiable benefits that have resulted for both the public and private sectors. More of the scarce public revenues of these three small developing island states has had to be diverted towards regulating their international financial services (IFS) sectors. The majority of private firms and banks operating in the IFS sector in all three countries have experienced a significant increase in compliance costs, in some cases sufficient to threaten their future business viability.

A few specific examples illustrate these developments. In Barbados, over 27 per cent of corporate services providers (CSPs) state that compliance costs have increased so much that they are now thinking of exiting the market. Vanuatu now spends four times as much public money regulating the IFS sector in 2005 than it did in 2000, while the IFS sector now provides only half the government revenue it did in 2000. In Mauritius, CSPs (known locally as management companies or MCs) have witnessed a sharp decline in their profitability: in the four years 2002-05, the aggregate net profits of MCs amounted to about US$17 million, while incremental costs for meeting new anti-money laundering/countering financing of terrorism (AML/CFT) compliance requirements came to over $27 million.

Rather than reflecting local circumstances and priorities, the single most important factor explaining the adoption of these new international standards in all three countries has been fear of the consequences of being blacklisted by international organisations in the event of non-compliance. The most common benefit identified in adopting the new standards is enhancing the reputation of the IFC. That, in each case, is the perception of regulators, external interlocutors and many members of the IFS industry. Whether that is the perception of their global clientele is another matter altogether and constitutes an aspect that could not be confirmed by the availability of any hard evidence to that effect. Yet in each case, the significance of this benefit has been undermined by the inability of the same respondents to identify any associated increase in competitiveness or other tangible benefits. Despite these serious challenges, all three countries remain determined to retain their IFCs, and to meet whatever international standards are imposed on them to remain in the global market for IFS.

Although a relatively clear picture emerges on the broad impact of recent IFS regulatory initiatives in the three countries under consideration, this report calls for further research to be conducted to assess the extent to which the experiences of Barbados, Mauritius and Vanuatu are typical of other small state IFCs – and from the Commonwealth Secretariat's viewpoint especially, those that are members of the Commonwealth.

The authors wish to extend their gratitude and appreciation to all those who gave up their time to complete the questionnaires and participate in the regional workshops.

1

Introduction

....

1.1 Rationale for the study

The project *Considering the Consequences: the Developmental Implications of Initiatives on Taxation, Anti-money Laundering and Combating the Financing of Terrorism* assesses the costs and benefits of implementing new international regulations for small Commonwealth states with significant international financial services (IFS) sectors. The goal is to improve policy and operational outcomes by: (a) systematically assessing the impact of recent financial regulatory standards and reforms; and (b) providing this information to local stakeholders and governments, as well as multilateral organisations involved in improving the stability and quality of the international financial regime.

The project is important because IFS sectors provide an important source of external revenue and economic development for a large number of small Commonwealth member states that lack obvious alternative development options. Many such states were actively encouraged by donors and international financial institutions (IFIs), as well as by global accounting and law firms headquartered in Organisation for Economic Co-operation (OECD) countries, to set up international financial centres (IFCs) as a means of increasing their export income from high-value service exports. In combination, recent multilateral regulatory initiatives have often been see by IFCs as posing a threat to the viability of their IFS industries in particular, and to their economies in general.

Yet, until this project, no attempt had been made to study the overall impact of changes that have occurred in regulatory standards and practices, nor of their specific effects in IFCs. The project seeks to correct this lacuna by undertaking the equivalent of what is referred to in OECD member states as a regulatory impact assessment (RIA) in three small Commonwealth IFCs.

To address at the outset a key concern expressed by the agency that funded the study (FIRST) and its sponsors, it bears emphasising that the project is not aimed (implicitly or explicitly) at criticising or undermining new international regulatory standards. The project takes the new standards that have been put in place as a given. Its focus is, instead, to make an overdue *empirical* assessment of their costs and benefits. On the other side of the coin, to address a different, but even more strongly expressed, concern on the part of many small jurisdictions, the project was not intended or designed to convince small states to exit the market for IFS.

The project as a regulatory impact assessment

The cost-benefit assessment attempted under the project in the three countries concerned is similar to a regulatory impact assessment (RIA) of the kind undertaken in many OECD countries. An RIA is a systematic assessment of the costs and benefits resulting from government regulation. Such an exercise can either be conducted *ex ante* to determine the possible costs and benefits of a number of potential regulatory solutions to a given policy problem, or, as with this project, *ex post* to discover the costs and benefits of already existing regulation and communicate these to policy-makers for them to examine whether course-corrections might be in order. Such *ex post* policy monitoring can lead to revisions to existing policies to improve their effectiveness and efficiency, and to ensure that regulation achieves its intended aim rather than generating unintended and undesirable consequences.

Assessing the wider impact of regulation – i.e. beyond its direct cost to government – is a goal strongly endorsed by the OECD, World Bank and other multilateral bodies as constituting best international practice. In a majority of OECD member states, RIAs are routinely used, if not legally mandated, for all new regulatory proposals before policies are enacted. Moreover, periodic *ex post* reviews are conducted in almost all OECD countries to examine whether the regulation that has been put in place (in terms of laws, rules and so on as well as the practices and behaviour of regulators) is achieving the purposes for which it was intended, or whether it is resulting in unnecessary costs and unintended consequences. The uptake of the RIA has been slower in developing countries. However, there is a similar trend towards seeking a broader understanding of the impact of regulation both *ex ante* and *ex post*, including the indirect economic, social and environmental costs of compliance.

The information gathered in an RIA can be useful in promoting accountability and transparency in line with the overall priority of 'good governance'. It can achieve these goals by encouraging feedback from firms and individual citizens on the effects of regulation, and make clear the magnitude and distribution of costs and benefits produced.

Assessing the costs and benefits in the current project is particularly important given the prominent role outside multilateral institutions have had in designing the current financial standards and procedures in place in each of the three countries. Because such institutions do not have direct links with those affected by the regulatory standards they propagate, studies such as this are especially important in promoting transparency and accountability. These circumstances also put a premium on findings and local feedback reaching multilateral standard-setting bodies so as to facilitate policy improvements.

Relevant multilateral regulatory initiatives

The project was commissioned to examine the impact of new regulations affecting the IFS sector in small Commonwealth states with particular reference to the Organisation for Economic Co-operation and Development's (OECD) Harmful Tax Practices initiative in the area of international tax information exchange, and the activities of the Financial Action Task Force (FATF) relating to anti-money laundering/countering financing of terrorism (AML/CFT).

There is a large degree of overlap in the requirements of the OECD for international tax information exchange and the FATF's standards in relation to AML/CFT. At most basic, both require that public and private entities collect more information on the consumers of financial services than they did before and are more willing to share this information internationally.

Indeed this overlap goes deeper in that organisations such as the International Monetary Fund (IMF), Bank of International Settlements (BIS), Financial Stability Forum (FSF) and others have either designed, replicated or endorsed similar regulations. Thus, for example, the requirement for offshore banks to have 'mind and management' in-country was originally specified by the BIS, before being endorsed by the FATF and the OECD, with the monitoring of compliance with this requirement being jointly the responsibility of the IMF.

This report and each of the country studies gives much more attention to the FATF and AML/CFT regulations than to issues of international tax information exchange. In part this reflects the concrete measures undertaken with respect to AML/CFT compared with the commitments made, but not yet implemented, in relation to the exchange of tax information. However, it is important to stress that the specific FATF regulations that have had an important impact (such as 'know your customer/due diligence' (KYC/DD) requirements) are also key elements of the OECD initiative.

1.2 Design and methodology of the study

The project was originally intended to include seven countries. However, in order to fit a reduced budget, keep the report to a more manageable size and ensure early results, this intention was subsequently reduced to three countries. In selecting the three countries assessed, several factors were taken into account. To ensure that the project's results were valid and broadly comparable, it was decided to cover IFCs in three island regions: the Pacific and Indian Oceans and the Caribbean Basin. As the project was undertaken under the umbrella of the Commonwealth Secretariat, the countries had to be Commonwealth members. There was also a strong presumption that they should also be eligible for FIRST funding[1]. This condition restricted the project's focus to sovereign states. For that reason it excluded United Kingdom Overseas Territories or Crown Dependencies such as the Cayman Islands, Jersey, Bermuda etc. Within these constraints, it was decided to focus on larger, more established IFCs in each region.

In Africa and the Indian Ocean the field was narrowed to Mauritius and the Seychelles. Botswana was discussed as a possible substitute if political approval from either of the two Indian Ocean nations was not forthcoming, though this fallback proved unnecessary. Mauritius was selected because of its larger financial centre.

In the Pacific there are three Commonwealth IFCs: Samoa, Vanuatu and the Cook Islands. Once again, Vanuatu was selected because it is a more established IFC (being set up in the early 1970s), and because IFS are a larger component of the economy. Moreover, as the Cook Islands are in free association with New Zealand rather than a sovereign state, it was not eligible for FIRST funding.

The Caribbean region offered a wider range of independent Commonwealth IFCs, including Antigua and Barbuda, the Bahamas, Barbados, Belize, Dominica, Grenada, St Kitts and Nevis, St Lucia, and St Vincent and the Grenadines. With only a limited subset of this sample being eligible for FIRST funding, Belize and St Vincent and the Grenadines were initially selected. Although not on the FIRST list, Barbados was included in the study later with the permission of FIRST, as it was felt necessary to instead include a Caribbean country whose IFS sector was more significant in size and well-established than either of the other two states.

These decisions should not be taken as suggesting that a similar project including such IFCs as Samoa, the Seychelles or Eastern Caribbean states would not produce equally valuable results. On the contrary, the authors believe that both the countries concerned and multilateral standard-setting institutions would derive considerable benefit from a fuller picture generated by similar studies covering all the smaller Commonwealth and non-Commonwealth jurisdictions.

The three Commonwealth IFCs chosen – while large in comparison with many other Commonwealth IFCs – are not of the same size as the Channel or Cayman Islands or Bermuda. Yet the three 'mid-size' IFCs chosen do represent a broadly representative sample of the characteristics of most Commonwealth IFCs. For that reason, it can be asserted with a degree of confidence that the findings of the project (distilled in this report) would probably apply with equal force to other Commonwealth IFCs without any significant exceptions, though once again the report endorses the need for further research to confirm this hypothesis.

Questionnaire design

In assessing the impact of new financial and tax regulation, the project aimed to take into account as wide a range of costs and benefits as possible. This breadth was in keeping with the RIA rationale of measuring the total impact of regulation insofar as that was possible. Thus, early on the in the project, it was decided to include banks, corporate service providers (CSPs), insurance and asset management companies, accounting firms, securities firms, auditors, law firms, regulators, ministries of finance, central banks and financial intelligence units. There is therefore comprehensive coverage of the public and private financial sector players that are involved in providing IFS in Barbados and Vanuatu, although in Mauritius a local decision was taken to exclude all operators other than management companies (MCs) and banks providing offshore banking services.

Each of the relevant multilateral organisations has issued guidance as to how countries are to comply with general standards on tax information exchange and AML/CFT. For the FATF these are the 40+9 Recommendations[2], which have been bolstered with extensive guidance and interpretive notes compiled in co-operation with the IMF and the World Bank, and have been refined in an ongoing programme of peer assessment among the regional AML bodies. For the OECD, these are the similar guidelines drawn up by the Joint Ad Hoc Group on Accounts and the Global Forum on Taxation.

For the purposes of this study, **costs** were disaggregated into human resources, office space, training, IT systems comprising software and hardware, risk procedures, legislative design, internal audit, external audit and compliance procedures. Measuring and quantifying **benefits**, in particular, posed particular methodological challenges. These were separately identified in the questionnaire as including increases in competitiveness, volume of business, fees and levies, productivity as well as more specific AML/CFT-related variables.

It proved easier to measure the costs of new regulations associated with multilateral initiatives than to quantify benefits. The benefit to jurisdictions and firms was primarily that of preserving or enhancing reputation, and thus difficult (if not impossible) to quantify except perhaps in an indicative or illustrative sense. Nevertheless, it was important to get at least an approximate idea of benefits to ensure a balanced study and to come to an assessment of the net effect of the new regulations. Note that although the last section in the questionnaires covers benefits, it was possible for respondents to register 'negative benefits' quantitatively, e.g. a decline in business or profits in certain years as a result of regulatory initiatives.

Separate versions of the questionnaire were designed for the public and private sectors. In each case it proved necessary to strike a balance between sufficient detail to provide for a comprehensive RIA, but also sufficient 'user-friendliness' so as not to over-burden respondents and depress response rates. This latter concern was particularly pertinent in an atmosphere of 'initiative and survey fatigue' in all three jurisdictions, where demanding reporting and compliance requirements from the OECD (the Template for the Harmful Tax Practices initiative) and the IMF (the Offshore Audit) have already taken a great deal of participant time and energy. To add to these burdens, the Financial Intelligence Unit (FIU) in Mauritius decided to launch its own 'counter-survey' at the same time the study was being undertaken in that country. Fortunately, judging by the very encouraging response rate (higher than in Barbados or Vanuatu), this did not seem to affect the number of those willing to complete the survey. A qualitative version of the questionnaire for the private sector was also drawn up for those firms unable to answer the full quantitative version.

The response rate for the qualitative questionnaire was very high, on average at least 90 per cent, but the response rate to the quantitative survey was much lower, as the private sectors in Barbados and Vanuatu and the public sector in Barbados in particular were unable/unwilling to provide the detailed statistical material requested.

In designing the layout of the questionnaire, the first step was to look at the requirements of the two most important regulatory initiatives affecting the three states in question: the OECD Harmful Tax Practices initiative (formerly know as the Harmful

Tax Competition initiative) and the Financial Action Task Force's (FATF) efforts to improve AML/CFT standards.

In light of the confusion over reputational effects (see below), some members of the IFS industry pointed out that questions on reputation might more profitably have been directed at foreign consumers of the IFCs' services; however, budget and time constraints prevented modification of the questionnaire design and administration along these lines.

Regional workshops

Regional workshops were held in Vanuatu (10 March 2006), Mauritius (10–11 April 2006) and Barbados (21 April 2006) and comprised a vital part of the overall project. The aim in each case was to preview the results drawn from the earlier interviews and surveys, to refine the accuracy of the preliminary findings and to ensure the final conclusions of each country report faithfully reflected local opinions. The workshops also enabled lead and local consultants to clarify those points on which survey data had provided only vague or contradictory results.

The workshops were organised as half-day (Barbados), full-day (Vanuatu) or three half-day (Mauritius) events. Invitees were drawn from public sector regulators and the IFS sector. The authors would particularly like to express their gratitude to the Central Bank of Barbados and the Bank of Mauritius for generously agreeing to co-host these events in their respective countries. Their hospitality and the efficiency of their staff in organising these events were most impressive.

Although the organisation of each workshop differed in line with local circumstances, each featured a brief summary of the preliminary results, set-piece responses from prominent representatives from both the private sector and local regulatory bodies in the IFS sector, and more general discussion. In each case the feedback generated was invaluable in sharpening the conclusions of the country studies, and in informing this report.

1.3 Structure of this report

The remainder of this report is structured as follows. Chapters 2 to 5 comprise an introduction to and regulation of the international business and financial services sector in Barbados, overall findings from the case study questionnaires, interviews and workshop, and conclusions for that country.

The Mauritius case study is considered in chapters 6 to 9, which includes development of the IFS industry in that country, the importance of the industry and its regulation and supervision. Chapter 9 forms a substantive part of the overall report, presenting as it does the findings of the cost-benefit analysis that took place in Mauritius in some detail; the chapter also includes broad conclusions from the Mauritius case study.

The case study of Vanuatu is presented in chapters 10 to 12, which include an introduction to the IFS sector in the country, its regulation and supervision and a summary presentation of the findings from the questionnaires, interviews and workshop.

The final chapter, chapter 13, presents a synthesis of the three country case studies, including a summary analysis of the overall costs and benefits of enhancing the regulatory regime for international financial services to the public and private sectors in Barbados, Mauritius and Vanuatu, and general implications for the countries' international financial centres. The chapter goes on to formulate some broad conclusions, emphasising the importance of further research to assess the developmental impact of recent international tax and AML/CFT initiatives to the much larger number of IFCs worldwide.

Notes

1. See FIRST website: http://www.firstinitiative.org/ [accessed 15 February 2008].
2. See Financial Action Task Force website: http://www.**fatf**-gafi.org/ [accessed 15 February 2008].

2

The Barbados International Business and Financial Services Sector

2.1 Origins and development of the IFS sector in Barbados

The Barbados international financial services (IFS) sector, of which international business companies (IBCs) are the dominant area of activity, has grown steadily over the last decade. Even with the slowdown in the year 2000, resulting from the uncertainty surrounding the Organisation for Economic Co-operation and Development (OECD) initiative and other global economic developments, the level of activity in the sector has grown considerably since 1965 when the first International Business Company (IBC) Act was passed.

The IBC Act was designed to allow non-residents of Barbados to invest or trade internationally from Barbados. These non-resident entities were afforded a low rate of taxation, but prohibited under the Act from trading goods or services in Barbados or the Caribbean Community (CARICOM) Area. The primary beneficiaries of the Act were residents of the UK, who were allowed tax refunds from the UK Treasury under the provisions of the tax treaty (1970) between the two countries (see table 2.1).

In 1977, the IBC Act was modified in order to make its provisions more attractive to global investors and thereby expand the sector. As the needs of the sector changed, amendments were made in 1979, 1981 and 1985. In 1991, the Act was further amended to allow IBCs to conduct a broader range of activities. An IBC was redefined as: 'a company that is engaged in manufacturing, international trade and commerce from within Barbados'. Registered IBCs received a number of tax incentives and unlike companies registered under the Companies Act[1], IBCs pay tax on income on a sliding scale, with rates varying between 1 per cent on profits over US$15 million and 2.5 per cent on profits under US$5 million. IBCs are also exempt from exchange control regulations and from import duties, Value Added Tax (VAT) and stamp duty on the import of plant and machinery and business inputs.

The climate was further enriched by a number of tax and bilateral investment treaties that encouraged an investment and commercial presence by foreign companies. Subsequent legislation aimed at capitalising on new opportunities has expanded the product offering of the sector, which is now comprised of international business companies, international (offshore) banks, exempt insurance companies, exempt insurance management companies and societies with restricted liability. From its inception, Barbados' highly reputable and well-regulated IFS industry has benefited from a partnership between government and the private sector on legislative reforms and promotion.

The International Financial Services Act (IFSA) 2002–05, which replaced the Offshore Banking (1979) Act, establishes the regulatory framework for the operations of licensed offshore banks. Under the IFSA, licensing requirements are fairly rigorous and the degree of regulation and supervision is high, as was confirmed by the favourable reviews during the Financial System Stability Assessment (FSSA) completed by the International Monetary Fund (IMF) and the World Bank in February 2003. A wide range of activities is conducted within the offshore banking and wider financial services fields, including investment wealth management, investment banking, portfolio management, derivative and commodity trading and foreign currency lending, investment advisory fiduciary services, trustee services and estate and tax administration. The majority of offshore banks in Barbados are private banks, and the remainder either branches, subsidiaries or affiliates of international banks.

The insurance industry is a vibrant and growing part of the global economy and so the addition of insurance services to the offering of the IFS sector was a natural extension. In Barbados, international insurance business is defined as: 'the business of insuring risks located outside of Barbados, in respect of whether premiums originate outside of Barbados or CARICOM'. This includes the business of an underwriter, broker, agent, dealer or salesman, where beneficial ownership is outside CARICOM. These entities are established under the Exempt Insurance Act Cap308A, which was designed to allow Barbados to develop as a meaningful alternative to Bermuda for international insurance purposes, particularly captive insurance companies. Exempt insurance companies are regulated and supervised by the Supervisor of Insurance and Pensions within the Ministry of Finance.

In recognition of the possibility for further growth within the IFS sector, through the provision of other vehicles to minimise the tax burden of companies, the Society with Restricted Liability (1983) Act was passed establishing societies with restricted liability (SRLs) or hybrid entities that have the status of a corporation in Barbados, but are classified as a partnership in the US for tax reasons. An SRL can be set up either as an exempt or a non-exempt company, with limited liability status and are required to maintain a registered office and agent in Barbados. Exempt SRLs, which are used mainly for international transactions, benefit from a similar range of duty and tax concessions as IBCs and offshore/international banks (OSBs) and are prohibited from transacting business in Barbados or CARICOM. Non-exempt SRLs are not subject to these prohibitions and pay tax on profits at the domestic corporate rate.

During the past two decades, the Barbados economy has been challenged by the mounting pressures of an increasingly competitive global environment. Indeed, with the traditional sectors, agriculture, manufacturing and tourism, grappling with the harsh realities resulting from trade liberalisation, the need to maintain Barbados as a high-branded international financial services centre becomes even more critical in the efforts to further restructure and diversify the economy. Against this backdrop, the creation of a

Considering the Consequences

more effective and enabling environment for the expansion of international business, financial and other services is necessary to generate increased employment and to enhance the country's foreign exchange earning potential.

Unlike a number of 'offshore' jurisdictions, which depend upon zero tax rates to attract international business, Barbados offers low tax rates supported by a network of tax treaties and bilateral investment treaties that allow companies to benefit from aspects of the tax code in the source countries relating to foreign source income. The attractiveness of the treaties varies. For instance, the treaties with the Scandinavian countries (Finland, Norway and Sweden) contain extensive limitation on benefits articles and include provisions excluding international business sector entities from the treaty. On the other hand, treaties with Cuba and China have few limitations on benefits clauses, which make these treaties more attractive. The Cuba treaty (April 1999), in particular, positions Barbados to be a major conduit for investment funds to Cuba. A list of tax treaties and investment agreements is shown in table 2.1, below.

The Canadian treaty is the most widely used, with international business activity heavily skewed towards the Canadian market for this reason. The attractiveness of the Canada-Barbados taxation treaty is largely due to the fact that it allows Canadian parent firms of Barbados IBCs, SRLs and other corporate entities to earn and repatriate 'exempt surplus' (that is, profit which is not subject to Canadian corporation tax) from their Barbados-based operations, under the 'foreign affiliate' rules of the Canadian tax code. In recent years the treaty has come under close scrutiny by Canadian authorities and

Table 2.1 Tax treaties and investment agreements

Investment Agreement	Tax Treaty
Canada – May 1996	Botswana – February 2005
China – July 1998	Canada – January 1980
Cuba – February 1996	CARICOM – July 1995
Germany – December 1994	China – 2000
Italy – October 1995	Cuba – April 1999
Mauritius – September 2004	Finland – June 1989
Switzerland – March 1995	Malta – December 2001
United Kingdom – April 1993	Mauritius – September 2004
Venezuela – July 1994	Norway – November 1990
	Sweden – July 1991
	Switzerland – Extended to Barbados from UK, 1954
	United Kingdom – March 1970
	United States – December 1984
	Venezuela – November 1998

Source: http://www.barbadosbusiness.gov.bb/miib/legislation/treaties/bilateral.cfm

negotiation of a protocol to the tax treaty commenced in 1997. There are also substantial non-tax benefits for Canadian firms domiciled in Barbados[2].

Discussions with industry participants also revealed that generally US multinational firms only use Barbados in special circumstances, largely because the US authorities do not allow the tax-free repatriation of profits. Consequently, few of the US-parented firms operating in Barbados are believed to be tax-driven. One previous exception to this was in the case of foreign sales corporations (FSCs). At the end of 2000, almost 3,000 FSCs were domiciled in Barbados. However, a World Trade Organization (WTO) ruling against the use of these 'offshore' entities by US exporters, which followed complaints from the EU that such arrangements constituted an unfair export subsidy, and subsequent revisions to the US tax code, have ended the use of FSCs.

The opportunities created by the network of tax treaties and other legislative support, coupled with the Barbadian government's business facilitation efforts, have resulted in fairly decent growth of the IFS sector over the last two decades. Apart from its contribution to employment and foreign exchange earnings, the sector is also an important contributor to government revenue, even with the low rate of taxes paid. In 1985, around 500 active companies made payments of US$0.25 million for incorporation and US$0.50 million for licence fees. By end-2003, approximately 5,403 offshore companies were licensed with annual application and licensing fees totalling US$4.9 million and tax revenue of US$93.6 million[3].

Notwithstanding the gains achieved over the years, the IFS sector in Barbados faces a number of challenges. Apart from the highly competitive nature of this market in the Caribbean/Atlantic region, there have been a number of adjustments to doing business, which have arisen from concerns advanced by the international organizations, particularly with respect to terrorism financing and other illegal financial activities (anti-money laundering and countering the financing of terrorism [AMLA/CFT] initiatives). The OECD Harmful Taxation initiative, the implementation of the US Patriot Act and the globalisation process have also added to the complexity of the global environment for international business, prompting ongoing legislative and supervisory changes in the industry. The various tax treaties entered into by Barbados include provisions for the exchange of information relating to tax matters, and that international business income is generally fully declared to the domestic tax authorities. Consequently, meeting the OECD initiatives for information exchange and transparency requirements was not too onerous for Barbados. However, there have been increased costs related to these measures[4], including the increased paperwork needed for large financial transactions and the additional due diligence (DD) requirements for establishing companies and establishing client bona fides.

2.2 The importance of the IFS sector in Barbados

There is a paucity of available statistical information on the various aspects of activity in the IFS sector in Barbados. The agencies with regulatory and supervisory oversight collect basic data, such as new registrations, renewal of licences, partial employment information, national insurance contributions, fees and taxes paid to the government. However, the data is not compiled in a format that allows a proper analysis of the sector's contribution to the domestic economy to be readily undertaken[5].

The total number of registered companies, excluding foreign sales corporations, has exhibited a general upward trend since 1996, increasing at an average annual rate of approximately 4.7 per cent from 4,604 companies to 6,163 by the end of 2005 (see table 2.3). The number of new registrations was higher in the 1996 to 1998 period, moderating somewhat in the 1998 to 2000 period, but total new registrations fell sharply in 2001. This was largely because of the uncertainty created by the inclusion of Barbados by the OECD in its harmful tax competition list of tax havens in 2000, coupled with the fallout from the foreign sales corporations sub-sector (see table 2.2). On the positive side, this development brought into sharp focus the vulnerability of the industry and prompted the authorities to further enhance the regulatory and supervisory infrastructure in order to safeguard Barbados' high reputation and credibility as a clean jurisdiction. As a result, during the four years since 2005 new registrations were on the increase.

The international business company (IBC) as the dominant foreign business entity recorded the highest growth rate in new registrations, and at the end of 2003 accounted for roughly 80 per cent of active companies. Overall, the IFS sector continues to make an important contribution to foreign exchange earnings and government tax revenue.

Table 2.2 New registrations issued in the IFS industry, 1996-2005

Entity	1996	1997	1998	1999	2000	2001	2002	2003	2004	2005
International business companies	437	372	441	326	456	210	260	274	297	372
Foreign sales corporations	393	384	317	249	118	0	0	0	0	0
Exempt insurance companies	23	17	23	5	13	7	11	15	15	9
Exempt insurance management companies	1	3	0	1	0	1	3	1	1	3
Societies with restricted liabilities	14	18	33	32	47	22	26	31	64	42
Offshore banks	7	6	1	5	7	5	3	2	4	0
Total	875	800	815	618	641	245	303	323	445	426

Sources: Ministry of Industry and International Business, Central Bank of Barbados, Supervisor of Insurance.

The removal of Barbados from the OECD's harmful tax competition list of tax havens reduced some of the concerns of sector participants, but the subsequent growth of the sector slowed, with an average growth rate in registered companies of about 7 per cent in the period 2002–05 as compared to an average growth rate of 12.5 per cent between 1996 and 2000 (see table 2.3). Societies with restricted liability (SRLs) recorded the highest growth (71.3 per cent) during the period 2002–2005 while international business companies grew by 21.8 per cent. Exempt insurance companies (EICs) and exempt insurance management companies (EIMCs) increased by 9.8 per cent and 8.7 per cent during the same period.

The number of licensed offshore banks more than doubled from 26 to 54 between 1996 and 2005. It is estimated that approximately two-thirds of Barbados' offshore banks are from Canada and the remainder out of the US and Latin America. Canada

Table 2.3 Total number of registered companies in the IFS Industry, 1996-2005

	1996	1997	1998	1999	2000	2001	2002	2003	2004	2005
International business companies	2,260	2,632	3,073	3,399	3,855	4,065	4,325	4,599	4,896	5,268
Foreign sales corporations	1,907	2,291	2,608	2,857	2,975	2,975	....	....		
Exempt insurance companies	322	339	362	367	380	387	398	413	428	437
Exempt insurance management companies	61	64	64	65	66	66	69	70	71	75
Societies with restricted liabilities	14	32	65	97	144	166	192	223	287	329
Offshore banks	40	44	43	45	52	57	56	51	55	54[a]
Total registered	4,604	5,402	6,215	6,830	7,468	4,741	5,090	5,406	5,801	6,163
Memo Items:										
% increase in the number of registered companies		17.3	15.0	9.9	9.3	−36.5	7.4	6.2	7.3	6.2
Offshore banks: Total assets (% of GDP)	401	749	786	818	839	1,104	1,324	1,165	1,107	

Sources: Ministry of Industry and International Business, Central Bank of Barbados, Supervisor of Insurance and Pensions, Barbados FSSA 2003, IMF http://www.imf.org

Note: a. The operations of one offshore bank were terminated in 2005.

is reported to be the primary market for offshore banking business, with a number of licensees indicating that on average three-quarters of their business comes from this market. However, there was a more recent contraction in the number of licensed offshore banks, which reduced from 57 in 2001 to 54 at the end of 2005.

The total assets to GDP ratio of offshore banks rose from 401 per cent in 1996 to a high of 1,324 per cent in 2002, subsequently declining to 1,107 by 2004 (see table 2.3). Activity in the offshore banking sector is fairly concentrated, with the ten largest off-shore banks accounting for approximately 87.6 per cent of total assets in 2005.

Since the establishment of the SRL (1995) Act, the number of these licensed entities increased from 14 in 1996 to 329 at the end of 2005 (table 2.3). After 2000, there was a reduction in the number of new registrations, but growth picked up from 2003 following the country's removal from the OECD harmful tax competition list of tax havens, indicating a renewed interest in Barbados-domiciled SRLs within the global investment community.

The growth of EICs and EIMCs in Barbados was limited during the second half of the 1990s. Other jurisdictions, including the British Virgin Islands, have been more suc-cessful in attracting captive insurance companies, challenging Bermuda's market lead-ership position. The US market is the largest potential source of captives. However, given that the international insurance sector is driven primarily by the various taxation treaties between Barbados and, in particular, the US and Canada, the uncertainty sur-rounding the continuation of these taxation arrangements, which are currently being renegotiated, may have led to the reduction in the number of new licenses issued.

A number of current initiatives spearheaded by the public and private sectors should serve to rejuvenate sectoral growth in the international business and financial services sector over the medium term. A consultant's report focussing on the marketing of the sector internationally has been commissioned, which should chart the way forward, particularly with respect to improved targeting of the US market. In addition, innova-tive legislation designed to facilitate the development of 'protected cells' within captive insurance companies should increase the attractiveness of Barbados as a captive insur-ance domicile[6]. Combined with a number of other advantages, particularly the large pool of competitively priced skilled workers and professionals available in Barbados, which reduces the need for expensive expatriate professionals, this should provide some impetus for growth over the medium term.

Contribution to Gross Domestic Product

Based on the latest available data, unofficial estimates of the economic contribution of the IFS sector in 2000 put the value-added generated by the activities of international business and financial services firms at approximately 400 million Barbados dollars (Bds$), or approximately 7 per cent of GDP at market prices. EICs and IBCs were the main contributors to the sector's GDP, accounting for approximately 2.3 per cent and 3.1 per cent of total GDP, respectively. In contrast, while total offshore bank assets were sizeable, their contribution to GDP, as measured by their operating surplus and wages/salaries, was estimated to be relatively small.

Employment

Presently, labour force data collected by the Barbados Statistical Service (BSS) by industry group do not include a separate category for the IFS sector. The informatics sub-sector is the only area of international business for which employment data is available.[7]

Preliminary data suggest that IBCs, given their absolute number, are the major employers, with more than one-third of the persons employed in IBCs engaged in informatics. Although comparable wages information for other areas is not available, it is estimated that average wages paid by employers in the IFS sector is relatively high. The sub-sector with the most attractive remuneration appears to be EICs and SRLs.

Contribution to government revenue

A significant contribution of the IFS sector is to tax revenue. Based on the available information given in table 2.4, the industry accounted for approximately 6.5 per cent of the Barbadian government's tax revenue and more than 30 per cent of the total corporate taxes in 2000. More recent data obtained from the Inland Revenue Department, estimates the industry's contribution to total corporation tax revenue in 2004 at approximately 60 per cent, up considerably from the 34.1 per cent in 2000.

Unofficial estimates of personal income taxes paid are about 3.1 per cent of total personal income taxes collected. Personal income tax remittances from the offshore sector for the period 2003–2005 were reported at Bds$15.7 million. The majority of this income was collected from persons employed in IBCs and EICs. IBCs also provided the bulk of the corporate taxes collected from companies operating in the IFS sector.

Table 2.4 Estimated contribution to government revenue (income year 1999/2000)

Revenue categories	Government revenue (Bds$ millions)	IFS sector revenue	IFS sector (% of respective revenue category)
Corporation tax	223.1	76.1	34.1
Personal income tax	272.2	8.4	3.1
License fees	79.6	2.7	3.4
Indirect taxes and other fees	879.5	7.8	0.9
Total	1454.4	95.0	6.5

Sources: Inland Revenue Department, Government estimates 2001/2002.

Considering the Consequences

Linkages with other domestic sectors

Apart from its significant direct economic contribution, as measured by value-added, the IFS sector also has important linkages with other economic sectors. Services rendered to the sector include utilities, accommodation, restaurants and transportation. An unofficial estimate puts the contribution of the sector at in excess of Bds$45.0 million, or approximately 12 per cent of the tourism sector GDP at market prices in 2000. The telecommunication sub-sector was also a major beneficiary of business activity, as were other persons involved in the renting of properties to international companies, with contributions estimated at Bds$81.0 million and Bds$75.5 million, respectively.

Challenges facing the IFS sector in Barbados

In spite of a slow down in business activity immediately after being listed by the OECD, Barbados still enjoys a good reputation as an international business jurisdiction. The main incentives international firms cite for choosing Barbados for their business operations are its low tax rate, double tax treaties, good infrastructure and its highly educated and trainable workforce. However, there are some issues and challenges that need to be addressed to ensure that the sector remains viable and the related benefits accrue to Barbados.

The prescriptions of international agencies and some industrialised countries have had a profound impact on the industry through increasing the cost of doing business. Added to this challenge are the uncertainties surrounding changes to existing tax treaties and legislative reforms. The Anti-money Laundering and Countering the Financing of Terrorism (AML/CFT) initiative has increased the operating cost burden of companies and has been cited as a major concern among industry participants. The paperwork for deposits of Bds$10,000 (a small amount by most such companies' standards) or more and the increased due diligence required for companies to be licensed are two of the many complaints. The additional regulatory and supervisory requirements of this initiative have also been undertaken at a cost to the authorities, at a time when other international financial system soundness standards were required to be implemented.

The OECD ring-fencing issue prompted the Government of Barbados to explore tax convergence, which could remove one of the principal incentives for locating in this jurisdiction. Although the removal of the ring-fencing issue from the agenda of the OECD may have resulted in some loss of urgency for tax convergence, fiscal reform is still recognised as vital to the process of engendering a competitive private sector. While acknowledging that total convergence will not be feasible and that domestic companies will likely bear a higher tax burden, the Government of Barbados has implemented a systematic downward revision in the domestic corporate tax rate. In addition, policy officials are exploring other fiscal incentives that can be introduced without violating WTO free-trading rules. Characterised as a relatively high cost jurisdiction, the low tax rate currently enjoyed by offshore companies gives Barbados an edge over competing jurisdictions with lower operating costs.

Apart from the tax burden, entities desirous of doing business in Barbados also face an administrative burden related to setting up and doing business. As a jurisdiction with high telecommunications costs, Barbados is challenged to be competitive. However, with the ongoing liberalisation of the telecommunications sector some reduction in costs is expected. Further work is needed to expand the technical infrastructure to facilitate large digital transactions critical for exploiting business opportunities in e-commerce and software development.

Limited resources have impeded the Government of Barbados' ability to effectively deliver services to the industry. A computer information network that proposes to link 15 public sector entities responsible for facilitating and promoting foreign investment is intended to improve the efficiency of government services. Greater flexibility in the legal structure, to allow for more expeditious provision of services, would also enhance business facilitation.

The interaction between Government and the private sector has generally been good. The Barbados Investment and Development Corporation has been praised for its role in the initial setting up of international companies and its co-operative efforts with the private sector in the marketing of Barbados as a viable international business jurisdiction, but an overall strategic plan for further development of the sector is needed and this is currently being prepared.

Relevant tax treaties, particularly revisions to sections of the double taxation treaty between Barbados and Canada, need to be finalised and other pieces of legislation completed. Over half of the international business that Barbados has been able to attract is the result of a favourable bilateral tax treaty with Canada. However, the current uncertainty surrounding the outcome of the renegotiation of this treaty has slowed the flow of Canadian business and hence the rate of new business formations in Barbados. The conclusion of these negotiations with Canada is essential for the long-term growth of Canadian business in Barbados. Although Canada is a major source of business, additional marketing efforts should also be geared towards the US and European markets.

Labour market issues and human resource development also need to be addressed. The educational level in Barbados is good and generally fits into the needs of the sector. However, there is some room for more specialised training in areas such as investment trading, treasury operations, actuarial science and information technology, as well as for the creation of formal links between tertiary institutions and representatives of the international business sector. Greater private sector involvement in curriculum development and training at the tertiary level could assist in the matching of the human resource needs within the various sub-sectors. It is also important that the accounting/finance and legal professionals maintain strong international standards and continually strive to keep their knowledge and skills current in the constantly evolving international environment.

To address some of these issues and challenges, which constrain the growth of the IFS industry in Barbados, in March 2004, the Ministry of Industry and International Business formed a joint working committee with the broad mandate of identifying and recommending feasible solutions to improve facilitation and support for the international business services industry in Barbados. Through consultations with the Barbados Investment and Development Corporation (BIDC), the Barbados International Business Association (BIBA) and the international business community, the various sub-committees were able to ascertain that considerable work was still needed to facilitate an effective environment for international business activity. The working committee made a number of recommendations, including greater information sharing sessions between the Government and the private sector, the provision of comprehensive corporate information brochures or manuals, strengthening the registrar of corporate affairs' office and streamlining immigration and customs procedures to ensure efficiency. A review of the double taxation treaties, with a view to expanding the network of dual tax treaties and the current regulatory controls, particularly those restricting the flow of foreign currency funds, were also cited. With regard to the labour market, the key issues mentioned were high employment costs, such as hiring and firing costs, and the inability to work on public holidays. There was also a call to review the labour laws. A concise exposition of the constraints to the growth of the sector is given in a BIDC report entitled 'Constraints to Doing Business in Barbados'. The itemised operating costs included high data transmission and telecommunication costs, high utilities and transportation costs, as well as the high costs of funds. The future expansion of the industry therefore hinges on the ability of the Government to effectively address these issues.

Notes

1. During the period 2002–06, the nominal rate of corporate tax under the Companies Act was systematically lowered from 40 per cent to 25 per cent.

2. In interviews with Canadian industry participants, non-tax benefits cited included lower operating costs, ease of access from Toronto and cultural links with Canada.

3. See document 'Working Together – Stronger Together' produced by a joint policy working group set up to critically examine business facilitation in the international business and financial services sector, Barbados International Business Association.

4. Based on discussions with representatives of the private sector and regulatory agencies.

5. The problem of data unavailability is currently being addressed. The Barbados Statistical Services Department, in collaboration with the Central Bank of Barbados, The Office of the Supervisor of Insurance and Pensions, the Corporate Affairs and Intellectual Property Office, the Ministry of International Business and the Barbados International Business Association, is in the process of conducting an extensive survey of the sector, not only to fill the existing data gaps but also to establish a formal mechanism to have data readily available for policy analysis.

6. Protected cells are similar to the 'rent a captive' concept. They allow a number of parents to share the infrastructure and costs of a single captive insurance company, whilst protecting the

asset position of each participant and allowing separate identification of individual loss ratios and similar statistics for reinsurance purposes.

7. Employment data for this sub-sector is collected by the Barbados Investment & Development Corporation.

3

Regulation of the Barbados International Business and Financial Services Sector

3.1 Regulation and supervision of the IFS sector pre-1998

Barbados is characterised as a low-tax jurisdiction, with a long-standing reputation for a sound legal framework and high regulatory and supervisory standards. The success achieved to date in attracting international business is reflective of the extensive treaty network of double taxation agreements and bilateral investment treaties with several countries, including most importantly the United States and Canada, which encourage transparency and the establishment of a commercial presence. In addition, the industry benefits from effective co-operation between government and the private sector on legislative reforms and promotion. As such, legislative amendments have been implemented in response to changes in the international business environment in an effort to capitalise on new opportunities. A legal separation between the international business services industry and the onshore financial sector is maintained in Barbados, and any activity between the two requires the special permission of the Minister of Finance. This effectively limits the potential for the transmission of contagion effects between the international business and the domestic financial sectors.

As indicated above, Barbados' IFS industry comprises international business companies (IBCs), international (offshore) banks (OSBs), exempt insurance companies (EICs), exempt insurance management companies (EIMCs), exempt insurance holding companies (EIHCs) and societies with restricted liability (SRLs). Regulatory and supervisory oversight of the various international business entities is shared by various agencies. The Central Bank of Barbados regulates and supervises the operations of OSBs, the International Business Unit of the Ministry of Industry and International Business oversees the operations of IBCs and SRLs, and the Office of the Supervisor of Insurance and Pensions has regulatory and supervisory oversight over EICs, EIMCs and EIHCs. In addition, the Barbados Investment and Development Corporation (BIDC), a government investment agency, and Barbados International Business Association (BIBA), the private sector representative of the companies engaged in international business, support the Government in the marketing and promotion of international business activity in Barbados. It noteworthy that the Central Bank of Barbados and the Office of the Supervisor of Insurance have regulatory and supervisory oversight for both domestic and offshore entities in their respective areas.

Pre-2002 offshore banking activity in Barbados was conducted under the auspices of the 1979 Offshore Banking Act. Some offshore banks are subsidiaries of a parent bank, with customers generally afforded the full range of services of the parent. The Act specified that only non-residents are eligible to hold bank accounts with an offshore bank or trust company, or to hold investments, accounts and conduct their transactions in global currencies. The Act provided for offshore banks to benefit from a similar range of fiscal incentives granted to IBCs, including the taxation of profits on a sliding scale at rates of 1 per cent to 2.5 per cent, no direct or capital gains tax on profits and exemption from exchange control and payment of import and other duties.

Offshore banks domiciled in Barbados conduct a wide range of activities within the banking and wider financial services fields. These include wealth management (primarily the formation and administration of trusts), investment banking, retail banking in foreign currencies and corporate and trade financing through the issue of international stocks and bonds, acquisitions and mergers. These entities are licensed and supervised by the Central Bank of Barbados in keeping with international best practices. Licensing, due diligence and prudential requirements are rigorous and the degree of regulation and supervision of financial institutions is high. Risks for depositors are, to a large extent, contained by restricting the acceptance of third party deposits to those offshore banks that are owned by foreign banks.

The Exempt Insurance Act Cap. 308A, was designed to allow Barbados to develop as a meaningful alternative to Bermuda for international insurance purposes, particularly captive insurance companies. Exempt insurance companies are licensed, regulated and supervised by the Supervisor of Insurance and Pensions within the Ministry of Finance in keeping with international standards. Under the Exempt Insurance Act Cap. 308A, companies pay no tax on their income for the first 15 years, with a 2 per cent rate, to a maximum of only Bds$5,000, thereafter. They are also exempt from withholding tax.

3.2 Emergence and evolution of the post-1998 regulatory regime for IFS

There have been considerable external pressures for strengthening IFS regulation and supervision. The requirement to co-operate with the OECD in the highly contentious areas of information exchange, transparency and ring-fencing has been challenging. Barbados is well known as a 'clean', highly reputable jurisdiction that co-operates fully with international tax authorities and regulatory agencies. It is noteworthy that Barbados was not listed as one of the countries on the 2000 Financial Action Task Force (FATF) list of non-cooperative countries[1] with 'detrimental practices that seriously and unjustifiably hamper the fight against money laundering'. Therefore, there was little concern about the greater exchange of information for criminal and civil tax inquiries, more extensive availability of beneficial ownership and trust information, or the higher degree of auditing and filing requirements, which formed part of the Harmful Taxation Debate. The tax treaties between Barbados and other countries contain provisions that facilitate such queries. The principle contacts for information exchange in Barbados are the Inland Revenue Department, the Supervisor of Insurance and the Central Bank of Barbados.

There were, however, some additional reporting and due diligence costs which resulted from Barbados' enhanced AML/CFT requirements. Firms in the accounting and auditing field have also cautioned that while clients are aware of the extensive due diligence undertaken in Barbados, there is likely to be some disquiet if private information is required to be made available for public inspection.

According to an IMF report in 2003, Barbados has worked diligently to develop an effective regime for anti-money laundering and combating the financing of terrorism. The Money Laundering (Prevention and Control) Act was enacted in 1998 and amended in 2002, the Anti-Terrorism Act was enacted in 2002, the Mutual Assistance in Criminal Matters Act (1993) was amended in 2001 and Anti-Money Laundering Guidelines, in keeping with FATF recommendations, have been issued to all financial services providers. The institutional structure was also strengthened in 2000 with the establishment of the Anti-Money Laundering Authority (AMLA), which is charged with ensuring compliance of AML/CFT requirements by all financial institutions. The Authority is well organised and functions through its supervisory board, which includes representatives from the Commissioner of Police, Inland Revenue, Customs authority, Supervisor of Insurance, Corporate Affairs and Intellectual Property Office, Central Bank and the Solicitor General's Office. The Financial Intelligence Unit (FIU), which was also established in 2000, conducts day-to-day activities of the AMLA: namely, receiving, analysing and disseminating pertinent financial information and intelligence and investigating suspicious transactions. The FIU meets the Egmont Group's definition and Barbados was admitted to Egmont membership in June 2002[2]. The Unit works closely with the supervisory authorities of the various types of financial institutions in monitoring compliance with AML/CFT requirements.

Furthermore, Barbados[3] has demonstrated its commitment to AML/CFT through it membership and active participation in the Caribbean Financial Action Task Force (CFATF). This is an organisation of 30 states of the Caribbean Basin, which have agreed to implement common countermeasures to address the problem of criminal money laundering and the financing of terrorism. It was established as the result of meetings convened in Aruba in May 1990 and Jamaica in November 1992, with the main objective of achieving effective implementation of and compliance with its recommendations to prevent and control money laundering and to combat the financing of terrorism. The Secretariat of the CFATF has been established as a mechanism to monitor and encourage progress to ensure full implementation of the Kingston Ministerial Declaration[4] and works closely with the Co-operating and Supporting Nations (the Governments of Canada, the Kingdom of the Netherlands, France the United Kingdom and the United States of America), which are all members of the Financial Action Task Force on Money Laundering and the International Financial Institutions.

An AML/CFT supervision programme for offshore banking is in place. The Central Bank conducts off-site compliance reviews and has also implemented an on-site inspection programme.

The Financial System Stability Assessment (FSSA) report for Barbados (2003) confirmed the extent to which international standards and codes are observed by the financial sector. Detailed assessments of the following were carried out:

- The Basle Core Principles for Effective Banking Supervision

- The International Organization of Securities Commissions – Objectives and Principles of Securities Regulation

- The Committee on Payment and Settlement Systems – Core Principles for Systemically Important Payment Systems

- The International Association of Insurance Supervisors – Insurance Supervisory Principles

- The IMF's Code of Good Practices on Transparency in Monetary and Financial Policies

The report stated that Barbados' compliance with international standards in the onshore and offshore banking sectors was found to be generally high. However, some weaknesses in transparency and supervision in the insurance industry were noted. The issue of the definition of an insurance entity, licence classes and segregated cell companies were some of the concerns raised. The statutory requirement for the Supervisor of Insurance to determine on a contract-by-contract basis whether or not a transaction met the definition of insurance was also found to be not feasible administratively. The 2004 International Business (Miscellaneous Provisions) Bill included an amendment to the definition of insurance that resolved this matter.

One of the most important recent legislative changes has been the replacement of the Offshore Banking (1979) Act with the 2002 International Financial Services Act (IFSA), which introduced new requirements and restrictions in relation to the regulation of international financial services from within Barbados. The new act also enabled businesses organised under the Societies with Restricted Liabilities Act Cap. 318B to be eligible to apply for an offshore banking licence.

The IFSA (2002–05), which has improved supervisory compliance in the offshore banking sector, complements the Financial Institutions (1996) Act, the KYC ('know your customer') Guidelines and the regulations on Asset Quality and Capital Adequacy. Furthermore, the Act embraces the Core Principles for Effective Banking Supervision issued by the Basel Committee on Banking Supervision in 1997.

More specifically, the Act includes provisions which:

1. Permit the Central Bank of Barbados to conduct onsite inspections of offshore banks.

2. Permit entities other than those incorporated under the Companies Act, including societies with restricted liability, to be eligible for an offshore banking licence.

3. Remove the distinction between resident controlled and non-resident controlled international companies in determining capital, as done under the previous Act. (This distinction was inconsistent with the precepts of a single market and the requirement for non-discrimination based on nationality).

4. Make provision for the prescribing, through regulation, of capital adequacy ratios. Regulations are being drafted that will take into account the new Bank for International Settlements (BIS) Capital Accord as well as market risk.

5. Mandate offshore banks to have a physical presence.[5]

6. Raise the minimum capital to Bds$4.0 million for entities that take deposits and Bds$1.0 million for those that do not. (The Bds$4.0 million is in keeping with the requirement for commercial banks under the Financial Institutions Act).

7. Limit a bank's exposure to a person or group to 25 per cent of stated capital and published reserves, for banks which accept third party deposits.

8. Restrict the ownership or control of a bank by any person or group to 10 per cent of stated capital, except in cases where the approval of the Minister is granted for higher amounts.

9. Allow the Central Bank to examine any company, where there is reasonable cause to believe that the company is engaging in banking business without a licence.

10. Permit the Central Bank to inspect the books of any holding company, parent company or any other company that holds shares in a licensee.

11. Allow the Central Bank to disclose information to any supervisory or regulatory authority of a financial institution in Barbados and the appropriate supervisory or regulatory authority of a financial institution of another country at the request of that authority, where there is a branch, holding company or affiliate of the licensee operating in that country.

12. Permit entities that engage in intra-group treasury management, by lending and investing funds received from members of the group and where the liability is contained within the group, to elect not to be licensed under the International Financial Services Act (IFSA).

13. Require the prior consent of the home regulator before a licensee can establish a branch or subsidiary in Barbados.

In addition, the IFSA allows for more effective monitoring of the activities of offshore banks, including the requirement for prior Central Bank approval for changes in a bank's ownership structure, its articles of incorporation and any reduction in its capital and allows the Central Bank to request meetings, where appropriate, with external auditors and annual meetings with the directors and management of offshore banks.

The Exempt Insurance Act and the domestic Insurance Act establish capital requirements for a EIC/QIC (qualifying insurance company) based upon premium written. The Companies Act (Section 356.25 (b)) provides for the formation of segregated cell companies (SCCs), and during the last five years the legislation was amended to allow local insurance companies to conduct insurance business under an SCC. A 2004 amendment to the insurance legislation also requires EICs on conversion to a qualifying insurance company to pay income tax on an ongoing, forward basis and not retroactively as has been in the past.

Going forward

The international investment and financial services community is rapidly improving standards of regulation and supervision in response to growing concerns over money laundering and international crime. With the international business sector identified as a key area for potential growth in Barbados, continued improvements in regulation and supervision in response to growing concerns over money laundering and international crime is critical. The objective is to attain international best practice in all areas of international financial activity, but in a rapidly changing environment this is especially challenging for small resource-constrained economies like Barbados.

Fear of being blacklisted, with the potentially damaging effect on business in the sector, has prompted governments to expeditiously attempt to meet the requirements set out by the various international agencies. While acknowledging the importance of these initiatives, small developing countries like Barbados continue to be challenged by the level of resources required to implement them. However, Barbados is well aware that the costs of ineffective regulation and supervision, which could result in loss of reputation through potential sanctions and advisories from other jurisdictions, are likely to be far greater than the costs associated with achieving and maintaining an effective level of supervisory oversight.

Notes

1. In 1999, the FATF embarked on a project known as the Non-Cooperative Countries and Territories Initiative. It defined criteria by which a jurisdiction could be deemed 'non-cooperative' and, after investigating 31 countries, the FATF cited 15 jurisdictions, which it considered to possess serious, systemic, money laundering problems. Five CARICOM member countries appeared on this 'blacklist': the Bahamas, the Cayman Islands, Dominica, St. Kitts and Nevis, and St. Vincent and the Grenadines. Other Caribbean countries were eventually dropped from the initial pool of 31 suspects, but were asked to tighten up their practices. These included Antigua and Barbuda, the British Virgin Islands, and St. Lucia. In June 2001, the FATF released a second list of 'non-cooperative' countries. Four countries were eventually dropped, but six more were added. The Bahamas and the Cayman Islands were both removed, and in September 2001 Grenada was added.

2. See Egmont Group website: http://www.egmontgroup.org/ [accessed 15 February 2008].

3. Barbados is also a member of the **Caribbean Association of Regulators of International Business** (CARIB) formed by the members of the Caribbean Community to establish, in a precise and systematic forum, strategies which convey CARICOM's position on the G7's

continued attacks on Caribbean offshore financial centres (OFCs). CARIB's work programme consists of maintaining the integrity and transparency of international business transactions; increasing supervision of internationally mobile capital; ensuring appropriate standards and systemic stability; and enacting any other necessary financial intelligence activity. To perform its duties, CARIB is expected to foster a close relationship with the national authorities, since they will be the ones to negotiate with the G7 countries.

4. See CFATF website: http://www.cfatf.org/ [accessed 15 February 2008].

5. Defined as having at least one director who is a citizen of Barbados and who resides in Barbados.

4

Incremental Costs and Benefits of Enhancing the IFS Regulatory Regime in Barbados

4.1 Incremental costs of adopting new international regulatory standards

Barbados has continued to maintain its reputation as a well-respected international financial services jurisdiction with high regulatory and supervisory standards, despite being listed by the OECD as a 'tax haven' in 2000. Indeed, without having to make any commitments to the OECD, Barbados was removed from that list in 2002 and was subsequently identified as a significant international financial centre (IFC) in the OECD report A Process for Achieving a Global Level Playing Field[1]. As a result, Barbados was invited to participate in the Global Forum on Taxation and has been involved in providing information on transparency and exchange of information. It should also be noted that Barbados has a stand-alone information exchange agreement with the United States and in addition, all of Barbados' double taxation agreements provide for the exchange of information on all direct taxes between the parties unless the entities involved are specifically excluded from the treaty. Barbados' Financial Intelligence Unit (FIU) has also established formal Memoranda of Understanding with other FIUs relating to information exchange and is also part of an international network of FIUs that exchange information. These measures were all in place prior to the new international regulatory requirements.

Barbados supervisory and regulatory requirements are in keeping with international best practices and have been that way for some time. However, compliance with the new international regulatory standards, while imposing some incremental costs to the international financial services sector in the short term, has undoubtedly strengthened overall financial sector regulation and supervision in Barbados, thus further enhancing its reputation as a well-regulated IFC. To this end, Barbados implemented legislative/regulatory changes to make provision for greater disclosure of information by international companies, especially in respect of beneficial shareholders, in order to meet the additional international requirements relating to combating money laundering and financing terrorism. Service-providers were also required to provide the authorities with the know your customer/due diligence (KYC/DD) procedures followed in deciding whether to accept or reject a client and, with the assistance of the

Financial Intelligence Unit of the Anti-Money Laundering Authority, guidelines were also issued to ensure that service-providers meet the requirements of Barbados' anti-money laundering legislation.

The qualitative and quantitative survey data collected from government regulatory and supervisory agencies and private sector entities highlighted the main incremental costs resulting from the adoption of the KYC/DD regulatory requirements for compliance with AML/CFT rules. Based on the quantitative responses, the most significant costs related to the hiring of staff, the renting of additional office space and the purchasing of new hardware and software for the information technology systems needed to comply with the KYC/DD and AML/CFT initiatives. In addition, both public and private sector entities reported incurring higher costs relating to the training and retraining of staff, staff attendance at conferences and consultations with domestic accounting/auditing firms and local/foreign lawyers.

Significant non-quantifiable costs mentioned by private sector firms operating in the IFS sector were the increased burden placed on their clients in meeting the increased regulatory requirements and the additional demands placed on their own employees to ensure compliance with these requirements, which in some cases took away considerable time from other important firm-specific issues relating to growth and diversification. One regulatory agency also identified the non-quantifiable cost of being forced to be reactionary in terms of the constant diversion of resources from developmental to regulatory issues in response to OECD and other such initiatives.

Incremental costs incurred by government regulatory and supervisory agencies

Since 2000, the scope of the functions of government regulatory and supervisory agencies in Barbados have widened considerably to include, inter alia, the mandate of upholding the KYC/DD regulatory requirements for compliance with the new AML/CFT rules. In this regard, the implementation of the nine additional recommendations of the FATF, as well as the provisions of the Sarbanes-Oxley Act in the United States on corporate governance, has been given significant attention. With regard to the latter, government agencies with regulatory and supervisory oversight have reported that a number of company directors and other senior officers in the international financial services sector have embraced, implemented and are complying with the corporate governance provisions, as outlined in the Sarbanes-Oxley legislation.

The majority of government regulatory and supervisory agencies surveyed reported increased financial costs, stemming mainly from the hiring of additional staff, resulting in the need for additional office space, the purchase of new information technology (IT) systems and the cost of retraining and training personnel to effectively carry out their increased regulatory responsibilities. Most of the regulatory agencies reported having to assign additional resources to ensure compliance with the increased requirements. For instance, the Supervisor of Insurance hired an additional five persons in 2005, resulting in increased cost for wages and salaries of Bds$183,000, rent expenses of Bds$43,000 and in-house training of about 126 hours. The additional persons were needed to conduct broadened regulatory audits of companies, including on-site inspections, to ensure compliance with the enhanced regulatory guidelines, including KYC/DD requirements through the use of external audits and other administrative arrangements. Other financial costs incurred by government agencies were increased expenditure each year for staff attendance at special conferences, which averaged almost Bds$25,000 each year between the years 2000 and 2005. The costs of investment in additional information technology systems (hardware and software) for AML/CFT purchased between 2000 and 2003 was estimated by one regulator to be Bds$122,000. Associated with these financial costs, government agencies have identified other non-quantifiable costs, such as those resulting from being more dependent on external sources for assistance, training and advice.

Incremental costs incurred by private sector providers of international business financial services in Barbados

Private sector firms appeared to be somewhat uncertain regarding some of the questions relating to the new KYC/DD requirements. These included whether the adoption of the standards was detrimental to the reputation of Barbados as an IFC, the reputation of firms operating in the IFS sector or whether the additional costs incurred were likely to increase the competitiveness of private sector firms. In addition, most firms indicated an indifference to the question of whether excessive demands were being made on the capabilities of the managerial and other staff in government regulatory agencies to properly carry out their mandate.

However, approximately 50 per cent of the private sector firms surveyed expressed the view that excessive demands were being made on firm personnel, not only to meet the new compliance requirements, but also to deal effectively with government regulatory and supervisory agencies. This required the hiring and training of more front line and back office staff, as well as the purchase of new IT systems to deal effectively with KYC/DD compliance guidelines. Most noticeably, over 75 per cent of private sector firms were of the opinion that the financial costs incurred were higher than was necessary to promote the regular business growth of the firm. This was identified as a substantial burden to firms, with 81.8 per cent of them also indicating that AML/CFT compliance had diverted their attention away from other more important matters. This also resulted in an increase in the level of costs and attention being directed to the new regulatory requirements of local government agencies, as compared to that required for more important firm-specific issues, such as diversification and firm growth. The majority of private sector respondents (77.8 per cent) agreed that the enhanced measures required significant retraining of back office staff involved in AML/CFT compliance, while 55.6 per cent indicated that significant retraining of front line personnel was necessary. A summary of the responses by private firms and regulators to the qualitative questionnaire is shown in the appendix at the end of this report.

From the responses to the quantitative survey, private sector firms reported that either additional person-hours were necessary or additional persons were hired to comply with the new requirements for the KYC/DD guidelines. Most private sector firms indicated incurring higher wages and salaries over the five years since 2000, averaging approximately Bds$186,000 per firm, with the majority of the hiring being undertaken since 2003. To accommodate the new staff, firms reported renting additional office space, with on average around Bds$11,000 being spent annually on rent.

The majority of firms reported providing regular in-house training, amounting to approximately Bds$17,000 per firm, while only two firms reported receiving additional training from attending conferences, estimated at a total of Bds$63,000 in 2004 and 2005. One firm indicated that training was also conducted on new information technology systems for KYC/DD requirements. Most firms reported that the costs of external technical assistance by way of professional associations and advisers were about Bds$22,000 on average, and that there were added costs resulting from consultation with local accounting and auditing firms and with domestic and international lawyers. Approximately half of the firms cited investment in additional information systems, amounting to approximately Bds$65,000 per firm, with the bulk of spending going towards the purchase of hardware. Other costs incurred were payments for new licensing procedures, which were estimated at about Bds$100,000 per year since 2002, as well as the costs of external audits and the satisfying of KYC requests from external regulators and auditors.

4.2 Incremental benefits of enhanced IFS regulation and supervision

The survey results on benefits were somewhat conflicting, as no discernible consensus was reached on the incremental benefits accruing either to individual private sector firms or to the domestic economy. Contrasting views were evident among government regulators and private sector service providers of IFS (i.e. accounting and auditing firms, law firms, international banks and trusts companies), but there were a few common threads within these two groupings. An important caveat is that given the limited number of responses[2], particularly the few quantitative responses, generalising is not possible; however, the survey results can provide some preliminary indicators.

The enhanced reputation of Barbados as an international financial centre

The general view was that the new KYC/DD compliance requirements (to meet AML/CFT compliance) enhanced Barbados' reputation as an international financial centre (IFC). Although already considered a highly reputable jurisdiction because of its maintenance of international standards of best practice, the majority of the private sector service providers surveyed (over 60 per cent) as well as the regulators, perceived that Barbados' reputation as an IFC had been enhanced by the new KYC/DD compliance requirements. Accounting firms in particular, which comprised about 15 per cent of respondents, strongly agreed that the country's reputation had been enhanced by these measures. Similarly, regulators cited the increased number of licences issued in the last few years and the continued favourable reviews of various aspects of the sector's regulatory and supervisory framework by external assessors, as evidence of this.

The pattern of responses was generally the same on the issue of whether the new regulatory requirements strengthened overall financial system regulation in Barbados, with the majority of private providers of IFS and regulators in agreement. Again, the accounting firms were strong in their views on this issue, perhaps rightfully so given their extensive exposure in the international financial market, which better positions them to ascertain the extent to which Barbados' international reputation and regulatory system had been strengthened. Indeed, the review of the financial system by the IMF (FSAP, 2003) substantiated the view that Barbados' financial system is now relatively stronger. From the regulators' perspective, initiatives like the Sarbanes-Oxley Act, which emerged from closer attention being paid by the international community to the industry, have been beneficial to the jurisdiction by providing a catalyst for positive change. According to the regulators, Sarbanes-Oxley increased awareness of the sector to effective corporate governance and brought legitimate pressure to bear on directors and senior officers of organisations in understanding that they are responsible for their actions and could be held accountable for the fortunes of the organisation.

While there was broad-based agreement that both the regulatory system and the country's reputation had benefited from these changes, there was also some uncertainty among a limited number of respondents (approximately 30 per cent) on this issue. A negligible percentage of respondents (less than 10 per cent) disagreed that the overall financial system had been strengthened and the reputation of Barbados enhanced by the new KYC/DD requirements.

Enhanced competitiveness vis-à-vis other international business jurisdictions

Perhaps, the widest divergence of views was expressed on the extent to which Barbados' competitiveness relative to other 'offshore' financial centres had improved with the new KYC/DD compliance requirements. From the survey data, approximately 30 per cent of private sector service providers felt that Barbados' competitiveness had improved, while 23 per cent were uncertain and 38 per cent disagreed. This high level of uncertainty in responses perhaps reflects the industry's inability to adequately assess the impact on business activity arising from the various measures. Separating economic effects is a highly complex undertaking requiring a notion of the counterfactual, that is, what would have obtained in the absence of these measures. This may also explain the high level of non-response to some of these questions.

In examining the composition of respondents, accounting firms were among those expressing positive views on the matter of enhanced competitiveness, while regulators and other private service providers (including legal entities) offered mixed views.

Expectedly, most entities that responded affirmatively to the question of competitive gains made by Barbados also disagreed that the new regulatory measures imposed disproportionately high costs on firms relative to the likely benefits. Yet, these entities also opined that the upgrades made to their information technology systems and the improvement of staff capabilities may not have been necessary otherwise. This subset was mixed, comprising regulators, accounting firms and other service providers.

Similarly, the majority of respondents that disagreed on the issue of competitive gains also felt that the new regulatory measures had not imposed disproportionately high costs on firms compared to the likely benefits that could accrue. Yet, at least half of these firms suggested that the additional costs, although not disproportionately high relative to the benefits, were such that they were considering exiting the IFS business. Again, this was a mixed subset of the category of respondents (excluding legal entities) and comprised mainly service providers. This group (those disagreeing with competitiveness gains, agreeing that costs were not disproportionately high, but were high enough that leaving the industry was an exercisable option) also expressed the view that the measures made excessive demands on the managerial and staff capabilities of both government regulatory authorities and private sector firms. Regulators, although mixed in their views on the extent to which they were required to upgrade their systems and staff capabilities in a manner and at a cost that may have been necessary, were generally indecisive as to whether these demands were excessive (see appendix 1).

Over 50 per cent of entities (including regulators, but excluding accounting firms) noted that the KYC/DD compliance requirements for AML/CFT substantially increased their financial and staff costs for meeting the requirements of external auditors. The majority (over 80 per cent) considered that these new measures diverted their attention from more important matters concerning the diversification and growth of their IFS business. The latter view was also shared by some of those respondents who felt that the costs were reasonable and the measures necessary.

There was an equally mixed position on the issue of whether the costs associated with the new measures were reasonable to ensure Barbados' high reputation and increase the competitiveness of the firm as an IFS provider, with a high proportion of respondents neither agreeing nor disagreeing (61 per cent). About 20 per cent of respondents did not concur that these costs would have been necessary anyway.

The most commonly expressed view (over 50 per cent of respondents) was that the new measures required entities to undertake some retraining of staff and upgrading of their systems in a way that extended beyond what was necessary for regular business; the measures also increased costs, while diverting attention from regular business activity. Hence it could be concluded that the new requirements might have impeded business growth, albeit marginally.

Incremental flow of IFS business to Barbados

The discussion above provides some preliminary indications of the likelihood of firms experiencing any incremental flow of IFS business. Over 50 per cent of respondents to this question indicated that the KYC/DD compliance requirements for AML/CFT did not result in any increased business for the individual firms and commensurately for Barbados[3]. Furthermore, the majority of respondents also noted that they did not experience any decline in business as a result of these measures, which implies that there was no material impact on business activity in most cases.

An estimated 32 per cent of firms recorded an increase in business activity associated with these new measures. A minority of respondents engaged in banking services provided estimates of the incremental benefits derived from the enhanced IFS regulatory/supervisory regime at over Bds$2.0 million in business revenue and Bds$1.0 million in profit. This group also noted that product/service diversification was negligible, but reported that there were improvements in information technology capacity and knowledge base in providing global international financial services, with an estimated increase in business of between 15–30 per cent.

Accounting firms constituted 15 per cent of respondents, and estimated incremental business revenue of over Bds$200,000 (total for all accounting firms). However, this result was not fully representative of the group of accounting firms, as 50 per cent of this subset experienced an overall decline in business of 0–15 per cent and no change in customers.

Companies providing legal services accounted for a mere 7 per cent of total respondents; they, not surprisingly, reported experiencing a pickup in business of over 30 per cent, indicating a greater reliance on legal guidance in the enhanced regulatory environment. This subset also pointed to a greater geographic diversity in its customer base. Similarly, some regulators suggested that overall IFS business rose by between 15–30 per cent.

Increased growth and diversification of the IFS product and services

It is not surprising based on the above, that the majority of companies responding to the survey did not experience any increased growth or diversification of IFS products and services. Indeed, the majority of those that responded to this question disagreed that their business experienced any increase in the number of individual or corporate customers and/or achieved any product/service or geographic diversity resulting from these measures. Nonetheless, the high proportion of respondents (between 30–60 per cent) neither agreeing or disagreeing with these questions could suggest an inability to assess or separate the effects of the new measures from other influences and consequently to apportion benefit. A small number of firms (15 per cent) reported greater diversity in the geographical origin of their customers.

4.3 Overall assessment of net benefits accruing from the adoption of new international regulatory standards and strengthening the regulatory regime

The overall net benefit to the economy

The most challenging aspect of the study is the calculation of the net benefit to the Barbados economy. Conceptually, the net benefit of a policy change is equivalent to the total benefits less total costs associated with the new measures aggregated across affected firms and industries. For the purposes of this study, estimates of the costs and benefits resulting from the adoption of new regulatory standards and strengthening the regulatory regime were requested through the survey of key stakeholders in the IFS sector. Utilising the costs and benefits from the survey data should have allowed for the calculation of a net benefit, except that most respondents did not or were unable to quantify the benefits of the new measures. Indeed, over 60 per cent of respondents did not provide quantitative estimates of net benefits, but provided cost estimates, which were perhaps easier to measure. As a result, the ensuing analysis focuses on the costs aspect.

Notwithstanding the above, the qualitative responses can provide limited estimates of the benefits, which when combined with the costs data can provide some indications of the net benefits. Firstly, over 90 per cent of respondents mentioned that the new KYC/DD regulatory requirements resulted in greater diligence at knowing their customers, their needs and their motivations. Furthermore, over 60 per cent of respondents reported favourably that the new compliance requirements enhanced Barbados' high reputation as an IFC and strengthened overall financial system regulation. Tempering these benefits, however, are the costs to individual firms, which as previously mentioned ranged from Bds$25,000 to over Bds$200,000 per annum per firm.

In the absence of complete data, the pertinent question is whether the costs are disproportionately higher than the benefits? About 45 per cent of respondents felt that they were not, but 27 per cent expressed the view that the additional costs were so high that they were considering exiting the international financial services business.

Even those that felt that the costs were not disproportionately higher than the benefits, cited other downside risks to doing business, such as making excessive demands on staff and diverting attention from more important matters concerning the diversification and growth of IFS business, and consequently Barbados' competitiveness as an IFS jurisdiction. This is further supported by the number of respondents (55 per cent) that noted that the new KYC/DD compliance requirements for AML/CFT increased substantially their financial and staff costs for meeting the requirements of external auditors. As previously mentioned, approximately 50 per cent considered that these new measures made excessive demands on managerial and staff capabilities. Only 22 per cent noted that these measures required upgrades to information technology systems and staff that were necessary anyway, while 77 per cent noted that they were required to spend far more than would have been necessary for regular business.

A small percentage (less than 10 per cent) lamented being inundated with requests from the authorities for money laundering information on their customers, but over 50 per cent were concerned about striking the right balance between respecting confidentiality and meeting new compliance demands. A small minority (less 10 per cent) of respondents felt that they were being required to police financial transactions in an inappropriate manner and were focusing so much on KYC/DD requirements that it was possible that they could miss other major abuses of the system. Some 23 per cent of firms thought that the measures were more intrusive in requiring information, which irritated customers and could possibly drive them away. About 20 per cent of respondents noted that they were now more careful in dealing with regulatory and supervisory authorities, while 22 per cent considered that the measures were preventing them from meeting legitimate tax, AML and CFT concerns.

The above indicates that the new measures created some obstacles to doing business in Barbados; these could impede the future growth of the sector, but they were hard to quantify.

Government and the public sector

To the extent that some 32 per cent of companies recorded an increase in business activity resulting from the new measures, the increased earnings and profitability would have translated into higher government revenue. Indeed, the contribution of the sector to corporation tax revenue has increased over the years and is now over 60 per cent.

Another benefit arising from the increased scrutiny of the IFS sector has been the opportunity for non-OECD countries to participate in decision-making. The Global Forum identified Barbados as a significant financial centre and in the context of ensuring that the identification and review of significant financial centres was a dynamic process, invited Barbados to participate in the Global Forum. Consequently, Barbados has been involved in the process of completing a template/questionnaire on transparency and exchange of information together with all members of the OECD and other non-member participating partners. This development can only be beneficial to Barbados.

Regulators

Based on the regulators' responses to the survey, estimated incremental benefits accruing were over Bds$100,000 per annum (across all regulators) between 2000 and 2005, arising from improved technological capacity. A marginal increase in staff efficiency/productivity was reported, with costs over the period 2000–05 around Bds$200,000 per annum (not including the costs of additional person-hours, for which data was not provided). This would suggest a negative net benefit. Some regulators considered that the benefits to the jurisdiction were more evident from its ability to continue to attract new highly reputable business, while incurring reasonable costs in this regard.

Private providers of IFS

Most private providers of international financial services disagreed that the new measures impose disproportionately high costs on firms compared to the likely benefits that might accrue to the firm, supporting the hypothesis that the new regime may have enhanced competitiveness relative to other jurisdictions.

As indicted above, there was consensus that firms benefited from becoming better and more diligent at knowing their customers and their needs and motivations. Many firms were unable or unwilling to provide a quantifiable estimate of the benefits, while most provided cost estimates. Based on the limited information received, incremental business revenue was estimated at over Bds$200,000 per annum per firm with gains from increased access to foreign markets at Bds$95,000 and with their increased competitiveness netting Bds$30,000. These figures compare less favourably to the costs, which at the minimum were around Bds$220,000 per firm per annum over the past five years, if only the wages and salaries incurred by most private sector firms are considered. Additional costs related to training, upgrades and rental space would have contributed significantly to overall costs, so that for the average firm the reported costs exceed the quantifiable benefit to result in a negative net benefit.

This outcome is partly substantiated by the qualitative survey, where the sentiment expressed was that the measures made excessive demands on the capability of their personnel in meeting new compliance requirements, requiring training and increased financial and staff costs not commensurate with what is necessary for regular business growth. Furthermore, about 20 per cent of these firms felt the measures imposed very high and unnecessary administrative overhead cost burdens.

Measurement problem

Given the difficulty inherent in measuring benefits as opposed to costs, which relates to disentangling the effects of different policy changes and which may be responsible for the low response rate to the incremental benefits questions, it is likely that total benefits and consequently the net benefits are understated. This is partly reflected in the indication by some respondents that they experienced increased business activity. However, it would be misleading to infer from the limited data the nature of the distribution of the benefits.

Notes

1. Report produced by OECD Global Forum meeting at Berlin, Germany, 3–4 June 2004.

2. There was a 100 per cent response rate by the regulators, but the rate of private firms was 33 per cent while that of service providers was 50 per cent. Responses to the quantitative questionnaire by all respondents was generally poor.

3. The average response rate to this question was about 50 per cent.

5

Overall Conclusions for Barbados

The enhancement of the international business and financial services sector of Barbados is a key component of its long-term development strategy. Therefore, improving the standards of regulation and supervision in accordance with global developments, in particular the growing concerns about money laundering and the financing of terrorist activities, is critical if Barbados is to maintain its long-standing reputation for high levels of regulation and supervision and a highly branded jurisdiction. Indeed, the aim is to create a more effective and enabling environment in line with international best practices, without increasing the compliance costs of both government regulators and private providers of international business and financial services.

Against this backdrop, the main objective of the study was to ascertain how the adoption of the new KYC/DD regulatory requirements for compliance with the CFT/AML laws has impacted on the IFS in Barbados during the period 2000–2005. To this end, both qualitative and quantitative survey data was collected from government regulators and private sector service providers. From this data, estimates of the incremental costs and benefits that resulted from compliance with the new regulatory measures were examined for an overall assessment of the net impact on the respective stakeholders, the industry and the domestic economy.

Based on the survey responses, it appears that the incremental costs of adopting the new regulatory measures outweighed the benefits. The main costs cited by survey respondents were the hiring of staff, the renting of additional office space and the purchasing of new hardware and software for the information technology systems needed to comply with the KYC/DD and AML/CFT initiatives. Additionally, both public and private sector entities incurred higher costs relating to the retraining and training of staff, staff attendance at conferences and consultations with domestic accounting and auditing firms and local and foreign lawyers. Furthermore, most private sector firms reported that the measures exerted excessive demands on managerial and support staff to the extent that they have had to divert resources away from other important matters concerning diversification and firm growth. Most noteworthy was the response that compliance costs were at such a high level that some firms were considering exiting from the international financial services sector.

In terms of the benefits, however, it was difficult to find consensus among regulators and private sector entities. In particular, there were conflicting views on whether Barbados' reputation or its competitiveness as an IFC improved as a result of the KYC/DD requirements. Some private sector firms reported increased business activity, while government regulators reported a marginal improvement in efficiency/productivity.

Notwithstanding the preponderance of responses of higher costs relative to benefits, over 90 per cent of the respondents mentioned that the new KYC/DD regulatory requirements resulted in the greater due diligence/knowing their customers and the strengthening of overall financial system regulation.

Going forward: policy implications

The survey highlights the sensitivity of small economies to the prescriptions of international regulatory agencies and some industrialised countries. With their limited resources, small countries are particularly challenged to expeditiously implement changes in international best practices without compromising the achievement of their other development objectives. Indeed, the costs associated with these measures may exceed the incremental benefits, as appears to be the case with Barbados' international financial services sector. Barbados' high branding, its low tax rate, double tax treaties, good infrastructure and its highly educated and trainable workforce are among the reasons why many international firms have chosen Barbados to locate their operations. Nevertheless, there are inherent obstacles that have to be corrected if the purported benefits are to accrue to Barbados. Competitiveness is key to the success of this sector and greater emphasis must be placed on ensuring an enabling environment for business activity. Enhancing the ease with which firms can set-up and do business is critical and should form an important part of the overall strategic plan for further development of the sector.

As previously mentioned, labour market issues and human resource development also need to be addressed. The educational level of Barbados is good and generally fits into the needs of the sector, but there is some scope for more specialised training in areas such as trading, treasury operations, actuarial science and information technology. These should be coupled with formal links with tertiary institutions and representatives of the international business sector.

Fiscal reform will be vital to the process of engendering a competitive private sector. With the higher administrative costs, policy-makers must explore other fiscal incentives to encourage and attract businesses to Barbados.

Both the government and the private sector in Barbados recognise the importance of collaboration in addressing the critical issues facing the international financial services sector, as evidenced by the initiative of the Ministry of Industry and International Business to form a joint working committee with the broad mandate of identifying and recommending feasible solutions to improve facilitation and support for the IFS industry in Barbados. Already consultations with the BIDC, BIBA, the international business community and the various sub-committees have yielded some useful results and are expected to provide a road map for better positioning the industry. It is also important for there to be continued dialogue and consultation by international authorities with small states like Barbados, particularly in the initial stages of strategy formulation. This, coupled with ongoing technical assistance with the implementation of new initiatives, would ensure the continued growth and viability of the international financial services sector and would enhance the sector's contribution to the overall growth of the domestic economy.

6

Development of the IFS Industry in Mauritius

6.1 Inception and early regulation of the IFS Industry in Mauritius

The intellectual origins of the international financial services (IFS) industry in Mauritius are perhaps traceable to 1972 when the Export Processing Zone (EPZ) was established with tax concessions and exemptions, an export orientation and prohibitions on domestic market access. The creation of the Offshore Financial Centre (OFC) 20 years later, applied the same ideas to financial services. Although it materialised in 1992, studies on establishing an OFC were carried out by the Bank of Mauritius (BoM) at the request of the Prime Minister's Office (PMO) a decade earlier. However, the idea went into limbo during the mid-1980s; perhaps because of the debt crisis engulfing the developing world at the time, and the salutary experience of the Seychelles with its OFC. The OFC came up again for public discussion in 1988/89 when the findings of a study commissioned from an international firm became available and, concomitantly, the domestic financial sector was overhauled under a reform programme.

The first offshore banking and management company licence was granted in 1990, and operated under a specially tailored tax regime. However, that experiment performed below expectations triggering a review that led to the establishment of the Mauritius Offshore Business Activities Authority (MOBAA), the predecessor of the present regulatory authority – the Financial Services Commission (FSC) – for the IFS regime. The motives and objectives for establishing the OFC under MOBAA were the same as for the EPZ, that is: (a) economic diversification; (b) inward transfer of know-how; (c) expansion of services exports beyond tourism; (d) high-value employment creation; and (e) smoothing the path for the eventual integration of Mauritius into the global financial system and economy. In setting up the offshore regime, particular attention was paid to protecting the domestic economy with a clear line being drawn between domestic and offshore activities – though such demarcation later proved to be partly illusory.

OFC operations were favoured with a more flexible operational and legal environment. They also had tax advantages that the authorities were anxious to prevent from spilling into the domestic economy, in order to preserve the integrity of public finances and prevent them from deteriorating. Offshore finance was defined as an activity carried out within Mauritius, but transacted with non-residents in non-Mauritian currency. In addition, an offshore entity registered in Mauritius could not 'deal or transact' with a Mauritian resident. In stipulating these conditions, the authorities were concerned about the possibilities of leakage and other risks under a regime of exchange-control. They created an elaborate regulatory edifice within the Bank of Mauritius to ensure that the line between domestic and offshore business was not crossed.

During the 1990s, offshore business 'management companies' (MCs) were issued with a certificate of incorporation by the Registrar of Companies on the filing of the usual company registration documents. However, MOBAA was their regulator and licensor, issuing certificates authorising offshore operations only after scrutinising the qualifications of applicants. This two-step incorporation and authorisation process, which took time, was a bureaucratic irritant; it made Mauritius uncompetitive with other OFCs that were able to issue administrative approvals for entities to begin operating within 24 hours. This overlapping institutional and legal framework was thought necessary to prevent abuses of the OFC by **money launderers** and **arms-dealers** to which the statute made specific reference.

The bureaucratic approach to licensing and regulation of the IFS industry in Mauritius has been challenged by MCs since its inception in 1992. There has been continuing tension between the regulator and the industry to achieve a better balance between: (a) the need for sound supervision to ensure the integrity of the IFS industry and prevent the line between domestic and offshore operations from being crossed; and (b) for operational flexibility and user-friendliness. That tension has been heightened with the establishment of the FSC ten years later, with the ensuing avalanche of additional regulatory demands making the argument about more balanced and appropriate regulation as current and relevant as ever.

The creation of an IFS industry did not result in immediate demand for IFS in Mauritius from the global community. Mauritian firms did not have any domestic experience or capability in offering IFS to clientele from anywhere. The country opted to have its IFS industry develop indigenously and organically, rather than opening up to experienced exponents from abroad. In fairness, better known foreign corporate/bank providers of IFS had already established themselves in European 'offshore' jurisdictions (viz. Switzerland, Luxembourg, Liechtenstein and Monaco) and in Bermuda and the Caribbean (the Bahamas, the Cayman Islands etc.) to service their EU/US clientele. In Asia, OFCs like Singapore and Hong Kong had emerged rapidly to service clients from Japan and the Association of Southeast Asian Nations (ASEAN). At the time, South Africa was still a closed economy under apartheid with sanctions imposed on it. Established global providers of IFS were therefore uninterested in offering IFS out of Mauritius. There was no critical mass of clients from another geography that the country could tap.

Reciprocally, typical Organisation of Economic Co-operation and Development (OECD) clients for IFS would not come to Mauritius unless established firms were operating out of there. Extant offshore banks, even foreign bank branches, did not attract business, except for intra-bank, cross-border transactions aimed at achieving tax-efficiency. For a nascent OFC it was a Catch-22 situation. In other jurisdictions the local legal establishment had been at the forefront of offshore business development; but in Mauritius, legal practitioners kept aloof. They had neither the experience nor the interest in offering IFS; their client base was primarily domestic. It was mainly local and foreign accounting firms, networked internationally and with access to global contacts and clients, who nurtured the incipient IFS industry at the outset. They were ready when Mauritius' OFC was catalysed by the signing of the Mauritius treaty with India on the avoidance of double taxation in 1992. That treaty provided the main gateway for offshore investments into India and placed Mauritius on the global map as a legitimate OFC.

6.2 Development of the Mauritian IFS industry during 1992–98

During the period 1992–98, Mauritius was among the fastest growing OFCs in the developing world, building up its reputation as a treaty jurisdiction for channelling investments from clients in India, China and South Africa to the rest of the world. Despite tailored incentive regimes being created for attracting specialised offshore activities, such as ship registration and management, aircraft leasing and other similar industry-specific, cross-border financial arrangements, Mauritius was unsuccessful in attracting a share of these global activities away from established centres like Liberia (for ship registration). The most important attraction of Mauritius became its double taxation treaties with third countries. Administering (rather than actively portfolio managing) global investment funds benefiting from tax reductions/exemptions under these treaty arrangements became the mainstay of the Mauritian IFS industry. As a result of a requirement that investment funds in Mauritius had to have a local admin-istrator and a cash custodian, some local expertise developed within Mauritian firms for investment funds administration.

Such funds focused mainly on investment in listed and exchange-traded securities of neighbouring emerging markets and developed markets. However, the offshore finan-cial services offered by Mauritian MCs also involved direct investment through special purpose vehicles (SPVs) and joint ventures by Indian and ASEAN clients in China, South Africa and Indonesia.

Apart from these services, aimed at the corporate market for IFS, Mauritius has at-tracted a small share of the Indian market for private wealth management undertaken by portfolio managers on behalf of high net-worth individuals (HNWIs), but with the proceeds parked in Mauritius and administered by MCs. In many other Common-wealth OFCs, tax-exempt trusts have been the favoured vehicles for managing private wealth. However, in Mauritius the trust industry did not take off because it had no history of trust law application. For that reason, there was an absence of lawyers trained in trust law and local accounting firms had no experience in that arena either.

At the same time, there was no world-class global fund or asset manager located in Mauritius with real-time access to global market information and direct trading ability on the world's principal securities markets. But many HNWIs (mainly from India) were content to hold their portfolio investments in equities and bonds held by passive investment companies that benefited from advantageous tax treatment. This explains the rapid growth of licensed offshore companies from 2,000 in 1992 when the industry was set up, to 8,000 in 1998. Of these, the overwhelming majority were tax exempt and not reliant on treaty provisions. At the time of writing there were over 26,000 such global business licensees, although not all of them are completely tax exempt.

Though tax treaties were the foundations supporting the IFS industry in Mauritius, local MCs had to compete with other OFCs as well as financial centres in home jurisdictions for business generated by such treaties. That competition led them to expand their knowledge-base by recruiting from abroad, sending their staff for training/ secondment to foreign firms and investing in continuing programmes of on-the-job training and professional development of their human resources.

Better, more tax-efficient use of tax treaties was also made in designing outward Mauritian foreign direct investment in Africa and the Indian Ocean, e.g. in Madagascar and Mozambique. Financial engineering and structuring by Mauritian MCs and banks has become more sophisticated, as IFS knowledge has spilled over to the local capital market. Local investment fund products have become more effective and asset management techniques have improved considerably. The rules of the Stock Exchange of Mauritius (SEM) have been revised to encourage offshore fund listing. SEM is working towards adopting new London Stock Exchange listing rules.

Offshore vs. domestic financial market demarcation

The strict demarcation between onshore and offshore jurisdictions has been stretched regularly since 1998, as more Mauritian companies and professionals began to demand the same tax benefits as those granted to non-residents. The IFS industry has been pressing the government to migrate from a dual (offshore-onshore) tax regime towards a single, low-tax regime and to relax supervisory rules to enable the industry to conquer new markets, sharpen its global profile and increase its global market share. The argument for a single tax regime has the added attraction of averting the kind of opprobrium and over-intrusive attention from OECD (on exchange of tax information and harmful tax practices) that a dual tax regime inevitably attracts. Dual regimes often seem to home countries (especially in the high-tax environments of OECD countries) to be designed to exploit inter-jurisdictional tax arbitrage opportunities created artificially at their expense.

More relaxed regulation would theoretically attract a greater number of company incorporations. Rules requiring more substantive value-addition and employment in Mauritius, along with closer regulatory oversight, were traditionally thought to be indispensable in strengthening the capability of domestic firms. However, these rules are now viewed with suspicion under the World Trade Organization (WTO) regime for global trade in financial services and are seen to be unacceptably protectionist in nature. Such rules are also seen by potential foreign investors in the financial services industry to be an antediluvian deterrent restricting operational choice and flexibility.

Types of offshore entities/licensees

There are two forms of company incorporation in the Mauritian offshore sector:

- **Offshore companies** with regular company law features, qualifying for tax-treaty access but being subject to domestic tax. Mauritian residents investing abroad are allowed to set up or to hold a shareholding interest in such companies; and

- **International companies** that are exempt from taxation and are more flexible and relaxed than mainstream companies.

Trust settlements are open to foreign nationals when they have no Mauritian resident beneficiaries and no assets in Mauritius. **Partnerships** are rarely used. Special legislation for **protected cell companies** has been adopted to house 'fund-of-funds' structures, multi-class funds and the captive **insurance** business. Mauritius has not attracted much offshore insurance or reinsurance business, except for some from South Africa. To accommodate the needs of a wide variety of global clientele, tax rules now provide for myriad tax structuring possibilities. A voluntary option is available that allows offshore companies to choose a rate of tax along a scale from 0 per cent to 35 per cent.

One of the hallmarks of the Mauritian IFS industry was total protection of confidentiality, safe-guarded by legislation that prevented information relating to offshore clients from being disclosed, except by court order on specified grounds of suspected money laundering and arms-dealing. However, that legislation did not bar domestic regulators from conducting investigations and exchanging information with their foreign counterparts. Nor did it prevent foreign authorities from obtaining rogatory commissions or other forms of permission for disclosure of information on local MCs and offshore or international companies.

The Mauritian IFS industry is now well established. However, Mauritius has not yet attracted well-known foreign firms in the global investment or advisory business. Nor has it attracted well-known international law firms with global corporate and HNWI advisory practices. IFS space has been left uncontested to local MCs with comparatively limited global experience and few international connections, especially as far as OECD clientele are concerned. This may be because the Mauritian authorities have, until 2006, been inherently protectionist in practice. They have raised a number of invisible barriers, such as being excessively bureaucratic in granting operating licenses, and not granting resident visas to managers and staff of foreign firms quickly and easily. The general complaint of foreign firms seeking to locate in Mauritius is that the jurisdiction is far more protectionist in practice than it is in theory and much more so than its legislation suggests. For that reason, despite its rapid growth during 1992–98, the Mauritius IFS industry continues to suffer from: (a) geographic concentration risk in its dependency on clients from India, Indonesia, Greater China and Africa; and (b) excessive functional risk in being dependent on a limited range of products and services.

6.3 Post-1998 developments affecting the Mauritian IFS industry and its regulation

Growth of the IFS industry in Mauritius stalled when the OECD released its report on *Harmful Tax Competition* in April 1998. That report passed part of the burden of solving a problem created by OECD countries themselves onto OFCs. Since then, OFCs like Mauritius have been under constant pressure from the Financial Action Task Force (FATF), the OECD, international financial institutions (IFIs), and the G7's Financial Stability Forum (FSF) to improve the transparency and accountability of their operations. The accompanying threat of blacklisting, and applying sanctions to, jurisdictions deemed non-compliant with OECD demands, has stretched the limits of international relations. Institutions and countries with asymmetric power have browbeaten, quite unreasonably, many small jurisdictions without countervailing power into submission on questionable grounds.

Fear of being blacklisted, with an ensuing loss of credibility and reputation, has prompted a number of OFCs around the world into taking disproportionately drastic measures. OECD countries seem particularly concerned about the proliferation of smaller OFCs offering services based on confidentiality (perhaps, in part, because of the competition offered to their own financial services industries in global financial centres such as London). OFCs have been automatically, and in most cases quite wrongly, equated with the facilitation of money-laundering and providing a safe-haven for illicit tax-evading capital flows. It is interesting to note that upon release of the *Harmful Tax Competition* report, Luxembourg and Switzerland, two OECD members, objected to the bank secrecy and confidentiality provisions contained therein. After all, their financial services industries had been based on providing those two rights. However, these countries were not included in the 'tax haven' list, while non-OECD jurisdictions were faced with that stigma.

Harmful tax competition

The OECD report on *Harmful Tax Competition* was published with the aim of countering tax practices deemed harmful to the interests of high-tax OECD economies. The report took a prejudiced view of tax competition and set out criteria for identifying tax havens. These included, inter alia, a nil or nominal tax regime, legalisation of entities with no substantial business activity, lack of transparency and no or little provision for exchange of tax information.

In May 2000, the Mauritian government made a set of commitments to eliminate tax practices deemed harmful by the OECD Fiscal Committee. It committed to a programme of tax information exchange, transparency, the elimination of provisions aimed at attracting offshore businesses with no substantial domestic activities and to phasing out any practice deemed harmful by end-2005. In parallel, changes were made to remove the ring-fencing of the offshore sector. From 1998 onwards, offshore companies were deemed 'incentive companies' taxed at a flat rate of 15 per cent. By applying reciprocal foreign tax credit rules, however, this effective rate of tax could be brought down to 3 per cent. The final list of 'tax havens' published by the OECD on 26 June 2000 contained 35 jurisdictions. Mauritius was removed from the list for having committed to eliminating harmful tax practices. The OECD has since monitored Mauritius' compliance with commitments and conducted surveys to check adherence with its principles of international taxation. Mauritius was given 'participating partner' status at the Global Tax Forum after its commitment to the OECD process in 2000.

The Financial Stability Forum (FSF) report on OFCs

The report of the FSF Working Group on Offshore Centres (2000)[1] contained a list of OFCs categorised in accordance with G7 perceptions of each in terms of their quality of regulation/supervision, degree of co-operation with other jurisdictions and compliance with international standards. Category I included jurisdictions perceived as having supervision of a high quality. Category II included OFCs with procedures for good supervision in place, but weak implementation. Category III jurisdictions were defined as having supervision of a low quality, with little or no attempt to meet international norms. The classification of Mauritius in the third category led to an official protest by the government. Desperate steps were taken to meet the highest international standards at considerable financial and political cost. In particular, FSF was criticised because it had not given Mauritius an opportunity to make any representations on the findings of its Working Group on OFCs. The Mauritius government made forceful attempts to be removed from the third category without success, in spite of a favourable FSAP assessment on its banking and anti-money laundering regulation.

The FATF NCCT list

To avoid being blacklisted by the FATF, Mauritius pushed through a series of measures, tightened disclosure requirements of offshore companies and reduced its protection of confidentiality. The February 2000 FATF report on *Non Co-operative Countries or Territories* established procedures and criteria for identifying jurisdictions that failed to co-operate in implementing effective anti-money laundering (AML) regimes. To compel compliance, FATF compiled a list of non-co-operative countries or territories (the infamous NCCT list) that failed to meet its criteria for 'co-operation'. When Mauritius enacted its Economic Crime and Anti-Money Laundering (ECAML) Act of 2000, the FATF excluded Mauritius from the NCCT list. The ECAML Act (forerunner to the Financial Intelligence and Anti-Money Laundering Act of 2002) consolidated existing legislation on AML measures, although certain concerns regarding the identity of directors and beneficial owners of offshore trusts were raised.

By 2002, reacting to pressure from international bodies, Mauritius breached the legitimate long-term expectations of its IFS industry and offshore clientele by reneging on earlier promises and drastically curtailing tax privileges provided to registered offshore entities. It whittled down confidentiality protection, increased regulatory scrutiny and imposed substantially heightened, extremely costly, compliance requirements over the

IFS and domestic financial services industries. Government policy was to: (a) avoid confrontation with IFIs, FATF and the OECD on offshore financial centre issues; (b) make externally mandated changes at any cost, short of closing down the IFS industry altogether; and (c) implement the international standards and core principles set out in the modules of the IMF/FSF Compendium, regardless of whether they were contextually appropriate to Mauritius. That policy begs the question as to whether government made the correct trade-off in accommodating the extraordinary and inappropriate demands of international agencies, while risking the IFS industry's business competitiveness. The conclusions of this study provide an answer to that question.

Major regulatory developments occurred after the report of the Steering Committee on Financial Services Sector Reform in Mauritius (February 2001)[2]. That report recommended: (a) regulatory and industry consolidation and integration of the financial services sector; (b) establishment of the Financial Services Commission (FSC) as a unified regulator for all non-bank financial institutions (NBFIs) and for licensing global business entities (formerly known as **offshore** entities); and (c) adopting a functional, rather than product-based, approach to regulation. The FSC was supposed to be the first stepping stone towards having a single regulator for all financial services and was intended to bring about eventual integration of offshore and domestic financial services.

Previously, the regulation/supervision of financial services and institutions was fragmented, with responsibility being spread across different institutions. In addition to its responsibility for the conduct of monetary policy, the Bank of Mauritius (BoM) had responsibility for the supervision of banks. Insurance companies and brokers were regulated and supervised by the Controller of Insurance, located in the Ministry of Finance. The stock exchange and securities market were regulated by the Stock Exchange Commission (SEC), while the burgeoning offshore sector was regulated by the Mauritius Offshore Business Activities Authority (MOBAA).

Owing to this fragmented approach to regulation, some key financial service providers escaped regulatory oversight by falling between the cracks. Effectively unregulated entities included, inter alia, leasing companies, commercial credit institutions, pension funds, asset management companies and investment advisory services. Moreover, the legislative foundations for regulation and supervision were rarely updated in a timely manner. In many areas, current law inhibited supervisory authorities from taking timely action to prevent financial entities from becoming illiquid, insolvent or engaging in malpractices. The industry impression was that supervisory authorities were vulnerable to inappropriate political pressure exerted to prevent them from taking necessary actions, in order to protect privileged private interests. Because regulation was product-based and sector-based, the patchwork regulatory framework supporting it was ill-equipped to deal with rapid changes sweeping through the financial services industry worldwide. Growing linkages between banking, insurance and securities activities, coming together under the umbrella of large, complex financial holding companies on the one hand, and the proliferation of hybrid financial products and derivates on the other, posed a serious challenge to a fragmented group of regulators, especially against the backdrop of ongoing globalisation and the development of e-commerce.

Under evolving circumstances, the Steering Committee found that segregation between domestic and offshore business activities was no longer sustainable. The division created too much opportunity for arbitrage and led to misperceptions at the international level of how the system operated in Mauritius. The artificial division continued to be challenged by the OECD, FATF and the IFIs. More importantly, the Committee viewed such segregation as a handicap to the future development of the financial services industry in Mauritius. Its recommendation was to abolish the country's OFC and repeal the International Companies Act. That was intended not as a condemnation of the prevailing offshore regime, which had been quite successful until 1998, but as suggestive of the approach that needed to be taken to respond to changing global circumstances triggered by the OECD's 1998 broadside and subsequent developments.

It was thought that the establishment of a unified regulator for financial services, applying the highest international standards, would go some way toward alleviating external perceptions about regulatory gaps and shortcomings in Mauritius. A two-phase process was envisaged. The first was the establishment of the Financial Services Commission (FSC) as a single regulator for all non-bank financial institutions. It subsumed the SEC, MOBAA and the Insurance Division of the Ministry of Finance under a single regulatory umbrella. The creation of the FSC was also intended to facilitate smooth integration of the onshore and offshore regimes. The promotional functions of MOBAA were devolved to a Financial Services Promotion Agency. The second phase involved the FSC merging with the regulatory part of the BoM, to form a single regulator for all financial services. With the FSC being established in 2001, the first phase was completed. However, the second phase appears to have been dropped from official consciousness.

Since 2001, there has been a veritable tsunami of legislative changes governing financial services in Mauritius. Major subsequent enactments include: (a) The Companies Act of 2001; (b) The Financial Services Development (FSD) Act of 2001; and (c) The Trusts Act of 2001. The Insurance Act of 1987 and the Stock Exchange Act of 1988 were maintained until 2005 and administered by the FSC. This arrangement was kept in place until the enactment of further special legislation to consolidate the regulatory framework and harmonise the regulatory approach[3].

The new Companies Act eliminates ring fencing between the offshore and domestic sector by providing for incorporating both domestic and offshore companies under a single piece of legislation, with the incorporation process being streamlined. The Companies Act of 2001 repealed the International Companies Act of 1995, while the FSD Act repealed the Mauritius Offshore Business Activities Act of 1992, which had provided the legal regime for offshore companies.

In accord with a global proclivity for indulging in palliative euphemisms, the FSD Act introduced the term 'global business' and expunged the term 'offshore' from the statute books. The Trusts Act of 2001 repealed the Trust Act of 1989 and the Offshore Trust Act of 1992. It added to the *Code Civil Mauricien* in order to integrate the fiduciary concept into domestic law. Broadly speaking, the Trusts Act of 2001 extended features previously available to offshore trusts to all trusts created under the Act, with certain limitations on trusts set up by a Mauritian resident.

The distinction between domestic and offshore banks was removed under the Banking Act of 2004 and replaced by a two-tier licensing regime. Class A licences authorised banks to conduct domestic banking and open branches in Mauritius. Class B licences authorised banks to transact with non-residents and deal in currencies other than Mauritian currency[4]. This was the first step towards fuller integration, to be achieved through a single licence for domestic banking and for dealing with non-residents and global businesses. The distinction between the lines of business is, however, relevant for the purposes of tax treatment of income generated under either head.

The supervisory regime for global business has changed from 'registration' to 'licensing' with the name-change supposedly heralding closer monitoring of permitted activities in that area. Two kinds of global business companies (GBCs) are provided for; viz. Category 1 (GBC-1) and Category 2 (GBC-2) both drawing on the Companies Act of 2001. A GBC-1 license is issued to a corporation that carries on prescribed activities within Mauritius. It can transact with non-residents in currencies other than Mauritian currency and is subject to Mauritian corporation tax. As a resident of Mauritius, it can avail of the benefits of tax treaties entered into by Mauritius with other countries. GBC-1 licensees are subject to annual reporting requirements under the FSD Act. A GBC-2 license is issued to a private company that conducts approved global business only with non-residents and only in currencies other than Mauritian currency. A GBC-2 licensee is non-resident and tax exempt. Therefore, a GBC-2 company cannot avail of the benefits of the tax treaties entered into by Mauritius. GBC-2s are not subject to reporting obligations.

The enactment of the FSD Act was to be the first stepping stone towards meeting international standards and aims at improved supervision of the sector as a whole. The Act was to be a building block for eventually embracing other specialised pieces of legislation covering various financial services. In 2005, the Insurance Act and the Securities Act were passed by Parliament with a view to modernising the approach to regulation in both sectors respectively and to adopting international best practices and standards of regulation. Both these statutes provide for domestic and global business in their respective sectors under the same unified legislation. At the time of writing, the FSD Act was in the process of being revamped and amended to: provide for more comprehensive enforcement powers of the FSC; establish a right of appeal against its decisions and the imposition of penalties; and require greater transparency on the part of the regulator in explaining its decisions. At the time of writing, the relevant pieces of legislation had not yet come into force.

Financial Sector Assessment Program

In 2002–2003, a joint IMF-World Bank mission reported – in the context of the Financial Sector Assessment Program on the Observance of Standards and Codes for the FATF 40 Recommendations and 8 Special Recommendations on Terrorist Financing – that Mauritius had made significant progress in implementing a comprehensive AML/CFT regime. The mission took account of the efforts of the Mauritian Government to enhance the AML/CFT legal and enforcement framework by introducing major new legislation, including the Dangerous Drugs Act of 2000, the Financial Services Development Act of 2001, the Prevention of Corruption Act of 2002, the Prevention of Terrorism Act of 2002 and the Financial Intelligence and Anti-Money Laundering Act of 2002. The mission found that enactment of these laws represented key advances in bringing Mauritius toward full compliance with international standards, although it identified a few areas where further effort needed to be made. Accordingly, it recommended: (i) modifying confidentiality provisions that hampered information-sharing on suspected money laundering cases between supervisory authorities and the Financial Intelligence Unit (FIU); (ii) expanding the scope and focus of AML/CFT reviews during onsite inspection of financial institutions in line with the guidelines issued by the supervisory authorities; and (iii) better co-ordination of law enforcement efforts. The mission also recommended that financial institutions should: strengthen internal AML/CFT programmes by developing adequate internal policy/procedure frameworks to reflect guidelines issued by the supervisory bodies; increase compliance testing; and ensure that front line and compliance staff receive adequate training. These recommendations were implemented immediately with supervisory bodies over-emphasising AML/CFT in monitoring their licensed population.

Notes

1. Financial Stability Forum (2000).
2. Government of Mauritius/Ministry of Finance & Economic Development (2001).
3. The Securities and Insurance Acts were enacted in 2005. Legislation on Pension Funds and Trust & Corporate Service Providers were in the pipeline at the time of writing.
4. The Class A and Class B terminology was subsequently replaced by the Category 1 and Category 2 Banking License by the Finance Act 2002, without there being any substantive change in the regime.

7

Importance of the IFS industry in the Mauritian Economy

....

7.1 Introduction

In 2005 Mauritius' Gross National Product (GNP) was estimated at just over US$6.25 billion, with per capita income approaching US$5,300. As table 7.1 shows, its economy is primarily services-based, with government services, distribution, transport, health and education accounting together for the largest proportion. Tourism and financial services exports are significant, but appear to be reaching their potential growth limits requiring Mauritius to move further up the scale of sophisticated value-addition and geographic client (as well as product/service) diversification.

After 38 years of independence, Mauritius has progressively diversified its output and exports away from an overwhelming dependence on sugar. It faced a major economic crisis in 1979–81 when, faced with rapidly rising energy costs and falling sugar prices, its mono-commodity economy came close to collapse. That led to the Government of Mauritius undertaking a major economic adjustment and reform programme aimed at economic and export diversification. However, that period of liberalisation was partial

Table 7.1 Mauritius Economic Data (Source: *World Bank Development Indicators, 2006*)

	2000	2003	2004
GNI, Atlas method (current US$)	4.4 bn	5.0 bn	5.7 bn
GNI per capita, Atlas method (current US$)	3,690.0	4,100.0	4,640.0
GDP (current US$)	4.4 bn	5.2 bn	6.0 bn
GDP growth (annual %)	4.0	3.1	4.2
Inflation, GDP deflator (annual %)	4.7	6.1	6.0
Agriculture, value added (% of GDP)	5.9	6.1	6.1
Industry, value added (% of GDP)	31.6	30.5	29.7
Services, etc., value added (% of GDP)	62.5	63.4	64.3
Exports of goods and services (% of GDP)	63.3	59.1	55.6
Imports of goods and services (% of GDP)	65.3	57.0	56.2
Gross capital formation (% of GDP)	26.1	22.8	23.9
Revenue, excluding grants (% of GDP)	22.2	21.7	21.8
Cash surplus/deficit (% of GDP)	-1.1	-3.4	-3.2

and asymmetric, focused as it was on freeing restraints and prices influencing the export sector while keeping the domestic economy relatively closed. In the mid-1970s/ 1980s, Mauritius diversified into garment exports with its export processing zone (EPZ). That was followed by the rapid development of high-value tourism in the 1980s, and financial service exports in the 1990s with the country's offshore financial centre and the development of its IFS industry.

Through successful economic diversification and expansion, Mauritius enjoyed an average growth through the 1990s of around 6 per cent, an unemployment rate of 2–3 per cent and low inflation of 4–6 per cent, with a stable currency. However, since 2000 there has been relentless deterioration in the economy with the growth rate falling to below 4 per cent, the unemployment rate rising to over 10 per cent and inflation climbing to levels of 7–8 per cent, exerting some pressure on the Mauritian rupee. In 2005 Mauritius again faces a situation of stagnation, along with a rapid rise in energy costs reminiscent of the impasse it had arrived at in 1979–81. Falling growth, rising unemployment, rising energy prices, loss of guaranteed price support and EU market protection for sugar and garments, and slowing export income, have all resulted in the fiscal deficit expanding. To avoid political and social dislocations, levels of public consumption and social safety-net support have been maintained only by rapid increases in domestic and external borrowing.

The deteriorating trends affecting the economy are leading to concerns about the future as the country's sugar industry faces phase-out (unless Mauritius invests in ethanol production to become less vulnerable to external energy prices) and its traditional manufacturing industries become uncompetitive due to high labour and transport costs. There is a finite rate at which the Mauritian tourism sector can continue to expand without significantly increasing risks to the island's fragile ecology, although opportunities for attracting long-term 'retirement tourism' are now being explored. Increasingly, Mauritius' future is seen to lie in further exploitation of its marine resources, further expansion and diversification of its IFS industry, as well as exploitation of new service opportunities in the information and communications technology (ICT) space with emphasis on business process outsourcing (BPO) and knowledge process outsourcing (KPO) as well as developing its healthcare and education service exports.

The country now faces a serious strategic challenge. Another round of economic reforms are required urgently to: arrest and reverse the fiscal drain; improve labour and factor productivity; and address the politically sensitive social issues of growing relative poverty and an ageing population, with substantial emigration of qualified professionals. Mauritius needs to overcome continued overt and covert protectionism of its domestic business space, open up its economy symmetrically, attract higher rates of foreign direct investment (FDI), and re-instil a sense of confidence to stop the haemorrhaging of its human capital base to a point of irretrievability. The new government elected in 2005 is attempting to frame an appropriate policy mix for consolidating public finances by trimming back an unaffordable welfare state, creating an enabling environment, opening up the economy, diversifying into other service areas and enhancing export competitiveness, while creating a wide political consensus among stakeholders on the need for reforms to enhance Mauritius's competitiveness in a global economy without relying on externally guaranteed price supports and protected market access.

7.2 The financial services sector

Table 7.2, below, provides summary data gleaned from domestic data sources on value-added.

In the 1990s, financial services (comprising banking, insurance, capital markets, global business and other financial services) grew at an annual average rate of over 8 per cent. In gross value-added, the sector contributed over 13 per cent to GDP in 2000 with the contribution of the IFS industry estimated at about 2 per cent of GDP. However, as with growth in general, growth in financial services has fallen throughout the current decade, with the sector's contribution to total GDP declining to under 10 per cent in 2005.

The demands of enhanced financial regulation and growing business sophistication have necessitated more manpower. The financial services sector has generated more employment while average monthly earnings have increased. Banking and insurance have created the largest number of jobs. However, there was also across the board growth in financial services employment from 2002–05, reflecting an increasing cost base, while the relative value-addition of the sector to the economy has declined and overall employment has increased. The employment trend and regulatory developments may also suggest declining labour productivity in the financial services sector.

Table 7.2 Value-added in financial services

Amounts in US$ million	2002	2003	2004	2005	Total 2002-05
Macro-indicators: GNI at market prices	4,910	5,415	5,723	6,038	
Financial intermediation services: Gross Value-Added	411	469	555	605	2,040
Net Value-Added (NVA)	173	206	255	308	942
IFS industry: Gross Value-Added	45	56	71	85	257
Net Value-Added	28	33	39	43	143
Banking industry: NVA in domestic banks	104	124	163	204	595
NVA in offshore banks	21	25	30	33	109
Other financial services: Net Value-Added	20	24	23	28	95

Source: FSC and BoM Annual Reports for 2002-04 and National Accounts (estimates) for 2005.

Source: Annual National Economics Data[1].

Table 7.3 Financial intermediation: employment and earnings

	2002	2003	2004	2005(E)
Total employment in financial services *	7,347	7,494	8,401	8,856
Average earnings (MRs) *		17,734	20,225	21,478
Category 1 banks (domestic) **	4,353	4,586	4,697	5,371
Category 2 banks (international)**	512	562	588	643
Global business industry ***	510	600	785	950

Sources: *Central Statistical Office (CSO); ** Bank of Mauritius; *** Estimates based on FSC Sample Surveys.

One indicator of IFS growth is the rate of global business company (GBC) registrations. Other indicators are growth in the assets/liabilities base of international banks and of global business companies. At the end of December 2005, total assets of banks (both domestic and international) rose to US$14.7 billion, while total deposits were US$10.1 billion. The number of offshore banks grew from seven in 1996 to 14 in 2002, but diminished sharply to nine in 2005 although their aggregate asset base continued to grow (see table 7.4).

The IFS industry's (GBC licensees and management companies [MCs]) contribution to direct tax is becoming increasingly significant, as shown below. Growth in the IFS industry's contribution to public tax receipts is striking when its contribution to GDP is diminishing. The tax element may also be adding to the diminishing competitiveness of the IFS industry in Mauritius vis-à-vis other international financial centres.

Table 7.4 Number and assets of international banks

	1996	1998	2002	2005
No. of offshore banks*	7	9	14	9
Aggregate asset base: US$ million	847	1,022	4,320	7,886

* including banks conducting international banking under 2004 single licensing regime.
Source: Bank of Mauritius.

Table 7.5 Contribution to direct tax receipts

	Amount in MRs million	GBCs vs. MCs % contribution	As % of corporate tax
2003	150	75%	7%
2004	500	80%	20%
2005	700	80%	21%

Source: Ministry of Finance, Government of Mauritius.

Indicators for the IFS Industry (excluding Category 2 banks)

The non-bank part of the IFS industry in Mauritius comprises principally the MCs and their GBC clients. Whereas the number of international banks operating in Mauritius dropped from 2002 to 2005, the number of MCs has increased marginally, although the annual growth of GBC licenses issued decreased noticeably from 2002 to 2004. The average annual growth rate in GBC-1 licensees was a high 59 per cent from 1996 to 2002, but slowed down to 20 per cent between 2002 and 2005. That slowdown was more pronounced with GBC-2 licensees. These grew at an average annual rate of 173 per cent from 1998 to 2002, but at a much reduced 42 per cent between 2002 and 2005.

Likewise, the average annual rate of growth decreased substantially for global investment funds, although their asset base as at 31 December 2005 showed a staggering increase of above 400 per cent owing largely to the revaluation of their portfolios.

Passive investment holding companies predominate in the global business sector. In 2002, they accounted for 57 per cent (increasing to 66 per cent in 2004) of the activities of GBC-1 licensees and 37 per cent of those of GBC-2. Investments through Mauritius are now driven to the Indian stock market because of the favourable tax treaty between the two countries. Investments in Indian stocks through Mauritian GBCs increased from 19 per cent in June 2003 to 54 per cent in December 2004. Apart from India, other countries benefiting from the influx of funds were Indonesia, China, Hong Kong and Singapore.

Table 7.6 Average growth rate of global business company (GBC) incorporations

	1996	1998	2002	Growth	2005	Growth
Offshore companies: **GBC-1**	2,652	4,202	6,726	59%	8,068	20%
International companies: **GBC-2**	1,898	4,307	13,670	173%	19,348	42%

Source: Financial Services Commission Statistics.

Table 7.7 Global investment funds

	1996	1998	2002	2005
Global funds	92	148	256	359
Aggregate asset base (US$ billion)	3.20	4.40	6.30	26.75

Source: Financial Services Commission Statistics.

Notes

1. The data in the national account series are not consistent from year to year when translated from MRs (Mauritian rupees) into US$. The translation from gross to net value added is unclear. So the figures provided above should be regarded as best estimates.

8

Regulation and Supervision of the IFS Industry in Mauritius

8.1 The pre-2001 regulatory framework

Introduction

As indicated earlier, prior to 2001 regulation of financial services was fragmented in Mauritius. Regulatory/supervisory responsibilities were shared by the Bank of Mauritius (BoM; for banks) and the Ministry of Finance (MoF), which had a dedicated department for the supervision of insurance services. In 1988, the Securities and Exchange Commission of Mauritius was set up to regulate the stock exchange and the securities industry, including authorised mutual funds and unit trusts. Offshore finance came under the purview of MOBAA, established in 1992. The idea of a single regulator for financial services was mooted in the 1994/5 Budget Speech and was studied by the Financial Services Reform Steering Committee in 1996. The idea was implemented partially in 2001, but went no further.

In 2001, as a response to the several pressures exerted by a variety of international agencies, the decision was taken to move toward dividing regulatory responsibility between two main pillars: i.e. the BoM for banks and a single regulator – the Financial Services Commission (FSC) – for all non-bank financial institutions. Alongside, new organisations were created with specific ancillary functions: viz. the Financial Reporting Council set up in 2005 and the Financial Intelligence Unit established in 2002 under the Financial Intelligence and Anti-Money Laundering Act. This section discusses the responsibilities of these institutions prior to 2001, before the new AML/CFT regulatory regime came into force.

The Bank of Mauritius (BoM)

Pre-2001, the Bank of Mauritius adhered to customer due diligence and confidentiality protection standards established under the 1988 Basel Concordat issued by the Basel Committee on Banking Supervision (BCBS). Since its establishment, the BoM has been the sole licensing, regulatory and supervisory authority for the banking sector, including offshore banking since its introduction in Mauritius in 1989. In addition, the BoM regulates foreign exchange dealers, money changers and non-bank deposit taking institutions.

Apart from being the banking regulator, the BoM is also the island's central bank. In that capacity it formulates and implements monetary and exchange rate policy. It is the government's banker and the banker of last resort for the domestic financial system. It issues currency and derives seigniorage. It maintains and monitors in real time a payment, settlement and clearing system between banks, and manages public debt and foreign currency reserves. It also advises the government on financial matters.

With the abolition of exchange controls in July 1994, and open market determination of exchange and interest rates, the Bank has moved from direct to indirect monetary control. Through transparent open market operations it buys/sells foreign currencies when there is a need to stabilise the exchange rate market and buys/sells instruments in money and treasury markets to achieve the desired level, term structure and yield curve for domestic interest rates at any given time. In doing so, it attempts to function in a predictable manner to avoid introducing risk premiums that reflect excessive market uncertainty about the future predictability of interest rates and exchange rates. The role of monetary management and the regulatory/supervisory role of the BoM are inextricably intertwined.

As far as the supervision of commercial banks is concerned, the Bank of Mauritius is required to: (a) maintain the stability and soundness of the financial system; (b) ensure that adequate and reasonable banking services are always available to the public; (c) impose a high standard of conduct and integrity in the management of the banking and credit systems; (d) ensure that banks maintain a solid financial structure in line with the minimum risk capital adequacy ratios prescribed by the Basel Committee; and (e) protect the interests of depositors and consumers of banking services. The BoM derives its regulatory authority and supervisory charter from the Banking Act of 1988, passed when the Basel-1 capital adequacy regime came into force. The 1988 Act replaced the Banking Act of 1971 with a view to strengthening and modernising the regulatory and supervisory system as well as to providing for the legal framework for the establishment and operations of offshore banks domiciled in Mauritius. The 1988 Act incorporated principles of prudential regulation and supervision of banks, namely: licensing, capital adequacy, good governance, liquidity control, risk diversification, onsite and offsite monitoring and due diligence.

The Insurance Division

Before 2001, a Controller of Insurance with the status of a public officer supervised the insurance industry. The Insurance Act of 1987 provided the legal framework for the registration of insurers and intermediaries and the prudential regulation of insurance companies. That statute allocated to the Minister of Finance the regulatory responsibility for insurance services, gave the office a number of decision-making powers, as well as appellate jurisdiction over the regulatory decisions of the Controller. Before the Financial Services Commission (FSC) was created in 2001, the Insurance Division was manned by a Controller and a staff of about six inspectors. Due to staffing problems, onsite inspections conducted during that time were limited in frequency and scope.

The Controller and his/her staff were recruited through the Public Service Commission (PSC) and the office was financed out of the Consolidated Fund. The insurance department was a member of the International Association of Insurance Supervisors (IAIS), but had too few resources and appeared to lack the motivation to ensure that the insurance core principles developed by the IAIS were applied properly in Mauritius.

The Securities and Exchange Commission (SEC)

Prior to 2002, no special rules existed in connection with customer due diligence or AML/CFT in the conduct of the securities business in Mauritius. The Securities and Exchange Commission (SEC) was set up in 1988 to regulate the stock exchange, the market's clearing and settlement facility (CDS), stockbrokers and approved investment institutions i.e. unit trusts, investment trusts and investment companies. SEC was a parastatal body financed partly from fees levied on stock exchange transactions and partly from the Consolidated Fund. It was managed by a board of directors and run by a chief executive. Recruitment of staff was carried out by the SEC independently subject to ministerial approval. It had no mandate in the fight against money laundering and did not undertake inspection visits to the exchange or to stockbrokers. Neither the SEC nor the exchange or market operators (e.g. stockbrokers) had any mandate to verify client information or exercise customer due diligence based on know your customer (KYC) principles.

The Mauritius Offshore Business Activities Authority (MOBAA)

The structure of the Mauritius Offshore Business Activities Authority (MOBAA) when it was set up incorporated a fundamental conflict of interest. Its mandate combined a promotional role with a regulatory function. MOBAA was set up to encourage the rapid expansion of, and at the same time regulate/supervise, the non-bank offshore sector with a predominately developmental perspective. In parallel, tax incentives were provided to add impetus to the growth of offshore finance. MOBAA had to establish a fine balance between the stringency of its regulation and its mission to develop offshore business as rapidly as possible. Consequently, MOBAA adopted a 'pragmatic' regulatory approach. It was managed by a board of governors appointed by the minister responsible for financial services. The Authority was administered by a Director appointed by the board and funded by licensing fees paid by registered companies. The MOBAA Act (passed at the same time as the Offshore Trusts Act) provided the legislative framework for overcoming problems constraining the growth of the offshore sector. It provided for the registration of offshore companies and offshore management companies after full investigation of applicant qualifications. The Offshore Trusts Act, on the other hand, required only that a declaration of trust be registered with the Authority. The MOBAA Act allowed for two types of corporate vehicles, i.e. ordinary and exempt offshore companies. The regime applicable to exempt companies was more flexible and provided greater confidentiality as these companies dealt with private or personal assets. However, ordinary companies were taxable entities and could therefore avail themselves of double tax treaty benefits.

The International Companies Act of 1994 was passed to revamp legal provisions relating to exempt offshore companies, previously treated in the same way as any company registered under the Companies Act of 1984. The new international company had attributes that gave it more flexibility as an offshore business vehicle. It allowed for maximum confidentiality with minimal filing and reporting requirements and bearer shares provision. However, the OECD's 1998 report on *Harmful Tax Competition* forced this accommodating supervisory framework to be restructured in order to bring more transparency, accountability and supervision to the activities of offshore and international companies. Departing from the stereotype provisions of International Business Companies (as in the British Virgin Islands), requirements to file the company's share register and register of members and directors were made mandatory. The requirement to file accounts and the power of MOBAA to site-inspect all offshore service providers was introduced in 2000. Bearer shares were prohibited and the Economic Crime and Money Laundering Act (ECAMLA) that was passed in 2000 made amendments to provide gateways for the full disclosure of confidential information in cases of enquiry into money laundering.

The new tax approach

Exemption from domestic tax was a *sine qua non* for the development of the offshore sector, along with a flexible framework for 'light-touch' regulation. In addition to exemptions from domestic tax, key provisions in double tax treaties were exploited fully and the treaty network was expanded to gain a competitive advantage in maximising the range of cross-border tax optimisation opportunities that could be offered. Initially in 1990, offshore companies had been taxed on a par with offshore banks, i.e. at flat rate of 5 per cent; this was until offshore companies were permitted in 1994 to elect a rate of tax between 0 per cent and 35 per cent. This regime endured till 1998, when offshore companies were to be treated for tax purposes as 'incentive companies' taxed at a flat rate of 15 per cent with a generous provision for foreign tax credit. The previous tax regime was grandfathered so that existing offshore companies in operation before 1 July 1998 could choose between the sliding scale of tax or move to the new regime. Repeal and reform of the tax exemptions previously offered to the offshore sector was undertaken by Mauritius in response to pressures from the international community, more specifically the OECD, which declared, as part of its avowed fight against harmful tax practices, some jurisdictions offering fiscal advantages and secrecy regimes to attract business to be 'tax havens'.

The Economic Crimes Office

The Economic Crime and Anti-Money Laundering Act (ECAMLA) was the precursor of the present Financial Intelligence and Anti-Money Laundering Act (FIAMLA). It criminalised money laundering and established the Economic Crimes Office (ECO) as an investigatory and enforcement agency. The main function of ECO was to investigate economic offences and suspicious transaction reports (STRs) involving money laundering. Additionally, ECO was responsible for gathering and processing information related to suspicious transactions, analysing it, and disseminating it to law enforcement agencies. The mandate of ECO included co-operation with foreign authorities in the fight against money laundering and economic offences involving serious or complex fraud requiring expert investigators. Under ECAMLA, money laundering offences extended to any crime under the Criminal Code. The Act further defined an economic offence as any offence or fraud in respect of which money or other property at risk, gained or lost, exceeded MRs500,000 in value and whose investigation required specialised financial, information technology, accounting or legal expertise. The ECAMLA provided for a parallel two-tier system of STRs. STRs from banks were referred to the BoM, whose assessment was required before the report was passed to ECO. Other financial institutions not regulated by the BoM were required to report directly to ECO.

The director of ECO had the power to obtain permission from a judge in chambers to search banks or financial institutions when there were reasonable grounds for believing that these institutions had failed to keep proper business records or to report suspicious transactions. The director could obtain a judge's order to search any premises or place of business when he/she had reasonable grounds to believe that an offence had been, or was about to be, committed. ECO was headed by a director with a staff comprising a team of four accountants, an assistant superintendent of police, fourteen police officers and nine other public officers as investigators as well as customs officers, tax officers and VAT officers. There was no trained lawyer on ECO's staff. Legal advice was sought from the State Law Office. The ECAMLA also enabled the director of ECO to commandeer the services of police officers or other public officers designated by the commissioner of police or the head of the civil service. This in practice proved to be a source of conflict between the various persons involved.

Offshore Group of Banking Supervisors mutual evaluation

In early 2001, Mauritius was subject to an evaluation of its AML environment conducted by the Financial Action Task Forces' (FATF) Offshore Group of Banking Supervisors (OGBS). The evaluation report identified areas of concern, including the absence of a level playing field in the regulatory regime in the financial services sector. In the absence of regulations and guidelines, the report found there were no common standards to prevent money launderers shopping around and placing their business with the operator who applied the lowest standards. Moreover, evaluators found that the parallel, two-tier system adopted under the ECAMLA, whereby reports of banks were required to be made first to the BoM, impeded the speed with which action could be taken by the director of ECO. The evaluation team recommended that all STRs should be directed to ECO. Additionally, the evaluation team identified weaknesses in international co-operation and recommended that an Extradition Act be introduced as soon as possible to enable Mauritius to ratify the Vienna Convention. Further, it recommended that comprehensive AML training should be provided throughout the entire finance industry. The report also recommended that each supervisory authority conduct on-site inspections to ensure that institutions subject to its supervision complied with ECAMLA and that an AML officer be appointed for each.

8.2 The post-2001 regulatory framework for the IFS industry

FIAMLA

The Financial Intelligence and Anti-Money Laundering Act of 2002 (FIAMLA) replaced the ECAMLA and is now the centrepiece of post-2001 AML/CFT legislation in Mauritius. It established the Financial Intelligence Unit (FIU) (in place of ECO) to deal with AML offences, STRs and to exchange information on AML/CFT.

The Financial Intelligence Unit (FIU): is the principal intelligence gathering agency for anti-money laundering and countering the financing of terrorism (AML/CFT), acting as an independent interface between reporting institutions and law enforcement agencies. It receives and analyses all STRs from financial institutions and, if it judges appropriate, passes on its findings to law enforcement agencies for further action. Information is disseminated to the two supervisory bodies, namely the FSC and the BoM, for follow-up regulatory action. The statutory functions of the FIU include exchanging information with overseas FIUs and comparable bodies. The FIU became a member of the Egmont Group of FIUs in July 2005 and was appointed regional representative of Africa on the Egmont Committee for 2003–2005[1]. All technical staff of the FIU are trained in the AML/CFT framework of Mauritius, security awareness and the protection of information. Key members of staff are given specialised training overseas on the global AML/CFT regime.

Matters in which the FIU establishes a *prima facie* case are referred for investigation and prosecution to the Independent Commission against Corruption (ICAC), which has extensive powers of investigation and enforcement in the AML/CFT field. It can investigate any matter concerning the laundering of money or suspicious transactions referred to it by the FIU, institute criminal proceedings and can collaborate with international enforcement agencies. It has powers of arrest, search and seizure. FIU and ICAC share a common objective, although there is a clear distinction in their respective roles.

Legislative features of FIAMLA: The new Act criminalises money laundering and imposes high criminal sanctions for money laundering offences. It has a net of 'predicate' offences that include any crime (in the widest sense) with provisions that permit conviction for both the money laundering offence and the predicate offence. Under the Act, the offence of money laundering may still be established in the absence of conviction for a predicate offence. The Act requires all financial firms to have an internal framework for coping with AML/CFT risks. Banks and other financial institutions must, under threat of severe fines and imprisonment of key managers, put into place the measures necessary to ensure procedural and substantive AML/CFT compliance. They are expected to have internal controls, other AML/CFT measures including programmes for assessing AML /CFT risk and enhanced due diligence measures, with respect to their dealings with high-risk entities and with legal persons in jurisdictions that do not have adequate AML/CFT systems. The critical obligations of banks and financial institutions are: verification of identity of all customers and other persons with whom they conduct transactions; verification and keeping of identity records, transaction records and staff training records; appointment of a money laundering reporting officer; reporting of suspicious transactions to the FIU; training of employees; and documentation of the compliance procedures. Together these are known as know your customer (KYC) and due diligence (DD) requirements. The FSC and BoM have issued additional guidelines on the AML/CFT preventive measures that their respective licensees must put into place. These supervisory bodies conduct regular on-site compliance visits to their respective licensees to ensure that they are complying with their AML/CFT obligations.

Adapting to new international standards

A detailed assessment of the AML/CFT regime in Mauritius was conducted by a joint IMF/World Bank mission in late 2002 under the Financial Sector Assessment Program (FSAP). An Anti-Money Laundering (Miscellaneous Provisions) Act was passed in 2003 to remedy weaknesses identified by that mission to bolster the AML/CFT regime. The 2003 Act amended the FIAMLA of 2002, the Banking Act of 1988 and the FSD Act of 2001 to allow the disclosure of information to the FIU and eliminate impediments to the transmission of information by supervisory authorities to the FIU. Additionally, the Act widened the supervisory mandate of the FSC and BoM, making them responsible for ensuring that their respective licensees complied fully with AML/CFT preventive measures. It formalised officially the status of the National Committee for AML & CFT, which had previously been operating on an informal basis to ensure co-ordination between intelligence gathering, investigation, law enforcement and policy-making. In the later half of 2003, two other pieces of legislation were enacted: (a) the Mutual Assistance in Criminal and Related Matters Act, which provides for mutual legal assistance between Mauritius and a foreign state or an international criminal tribunal in relation to serious offences; and (b) the Convention for the Suppression of the Financing of Terrorism Act which ratified the same UN International Convention.

Based on the recommendations of the IMF/WB mission, Mauritian legislation was further enhanced by enactment of: (a) The Bank of Mauritius Act of 2004; (b) the Banking Act of 2004; (c) the Insurance Act of 2005; and (d) the Securities Act of 2005. These enactments embrace international standards set up by the BCBS, IAIS and IOSCO. Mauritius has signed, ratified and implemented UN Conventions against (a) Illicit Traffic in Narcotic Drugs and Psychotropic Substances, 1988 i.e. the Vienna Convention; and (b) Transnational Organised Crime 2000 (the Palermo Convention).

The Financial Services Commission

As an international financial centre (IFC), Mauritius is perceived (in generic rather than specific terms, substantiated by a proper AML/CFT risk assessment) as facing major money laundering and terrorist financing risks. One of the functions of the Financial Services Commission (FSC) is to take measures to suppress illegal, dishonourable and improper practices, market abuse and financial fraud in relation to any activity in the financial services sector. Money laundering and terrorist financing have been identified as crimes that can affect adversely the soundness and stability of the financial system and damage the reputation of Mauritius.

In exercising its licensing authority, the FSC seeks to be satisfied that applicants for global business company (GBC) and management company (MC) licenses are 'fit and proper' persons. Its guide to meeting the 'fit and proper person test' is extremely comprehensive. It has been designed to deter the abuse of Mauritius and its financial markets and also to deter dishonest, incompetent, unskilled or otherwise inappropriate operators in Mauritius. In processing applications for GBCs, the FSC works on the assumption that the MC (as a licensee of the FSC) has fulfilled pre-licensing customer due diligence requirements and that requisite information on the beneficial owners and promoters of their clients are in the possession of all MCs.

The FSC has introduced a compliance testing regime that involves on- and off-site inspection of all MC licensees, to ensure compliance with licence conditions and with AML/CFT obligations. In cases of non-compliance, the FSC is empowered to apply a variety of graduated sanctions including revocation of the licence. It can make inquiries into the business of licensees when the FSC receives a complaint or where it has reasonable suspicion that a licensee has or may carry out any activity that prejudices the integrity, soundness and stability of the financial system or damages the reputation of Mauritius.

In line with international trends, the enforcement powers of the FSC have been enhanced to give it 'sharper teeth'. It can now impose a range of disciplinary sanctions apart from license revocation. Under new powers, the FSC can impose administrative fines on any person licensed by it and to any person who is a present or past director, manager, partner or shareholder or controller of a licensee. Appropriate mechanisms for the protection of human rights and rights of appeal have been incorporated as well. All administrative fines collected by the FSC are to be paid into a Financial Services Fund, which will be used partly to promote the education of consumers of financial services and partly to fund a compensation scheme for those who have, upon appeal, been found to be wrongly treated.

New powers of the Bank of Mauritius (BoM)

A new Banking Act was passed in 2004 implementing recent international developments in the prudential supervision of banks. Apart from adhering to international standards set out by BCBS in its 25 Core Principles for Effective Banking Supervision[2], and evolving towards risk-based regulation and supervision of banking institutions, the BoM is also responsible for monitoring AML/CFT compliance by banks. Its AML Guidance Notes were updated in 2003 to meet the requirements of the FIAMLA and new FATF recommendations. The on-site inspection programme of the Bank of Mauritius includes monitoring compliance with AML/CFT requirements. Any weaknesses in a bank's AML internal system is identified and the bank is required to take remedial action within a specific time frame.

The BoM has also acquired new powers of regulation and supervision under the 2004 Act. It is entitled to impose fines, among the other sanctions, for dealing with breaches of banking rules and regulations. Its role in the protection of consumers of banking services has been enhanced and an Ombudsman for banking services has been provided for. The BoM's powers to exchange information with other banking supervisors were also clarified under the 2004 Act. It has always participated actively in central bank fora at global and regional levels and is a member of the Offshore Group of Banking Supervisors (OGBS). The new legislation builds clear gateways for exchange of information with local institutions (such as the FSC and FIU) engaged in financial supervision and with an AML/CFT mandate, as well as with foreign supervisors. To eliminate ring-fencing between onshore and offshore banking activities, the BoM's licensing procedures have been streamlined and a single licence is issued to banks with no distinction between domestic and offshore business except in their accounting presentation of foreign transactions.

The AML National Committee

The National Committee for Anti-Money Laundering and Combating Terrorist Financing was set up in the wake of the IMF/World Bank mission report, which recommended the setting up of a task force to map out the workflow plan and to prepare written procedures and guidelines for investigating and prosecuting money laundering and terrorist financing. The National Committee ensures co-ordination in law enforcement efforts and policy-making. It formulates the national strategy and advises government on policy and legislative actions. With the assistance of the FIRST Initiative, the National Committee engaged the services of a US consultant to prepare a money laundering investigation and prosecution handbook to assist those involved in investigating and prosecuting money laundering and terrorist financing.

Notes

1. See Egmont Group website: http://www.egmontgroup.org/ [accessed 15 February 2008].
2. BIS (2001). Available at: http://www.bis.org/pub/bcbs30a.pdf [accessed 15 February 2008].

9

Incremental Costs and Benefits of Enhancing the IFS Regulatory Regime in Mauritius

....

Background to the analytical part of the cost-benefit study

After five years of Mauritius' passing new laws, creating new regulatory and investigatory agencies (i.e. the Financial Services Commission [FSC], the Financial Intelligence Unit [FIU] and the Independent Commission against Corruption [ICAC]) and applying a series of complex additional rules and regulations to providers of financial products/services (i.e. banks, insurers, trusts, management companies etc.) it is timely to ask whether the incremental **benefits** derived from 'enhanced' regulation have been commensurate with its **costs**.

Representations made at the joint Commonwealth Secretariat-Bank of Mauritius Seminar on IFS Regulation held in Mauritius on 10–11 April 2006 (referred to as 'the seminar' throughout) suggested strongly that the Mauritian financial services industry was egregiously overburdened. The incremental regulatory load imposed on it since 2002 to meet **anti-money laundering** (AML) and **combating the financing of terrorism** (CFT) concerns, through more elaborate **know your customer** (KYC) and **due diligence** (DD) requirements, was felt to have been excessive.

Mauritian regulators retort that additional regulation, imposed from abroad, has had to be adopted (unquestioningly) for Mauritius to survive as an international financial centre (IFC), avoiding the stigma of being blacklisted and thus being put out of business. They assert that the cost of additional regulation has to be regarded by the international financial services (IFS) industry as an extra cost of doing business, one that has to be absorbed within the industry's extant operating margins or, if that is not possible, passed on to IFS customers.

The outcome of these two viewpoints may be something that neither the IFS industry in Mauritius nor its regulators (or government) would wish to see. That is, a relentless increase in regulatory costs resulting in no tangible benefits, but undermining the IFS industry's global competitiveness. That would result (as is already happening) in the loss of extant and potential IFS business to other jurisdictions, both established (e.g. London and Singapore) and emerging (e.g. Dubai) ones.

Hence the need for a more considered review of costs versus benefits, along with a necessary reflective pause for contemplating (dispassionately/impartially) whether the last few years have witnessed a degree of regulatory over-exuberance that needs to be reined back into balance. This study attempts to meet that need, along the same lines as efforts aimed at analysing the costs and benefits of additional AML/CFT regulation that have recently been made in the UK and US. These efforts have yielded disconcerting findings about costs far exceeding any discernible benefits. They suggest the need for more studies and regulatory impact assessments (RIAs) to be undertaken across all jurisdictions, especially in small offshore financial centres (OFCs) like Mauritius.

Mauritius has yet to migrate towards the Basel-2 regime for establishing risk-based capital adequacy requirements for its banking system. Regulatory 'enhancements' between 2002 and 2005 have therefore focused mainly on AML/CFT measures. The exchange of tax information under the OECD's *Harmful Tax Practices* initiative is being approached in a more gingerly fashion given the sensitivities and multiple legal risks that financial service providing entities in Mauritius feel they would be exposed to by exchanging information under regulatory duress in a way that violates privacy, confidentiality and fiduciary trust when no wrongdoing is alleged or proven.

As observed, the pressure for additional regulation on small OFCs like Mauritius has emanated mainly from external sources (principally the Financial Action Task Force [FATF] via the IMF and World Bank) rather than from within the IFS industry or from national regulators. The reasons for external interlocutors applying such pressure on Mauritian regulators have been many. They range from: (a) avoiding global and regional financial crises by curtailing volatile 'hot money' flows through OFCs; (b) discouraging OFCs from providing a venue for tax avoidance and tax evasion by corporate/individual taxpayers in OECD countries concerned about revenue leakage in the face of rapidly increasing (but questionable and wasteful) public spending; (c) minimising transfer pricing; (d) closing avenues for the laundering of money from large, but well-established illicit global industries, such as trafficking in weapons, narcotics and humans; and (e) preventing terrorism from being financed through the global financial system. These pressures have become particularly pronounced since the events of 11 September 2001 and the 'war on terror' that has been unleashed with much retaliatory emotion, accompanied by the loss of any sense of proportion in applying remedies that are proving to be worse than the disease.

After nearly a decade of argumentation these reasons remain contentious as a basis for the regulatory burdens that are now being globally imposed. Questions are being raised about whether global regulatory authorities and IFIs are not (unwittingly) using traumatic events opportunistically to legitimise intrusions into privacy and confidentiality – two bedrocks of fiduciary trust – that were impermissible before. Most of all there is questioning of whether a 'one size fits all' approach to financial regulation for AML/CFT, and the setting up of costly Financial Intelligence Units (FIUs) in every country, is appropriate or affordable. There is even suspicion in some circles about whether excessively burdensome financial regulation being imposed by the FATF and IFIs is not being used as a non-tariff barrier against OFCs by OECD governments anxious to protect their own IFS industries and eliminate the competition that OFCs are threatening them with.

In trying to achieve over-ambitious global social, economic and political goals through financial regulation, and highlighting the escape valves that OFCs (all of which have axiomatically been tarred with the brush of being ill-regulated, regardless of evidence to the contrary in specific instances) allegedly provide unscrupulous entities and terrorists with, the point often appears to be lost on the FATF, IFIs, OECD governments and their regulators, that the intractable, underlying problems that such regulation is meant to address have been created largely by the unintended consequences of their own policies, as well as by their failures of governance, interdiction and law enforcement. These problems have not been created or encouraged by OFCs; least of all by OFCs that have traditionally been as well regulated as Mauritius. Such issues are ill-suited to being tackled tangentially through the creation and application of elaborate, but ultimately ineffectual sieves in OFCs as a palliative. That arabesque only diverts attention from where the real solutions to these problems lie.

In such instances, the imposition of additional regulatory burdens on OFCs, accompanied by the threat of blacklisting if they are not complied with, raises fundamental questions about fairness, perspective and integrity in the conduct of international relations between large and small states with unequal bargaining power. Such questions become more troublesome when there is no recognition on the part of the OECD or IFIs that substantial costs are being imposed on parties who may not (directly or indirectly) benefit from their incurrence. Nor is there any recognition that under such circumstances there may be a powerful moral and legal case (under international law) for compensatory redress when costs and benefits might be so asymmetrically distributed.

Where the problem of **money-laundering** is concerned, it is simply not credible to believe or assert (as the FATF, IFIs and OECD governments implicitly seem to be doing) that illicit global financial flows from a variety of proscribed activities, estimated by various agencies to total $3–4 trillion a year, are amenable to being even temporarily or slightly inconvenienced by adding to a mountain of AML legislation and regulation in OFCs. Nor is **terrorist financing** – more easily handled through pervasive *hawala* markets, barter and cash transactions financed from the opium, arms and human trafficking industries – likely to be prevented by OFCs adhering to the FATF's *obiter dicta* on CFT.

Indeed the circumstantial and anecdotal evidence is mounting that more such AML/CFT regulation in OFCs might actually be counterproductive: creating a monumental, but ultimately useless, paralytic regulatory industry with its own codes, language and vested bureaucratic career and travel interests, while diverting attention from the real problems that such regulation is ostensibly attempting to address. As has been said, the attempt to contain such large volumes of illicit financial flows through AML/CFT regulation is akin to taming Niagara Falls with a tea strainer.

The approach taken so far by the FATF and the IFIs to the imposition of a plethora of new regulatory measures and standards concerning AML/CFT across all jurisdictions, and most forcefully in OFCs (whose guilt has been assumed before their innocence is proven), appears to be based on the presumption that the overriding benefit of such regulations is so obvious in safeguarding the integrity of the global financial system, that almost any level of cost incurred by anyone anywhere in applying them is acceptable and should not be questioned.

However, the evidence emerging from cost-benefit studies in developed jurisdictions is that: (a) the costs of additional AML/CFT regulation being imposed are much too high and spread across regulators, industry operators and consumers; (b) the benefits to jurisdictions incurring such costs are mainly reputational, albeit judged against arbitrary standards of probity, but such benefits are far too low, elusive, generally unquantifiable and probably accrued in jurisdictions different to those where very quantifiable and visible costs are being incurred without any provision for compensating for that asymmetry; and (c) the burden of surveillance and policing is being shifted decisively – and inappropriately – from regulatory and investigatory agencies to banks and other private financial service providers whose relationships with their customers are being compromised in the process.

Banks and financial institutions are now being obliged by AML/CFT regulation and KYC/DD requirements to become policemen, spies, informants and tax collectors vis-à-vis their customers. These roles involve major conflicts of interest. They leave financial institutions vulnerable to open-ended legal risk on both sides: i.e. on the one hand by customers who believe their basic rights to confidentiality and privacy in transactions involving fiduciary trust are being episodically infringed if not systematically violated and, on the other, by regulators who believe that financial institutions are not being enthusiastic enough in performing their policing and spying jobs for them.

The foregoing arguments are not made in the spirit of denigrating, or opposing for the sake of opposition, what is being done nationally and globally in order to safeguard the probity, integrity, stability and soundness of financial systems. That would be unreasonable. The argument instead is for the restoration of a sense of regulatory balance, perspective and proportion, taking costs and benefits into account, and assessing their impact before designing and applying new AML/CFT and other financial regulations. It is an argument that cautions OFCs like Mauritius against the dangers of interpreting and applying the FATF's standards and IFI recommendations in ways that are so meticulous, unthinking, rigid and draconian, that they threaten the viability and existence of the very system that these regulations are intended to safeguard and protect.

Financial regulation in Mauritius: background for the study

Contrary to general public opinion in the OECD world about the supposed laxity of regulation in all offshore financial centres (fostered and exaggerated by occasionally questionable observations made by official sources, and by sensationalist journalism about the risks that OFCs pose to global systemic integrity and stability) Mauritius has always been a relatively well-regulated OFC. This is a historical reality that the country has been given very little credit for by its external interlocutors. The Mauritian government was emphatic about putting in place sound regulation right at the inception of its OFC. Yet, it has been tarred (unfairly) with the same brush as other OFCs that are not so well regulated.

This part of the study tries to assess the costs incurred and the benefits derived by public and private institutions in the IFS industry from the adoption of AML/CFT regulation in Mauritius since 2002. It responds to a growing sentiment on the part of the IFS industry (and indeed on the part of some thoughtful regulators themselves, as reflected in the balanced views expressed by the incoming CEO of the Financial Services Commission [FSC] at the seminar cited above) that the evolving IFS regulatory regime needs to be re-examined in terms of both its overall cost-benefit ratio as well as its overall 'appropriateness', effectiveness and its impact on competitiveness.

Any regulatory regime has to be questioned that leaves those being regulated as dissatisfied and oppressed as the IFS industry in Mauritius appears to be. It also has to be readjusted to command the respect that is necessary for compliance to be helpful and voluntary rather than begrudging and resentful. For financial regulation to work as it should, those being regulated need to be convinced that it is being done in the best interests of their firms, their customers and the financial system. Internal compliance at the level of the firm, and peer-pressured compliance within the financial services industry, must be incentivised positively. It should dovetail seamlessly with the supervisory efforts of regulators to ensure *substantive* compliance of a kind that is meaningful, rather than *process* compliance that results in financial service providers filling out reams of useless forms in a desultory manner that is at cross-purposes with genuine compliance.

As explained earlier, Mauritius has always been eager (perhaps too eager) to comply with international standards established by recognised standard-setting organisations. To avoid the prospect of blacklisting by the FATF, it adopted all its recommendations promptly and applied them with a vigour that was demonstrably absent in many developed financial jurisdictions and most developing ones. The country has demonstrated its willingness to adhere to new principles of international co-operation and information sharing in the case of financial crimes. It was among the first six countries to have made commitments to the OECD after its report on harmful tax competition – modified to the euphemism 'harmful tax practices' after the internal contradiction of the proposition that tax competition among governments could be harmful was pointed out – was issued in 1998[1] (again perhaps an example of misplaced over-eagerness to please) and is now a participating partner at the Global Tax Forum.

Mauritius now has double tax avoidance treaties (DTAT's) with some 30 jurisdictions. It relies on the exchange of information clause in those treaties to provide/obtain tax information in deserving cases to/from foreign tax authorities. It has signed multilateral and bilateral conventions for mutual legal assistance in criminal matters. It was a founding member of the Eastern and Southern African Anti-Money Laundering Group

(ESAAMLG), a regional organisation styled on the FATF, in which it plays a leading role. The Mauritian FIU is a member of the Egmont Group, fully engaged in the exchange of intelligence with its counterparts in various jurisdictions by pursuing electronic and paper-trails to track the flow of suspicious funds. As a member of IOSCO, Mauritius adheres to the multilateral memorandum of understanding (MOU) on exchange of information on securities and market fraud. Its two main financial supervisors – i.e. the Bank of Mauritius and the Financial Services Commission – have signed numerous MOUs for exchanging information with their counterparts in a number of jurisdictions and have created the necessary legal channels to supply such information in confidence.

The country has regularly and actively participated in the IMF's Information Program, collecting and providing information on financial statistics and the aggregate flow of funds within the context of the General Data Dissemination System (GDDS). The willingness of Mauritius to participate in worldwide AML/CFT efforts and contribute to systemic financial integrity and stability at the international level cannot be doubted; especially as it has, so far, been willing to incur the very high costs involved without demur. However, the burden of incremental financial regulation since 2002 has been such that the question is now being asked – with increasing frequency and intensity by the IFS industry (and, as noted above, by some of the more thoughtful regulators themselves) – about the benefits that have been generated for the country from such collaboration and whether they have been commensurate with the costs.

The coverage of the Mauritius study

The Mauritius study focused on those local operators that are most active in the IFS business, namely the **management companies** (but not captive trusts) and **banking institutions** that are the main providers of IFS to offshore (and some affluent domestic) individual and corporate clients. Management companies (MCs) and banks are particularly vulnerable to international fraud and money laundering abuses perpetrated by clients they do not know well. However, Mauritian entities have a reputation for conservatism that disinclines them to do business with clients they do not know or who are not soundly referred.

Regrettably, the study in Mauritius did not cover insurance companies, securities brokerages, asset management companies, accounting firms or law firms. They were deemed, at the local level, not to be as involved in providing IFS, although many of them are involved in IFS indirectly. Nevertheless, as became apparent at the seminar cited above, representatives of these firms felt strongly that they should have been included in the study. They too have been dramatically affected by the application of AML/CFT regulations. They felt (correctly) that their inclusion in the study would have provided a better and wider picture of the total economic cost to Mauritius of applying externally imposed AML/CFT regulations. As matters stand, the total costs explicated below therefore represent only a significant fraction of the total economic cost that Mauritius has incurred in applying additional AML/CFT regulations at the behest of the FATF and the IFIs.

Of the 32 (37.6 per cent out of 85) **management companies** that responded to the questionnaire sent out, 82 per cent offered accounting and legal services, 61 per cent offered fund administrative services, while 30 per cent provided other non-bank financial services. All of the companies are required to exercise due diligence and to verify clients' identity under the Financial Intelligence and Anti-Money Laundering Act (FIAMLA). Further they are required to comply with the codes on the prevention of money laundering issued by the BoM (for banks) and the FSC (for trust and management companies, as well as other NBFIs) in line with FATF recommendations. Of the 15 (out of 18) banks that responded to the questionnaires some had, within their overall corporate holding company structures, affiliated captive management companies (some of which did respond to the survey).

Questionnaires were also sent to the Ministry of Finance (which is ultimately responsible for the financial system and IFS industry in Mauritius) the two principal regulatory authorities (BoM and FSC) as well as the Financial Intelligence Unit (FIU). These institutions deal directly with Mauritius' external interlocutors (i.e. the two principal IFIs, OECD counterparts and the FATF) and are the main transmission mechanisms for domestic regulatory shocks triggered/transmitted by external agencies.

The remainder of this chapter comprises three separate sections. The first (section 9.1) examines the costs incurred by public regulatory institutions as well as the private sector (i.e. banks and management companies) in Mauritius in implementing the new AML/CFT regime that has been evolving since 2002. The second (section 9.2) considers the benefits derived from implementation of additional AML/CFT regulation, while the third (section 9.3) attempts an assessment of the net benefits derived from application of the AML/CFT regime in the country. For obvious reasons, such an assessment is rendered difficult by the reality that compliance with AML/CFT regulations is inextricably intertwined with other regulatory compliance requirements that the institutions surveyed must also meet.

In a number of cases, respondents to questionnaires provided qualitative, impressionistic ratings (e.g. high or low) to specific questions asking them to specify in numerical (dollar or rupee) terms the costs and benefits of incremental AML/CFT regulation under particular categories (e.g. staff, training, IT systems, audit costs, legal costs etc.). However, in most cases respondents provided their best retrospective estimates.

Sample size and representativeness

The response to questionnaires sent out for the study to all management companies and banks was surprisingly large given the delays that occurred locally in sending them out and the limited time that respondents were given to complete and return them. Under the circumstances the response was gratifying. In the absence of those two factors, and with better guidance provided to respondents, the study would have yielded more thorough and accurate quantitative information on costs and benefits. A review of the questionnaire returns suggests that in some cases the questionnaires were referred to junior personnel who probably did not fully understand the business of the respondent or were unable to interpret the questions sufficiently accurately to provide responses that were consistent or comprehensible. However, such cases were the exception rather than the rule. In an impressive number of instances, the questionnaires were completed by senior executives of MCs who made many illuminating and informative annotations in their replies.

In that connection, the efforts made by the CEO of the Mauritius Bankers Association (MBA) to garner a maximum response rate from the banking community deserve special mention. She intervened personally on two separate occasions in March and April 2006 to ensure that as many banks as possible responded to the questionnaire. It was regrettable that, despite assurances provided by the MoF about extending full co-operation to the Commonwealth Secretariat and its consultants in undertaking the study, the response from the FIU on its costs was inadequate. The Ministry itself provided useful information before the seminar, as did the FSC and the BoM after the seminar.

Out of 85 management companies (MCs) operating in Mauritius, 32 responded to the questionnaires sent out. This understates the representativeness of the sample in terms of market coverage. When the 32 respondents are split into **small** (0–15 employees), **medium** (16-40 employees) and **large** (over 40 employees) MCs the response pattern was 21 out of 66 small MCs; 4 out of 9 medium-sized MCs; and 7 out of the 10 largest MCs. That distribution makes a significant difference in terms of market coverage. The ten largest MCs in Mauritius account for 60 per cent of the total IFS market, while the nine medium MCs account for a further 15 per cent. The remaining 25 per cent is accounted for by the 66 small MCs, of whom nearly 33 per cent responded. Thus the response by MCs suggests market coverage of about 65 per cent, although only 37.6 per cent of the total **number** of MCs responded. The 15 out of 18 banks (83 per cent) that responded represent over 90 per cent of banking services market coverage for IFS in the country. Under the circumstances, despite some avoidable local hiccups, the response rate has to be considered satisfactory and the study's findings representative.

9.1 The quantifiable incremental costs of new AML/CFT regulation in Mauritius

Introduction

The study tried to determine quantitatively the incremental costs incurred in Mauritius (by private operators as well as public regulators) attributable to the AML/CFT regime introduced in 2002 (and updated regularly since). Costs were broken down into three main categories:

- Costs related to the formulation of the company's internal policies, rules and procedures on complying with AML/CFT regulations. This category covers the costs of developing and codifying corporate policies and procedures established to manage and mitigate AML/CFT risk in accordance with regulatory requirements. Respondents were asked to provide information on costs related to establishing the corporate regime for dealing with AML/CFT broken down into further sub-categories: staff, training, IT hardware and software investments, space, office overheads and other costs.

- **Costs related to the actual collection, processing, evaluation and safe storage of required information for KYC and DD purposes.** These costs cover: (a) collection and compilation of information about clients and its verification; and (b) the costs of exchanging such information with other institutions. Establishing and using the client information database developed as a result lies at the heart of meeting the requirements of the AML/CFT regulatory regime. KYC/DD regulations require management companies and banks (as well as other financial service providers) to obtain from clients detailed addresses and identities with proof of same, and to lift corporate veils by going behind the identity of named clients to determine the actual beneficial ownership of the entities being serviced. KYC/DD involves undertaking a thorough search on the background and integrity of clients and making a business decision on their soundness.

- **Costs incurred in dealing with regulators and enforcement authorities**: e.g. for filing suspicious transactions reports (STRs), submission of information to regulators for 'fit and proper person tests', for license applications, for meeting specific requests made by regulators, co-operating with ongoing investigations and the costs of litigation related to AML/CFT.

The questionnaire sought information on these three categories of total costs incurred by respondents for the four-year period 2002–05 and for the year 2005. It asked respondents to differentiate between costs of a recurrent (annual) nature, and one-off capital expenditures.

Costs incurred by public regulatory and investigative institutions

As noted earlier, the overall regime for IFS regulation in Mauritius is shaped by the Ministry of Finance (MoF) with the active participation of the Bank of Mauritius (BoM) and the Financial Services Commission (FSC). The latter two institutions also implement IFS regulation/supervision. The BoM regulates banks, while the FSC regulates other financial institutions and service providers. The Financial Intelligence Unit (FIU), an autonomous agency specifically dedicated to AML/CFT intelligence gathering, is not a regulatory body as such. It nonetheless collaborates with the BoM and the FSC. Each of these four public bodies has responsibility within its jurisdictional competence to apply the AML/CFT regime mandated by the MoF.

Ministry of Finance (MoF): In elaborating regulatory policy and related legislation, and co-ordinating actions at regional and international levels, the MoF has incurred substantial incremental costs (shown in table 9.1, below) so that it might put the AML/CFT regime in place; however, these costs do not appear to have been a major source of concern.

The single largest cost was that of designing the AML/CFT policy framework based on the FATF's 40+9 recommendations and drafting legislation to support its implementa-

Table 9.1 Incremental costs incurred by Ministry of Finance in US dollars (nominal)

Cost incurred for	One-off capital cost [02–05]	Annual recurrent costs
	US$	US$
Drafting AML law for NBFIs (+ interest on WB loan)	1,000,000	60,000
Drafting basic financial intelligence and anti-money laundering law	50,000	
Drafting AML/CFT amendments & handbook	60,000	
Dealing with local costs of IMF-WB FSAP	30,000	
Meeting local costs of external TA for enforcement	60,000	
Monitoring & adjusting AML/CFT regime (1-PY)		15,000
Attending regional meetings AML/CFT (ESAAMLG)		30,000
Cost of hosting ESAAMLG meeting in 2004	30,000	
Annual subscription to ESAAMLG		20,000
Other costs (overheads/contingencies etc.)		15,000
Total Costs	1,230,000	140,000

tion in line with international standards. That involved recruiting international consultants for developing financial legislation in line with the standards of IOSCO, IAIS and IOPS. The work was undertaken as a special project that cost about US$1 million and was financed by a World Bank loan on commercial terms. It aimed at setting up a non-bank integrated regulatory and supervisory authority (the FSC) and its governance structure as well as reviewing existing laws concerning securities and insurance business.

Further costs were incurred in drafting FIAMLA by a foreign expert, including an estimate of costs for the involvement of the State Law Office. These amounted to US$50,000. Amendments were made to the law and regulations on the recommendations of the IMF/WB FSAP mission, which required two foreign consultants at a cost of US$30,000 each. These consultants also developed an AML/CFT handbook. The development of enforcement procedures made a further call on technical assistance estimated to cost US$60,000 (financed in part by the FIRST Initiative). In addition to these one-off 'set-up' costs of US$1.23 million, spent mainly on the fees of foreign consultants, the Ministry of Finance also incurs annual recurrent costs for:

- Monitoring and adjusting the AML/CFT regime in line with international developments, which costs the MoF the equivalent of a full person-year along with associated overhead and support expenses at an annual cost estimated at US$15,000 equivalent;

- Attending meetings and conferences overseas by government officials, in particular the ESAAMLG and FATF meetings with each mission estimated to cost US$15,000 (assuming the participation of the Minister) – consisting of travelling costs, accommodation and per diem payments;

- Subscriptions to ESAAMLG, which amount to US$20,000 annually; and

- Interest costs on the World Bank loan that financed the AML/CFT project.

In all, the Ministry incurs an annual recurrent cost of about US$140,000 for AML/CFT-related expenditures. For the four years 2002–05, the total recurrent cost has amounted to US$560,000. Adding the one-off capital costs incurred over the same period, MoF's total incremental costs for AML/CFT between 2002–05 are thus estimated to amount to a total of US$1.79 million.

Financial Intelligence Unit (FIU) and ICAC

The FIU was created in August 2002, with its raison d'etre only to gather intelligence on suspicious transactions under AML/CFT regulations. Its entire budget is therefore attributable to incremental AML/CFT costs for the purposes of this study. The Independent Commission Against Corruption (ICAC) was established a year later, but became operational only very recently.

The FIU did not provide any quantitative estimates of its costs for this study. It provided qualitative information indicating that it considered its costs to be low, along with figures on staffing, number of STRs handled etc. It was difficult to discern why the FIU was unable to provide information that was publicly available. Table 9.2 was therefore derived from FIU's 2005 Annual Report, which provided information for only two years (i.e. FY2004 and 2005). No information was available for FY2003. However, given that the FIU only came into existence in August 2002, its expenses in FY2003 would probably not have exceeded 40 to 50 per cent of those registered for FY2004 (that is, about $200,000). As table 9.2 shows (and estimating start-up expenses incurred in 2003 at $200,000), the FIU has received capital and recurrent grants from

Table 9.2 Incremental costs incurred by FIU/ICAC in US dollars (nominal)

Cost incurred for		2004	2005	2004–05
Receipts from government:	Capital grant	253,333		
	Recurrent grant	465,137	686,460	1,151,597
Expenses from capital grant (for IT systems)		–	72,097	72,097
Annual Expenses:	Salaries & staff allowances	254,265	380,698	634,963
	Training & seminars	6,715	7,857	14,572
	Overseas mission & conferences	40,705	18,263	58,968
	IT-related expenses	12,094	9,229	21,322
	Other office & admin. expenses	100,397	106,458	206,855
	Depreciation & amortisation	65,537	101,057	166,594
Total annual expenses		479,713	623,562	1,103,275
Annual + capital expenses		**479,713**	**695,659**	**1,175,372**

Source: FIU Annual Report for 2005 posted on its website. Mauritian rupees (MRs) converted to US$ at MRs 30=1 US$

the central government budget amounting to a total of $1.61 million, from which it has spent a total of $1.38 million up to 30 June 2005.

In outlining FIU's raison d'etre and activities during the seminar, its representatives seemed overly defensive in overemphasising the supposed **social** benefits justifying the need for such an agency to prevent money laundering and terrorist financing in Mauritius (although there is little evidence of either) and anxious to deflect attention from its cost. That view was not shared by the IFS industry at large. Nor was it clear that the BoM and the FSC concurred with the need for a financial intelligence gathering function as large, elaborate and expensive as that of the FIU to meet the domestic and international needs of an OFC and domestic financial system the size of Mauritius.

At the time of writing, the FIU had 27 full-time staff to handle an average of about 70 suspicious transaction reports (STRs) a year (for 2004 and 2005) filed by financial institutions with an average of 32 referrals to ICAC for further investigation and possible prosecution. It has decided against referring a further 88 STRs, owing to lack of evidence. In 2005, FIU senior staff undertook or participated in some 19 missions abroad at a recorded cost to the FIU of over US$18,000. The overall benefit of these to Mauritius is difficult to establish. That number of missions was probably exceeded in 2004, when their total cost was recorded at over US$40,000.

Given that the BoM has absorbed the entire incremental cost burden of applying and supervising AML/CFT regime compliance within its existing budget by reallocating staff, the expenditures of the FIU and the extent of its external interactions stand out in contrast.

No cost information was obtained from ICAC. On the basis of personal knowledge, and discussions with staff involved, the local consultant for the study imputed a cost for AML/CFT enforcement by ICAC and the State Law Office (SLO) of about US$150,000 annually. ICAC accounts for the bulk of that cost as it is principally involved in investigation and seizure actions, with SLO only following up in the case of criminal prosecutions actually being made. In the absence of better information from ICAC, the SLO or any other source, that estimate has been included in the total costs to government of establishing, implementing and maintaining AML/CFT regulation up to June 30, 2005.

Financial Services Commission (FSC)

The FSC was established in late 2001 with a capital grant from the Government of Mauritius of MRs100 million (US$3.33 million), of which MRs24 million (or about $800,000) was utilised in 2001–02 to set up its initial institutional infrastructure. The FSC licenses and regulates non-bank financial intermediaries (NBFIs) in Mauritius. These include: insurance companies and brokerages, actuaries, management companies, corporate trustees, pension funds and contractual savings schemes, capital market operators (i.e. stockbrokers, investment funds, mutual funds, portfolio managers, investment advisers/agents and market infrastructure providers), leasing and factoring companies, credit and finance companies.

Table 9.3 FSC total expenditures for 2002–2005 in US$ million (nominal)

Costs incurred for	2002	2003	2004	2005	2002–05
Staff salaries & allowances	0.962	1.134	1.522	2.138	**5.756**
Staff training & overseas seminars (20:80)	0.074	0.102	0.267	0.250	**0.693**
Legal & professional fees	0.056	0.114	0.034	0.178	**0.382**
General office & admin. expenses	0.418	0.730	0.831	1.035	**3.014**
Depreciation & amortisation	0.064	0.223	0.406	0.248	**0.941**
Non-recurrent set-up costs	0.800	0.003	–	–	0.803
Total expenditures	2.374	2.306	3.060	3.849	**11.589**
Memo: Capital grant from government	3.333	–	–	–	–
From which expended for set-up costs	0.800	0.003	–	–	–
Balance of capital grant available	2.533	2.530	2.530	2.530	**2.530**
Memo: Revenues from license fees	3.090	7.890	6.127	7.403	**24.510**
Interest income from cash surplus	0.196	0.381	0.506	0.897	**1.980**
Memo: Capital expenses on IT	0.139	0.016	0.085	0.463	**0.703**
Total no. of staff	55	82	96	112(E)	
Targeted staffing in CEO's Report 2003			(126)		

As of 30 June 2005, the FSC had approved some 29,751 licensees. Of these, 25,900 were global business companies (GBCs), which constitute the core clientele that utilise the services of the IFS industry in Mauritius. Services are provided to GBCs by 85 management companies (and 24 captive corporate trustees, which account for an insignificant fraction of total IFS business) and some 14 (out of 18) banks. The remaining 3,851 licensees were domestic entities of various types. The total costs and expenditures of the FSC (translated into US$) since its inception are shown in Table 9.3, above, which has been derived from annual reports for 2003 to 2005[2]. The FSC is a self-financing authority that generates a surplus from revenues (principally from license fees) over expenses and accrues the surplus to its own general fund. However, while its revenues might be seen as a benefit to government (and to public finances), they represent a cost (of being allowed to do business) to the financial services industry.

Since its set-up in 2001, the FSC has incurred a total cost of about US$11.6 million (up to 30 June 2005). Nonetheless, not all of this cost in 2002–05 can be considered additional and attributable to post-2002 regulatory demands for AML/CFT. This is because the FSC assumed the functions (and costs) of the former Mauritius Offshore Business Activities Authority (MOBAA), Securities and Exchange Commission (SEC) and the Controller of Insurance division of the Ministry of Finance.

Given the depth and width of its regulatory/supervisory ambit, the FSC's costs do not appear to be out of line with experience elsewhere. However, the rapid increase in the FSC's costs and staff since 2002 may require further attention. They do not provide a cause for budgetary concern, because the FSC is self-financing and generates a healthy surplus. Still, FSC's staffing has more than doubled over the last four years, while its annual (recurrent) expenditures have increased by nearly 150 per cent from US$1.57 million in 2002 to $3.85 million in 2005. Over that same period the population and diversity of its licensees has grown by under 10 per cent annually (in aggregate by 34 per cent) from a total of 22,276 in 2002 to 29,751 in 2005. Employment in its regulated domain of NBFIs has increased from 2,663 in 2002 to 3,030 in 2005 (or by 13.5 per cent – i.e. less than 4 per cent annually) while the FSC's staff has increased by over 100 per cent over the same period (these figures being derived from table 4 in the FSC's *Annual Report* of 2005). Those disproportionate increases in the FSC over industry staffing suggest that a considerable amount of incremental effort has been required of the FSC since 2002 in coping with new regulatory demands; such demands are mainly attributable to the new AML/CFT regime, rather than any other identifiable factor.

This observation is made to put the figures in table 9.4, below, in context. The table provides the FSC's own estimates of incremental costs related to the regulatory and supervisory burdens imposed upon it by the adoption and application of new AML/CFT legislation, which it participated in drafting. Table 9.4 suggests that less than **7.5 per cent** of the FSC's total expenditures between 2002 and 2005 were attributable to cost burdens imposed by new AML/CFT demands. However, this (surprisingly low) percentage is open to further scrutiny. About 14 per cent of the FSC's total **staffing** costs, less than 5 per cent of the FSC's total costs for **overseas missions**, less than 3 per cent of the FSC's total **training** costs and less than 1.25 per cent of all **other** FSC costs

Table 9.4 The Financial Services Commission's estimates of incremental costs for AML/CFT in US$

Costs incurred for	FSC costs for 2002–05		
	Total (A)	AML/CFT (B)	%B/A
Staffing costs for			
1. Drafting AML/CFT legislation (one-off)		37,000	
2. Assessment & surveys		4,000	
3. Participating in AML/CFT National Committee		30,000	
4. Attending FATF & ESAAMLG meetings	554,400	26,700	4.8%
5. Monitoring/supervising AML/CFT regime		683,900	
Total staffing costs	**5,756,000**	**781,600**	**13.6%**
Other costs:			
Costs of technical assistance to FSC for setting up regime		51,700	
Provision for creation/operation of specialised agencies		2,100	
Training costs (for staff & NBFI industry)	693,000	20,000	2.9%
Costs of disseminating information on AML/CFT		4,850	
Total other costs	5,833,000	78,650	1.35%
Total staffing + other costs	**11,589,000**	**860,250**	**7.42%**

(i.e. office overheads, equipment etc.) were attributed by the FSC to AML/CFT between 2002 and 2005. Those proportions seem extraordinarily low, if not incredible, given that AML/CFT and related KYC/DD preoccupations have been at the forefront of regulation during those four years. They require further scrutiny in view of the staff/cost increase that the FSC has incurred. Closer analysis suggests that an estimate of **15 per cent** of the total supervisory costs incurred by the FSC between 2002 and 2005 (or about $1.74 million) being attributed to AML/CFT burdens might be closer to the mark than the FSC's estimate of 7.5 per cent[3]. However, as the FSC has undertaken specific analysis for the purposes of this study, the figures provided (rather than an adjusted estimate) are taken into account for the present analysis.

The Bank of Mauritius (BoM)

The BoM, which regulates and supervises all banks in Mauritius, has provided the following figures as its internal estimates for the incremental costs of coping with the enhanced AML/CFT regime (see table 9.5, below).

Excluding interest expenses and other charges on its monetary operations, IMF charges and coin and note issuance charges, the BoM's annual staff and other office expenditures in 2002–05 amounted to an aggregate US$38.5 million or an annual average of US$9.6 million. That is low for a central bank of this size and reflects tight control over management and administrative costs. Probably, around 25 per cent of the BoM's total administrative cost is attributable to regulation and supervision, given the number of other activities that the BoM has to undertake. Roughly, that would imply a total of US$9.6 million being spent on supervisory functions over the four-year period in question. However, the BoM has provided information for only three of those four years. Adjusting for that, the incremental cost incurred by the BoM for coping with

Table 9.5 The Bank of Mauritius's incremental costs for AML/CFT in US$ (nominal)

Costs incurred between 2002 and 2005 for	Total costs 2002–05
Non-recurrent	
1. Preparation of internal AML/CFT guide for bank examiners	1,613
2. Preparation of AML/CFT guidance notes for all BoM regulated institutions	3,387
3. Costs of training provided by external consultants to BoM staff	18,548
Total non-recurrent costs	**23,548**
Recurrent	
4. Staff and training costs attributed to AML/CFT: 2002–03	38,615
(BoM believes 15% of its S/T costs 2003–04	59,930
are attributable to AML/CFT) 2004–05	62,667
Total non-recurrent costs:	**161,212**
Total recurrent + non-recurrent costs	**184,760**

incremental AML/CFT burdens amounts to **2.6 per cent** of its imputed total costs for regulation and supervision.

Looking at the negligible increase in staffing, it appears that the BoM has coped with additional AML/CFT burdens by reallocating work among its extant staff base and has stretched its staff through overtime. That impression was confirmed in private discussions with the BoM senior management during the course of the seminar. Nonetheless, stretching staff resources can only be done up to a point. It is not an indefinitely sustainable proposition. Sooner or later the BoM will need to increase staff to cope with the additional regulatory burdens being placed upon it. That will mean that the incremental costs of AML/CFT burdens will not be fully reflected in the BoM's accounts until 2006 or beyond.

Total (incremental) public sector costs for AML/CFT

Putting these costs for all public institutions involved with AML/CFT together results in the following picture (see table 9.6).

For the four years 2002–05, the Mauritian government and public agencies have spent nearly $5 million in incremental costs for developing and administering its AML/CFT regulatory regime in accordance with recommendations made by the FATF and IFIs for bolstering that regime. A third of these expenditures have been one-off capital costs. The total cost, while high in the context of Mauritius, pales in comparison to the costs incurred by private sector operators in the IFS industry.

Management companies and offshore banks: summary profiles

Private sector institutions were more forthcoming than their public counterparts in providing quantitative estimates of their incremental costs for setting up their own internal AML/CFT compliance machinery and observing AML/CFT regulations. Before the seminar, some 32 management companies (MCs) had returned completed (or partially completed) questionnaires, while nine banks had done so. After the seminar, further follow up by the CEO of the MBA resulted in six more banks providing the required information.

Table 9.6 Total AML/CFT costs for public institutions in US$

Institution	Incremental AML/CFT costs for 2002–05 period		
	Non-recurrent	Recurrent	Total
Ministry of Finance (MoF)	1,230,000	560,000	1,790,000
Financial Intelligence Unit (FIU)	272,100	1,103,300	1,375,400
ICAC & State Law Office (SLO)	n.a.	600,000	600,000
Financial Services Commission	90,800	769,500	860,300
Bank of Mauritius (BoM)	23,500	161,200	184,760
Total Public Sector Costs:	**1,616,400**	**3,194,000**	**4,810,460**

Before going directly into an analysis of questionnaire returns, it is essential to establish a profile of the two main types of players engaged in providing IFS to offshore clientele (which mainly comprise the two types of global business companies – GBC-1 and GBC-2 licensees). These two main players are: (a) management companies and (b) banks. Summary profiles of both groups are provided in tabular form below.

As table 9.7 indicates, at the end of June 2005 there were 85 management companies operating in Mauritius (although more licenses were issued, indicating that some were dormant, defunct or in the process of being wound up) compared to about 70 operating in 2001. Together they employed just over 1,000 people and had a wage bill approaching US$12 million (compared to $5.4 million in 2001). From the different percentages of MCs responding to the FSC's annual surveys it is not easy to extrapolate figures for the MC industry as a whole without knowing the size distribution of the responses received. The larger companies generally showed a much higher response rate than the smaller companies. Nevertheless, wherever possible the table shows extrapolated figures for the industry based on best assumptions and estimates.

Similarly, Table 9.8, below, provides a summary profile of banks in Mauritius.

Table 9.7 Summary profile of management companies in Mauritius

Characteristics	2001	2002	2003	2004	2005[E]
Number of MCs operating	70	71	79	81	85
Number of MCs reporting in FSC survey	38	57	69	67	n.a.
Number of employees for reporting MCs	n.a.	457	n.a.	813	n.a.
Approx. total extrapolated for all MCs	510	600	785	950	1,015
Employee compensation (US$ million)	3.62	5.16	6.69	9.07	na
Extrapolated for all MCs (US$ million)	5.40	6.85	9.14	11.78	12.45
Other expenses (US$ million)	11.73	13.12	10.97	9.73	na
Purchases of goods & services (US$ million)	2.03	5.73	9.18	10.81	na
Total expenses incl. tax (US$ million)	16.38	24.01	26.84	39.61	na
Gross income (US$ million)	23.69	29.40	33.06	41.16	na
o/w accounted for by largest 10 (US$ million)	19.92	21.80	13.20	21.80	na
: as percentage	67%	63%	54%	59%	na
Growth rate of turnover		+24%	+16%	−28%	+54%
Profits before tax (US$ million)	10.48	9.84	6.19	10.79	na
o/w accounted for by largest 10 (US$ million)	9.80	9.50	5.30	9.20	na
: as percentage	87%	82%	77%	76%	na
Profits after tax (US$ million)	7.31	5.38	6.22	1.56	na
Gross assets (US$ million)	n.a.	38.16	36.99	43.09	na

Source: FSC annual reports for 2003, 2004, 2005.

Table 9.8 Summary profile of offshore banks in Mauritius

Characteristics	2001	2002	2003	2004	2005[E]
Number of banks	n.a.	12	11	18	18
Number of banks operating domestically (C-I)	n.a.	10	10	11	11
Number of banks providing IFS (C-II)	n.a.	9	12	12	12
Gr. value added by offshore banks (US$ mill.)	68.3	70.1	80.4	82.4	85
No. of employees for offshore banks	n.a	512	562	588	643
No. of employees in the banking sector	n.a.	4,353	4,586	4,697	5,371
Employee compensation (US$ million)	3.1	3.7	3.8	5.2	n.a.
Other expenses	5.8	6.3	6.5	9.8	n.a.
Operating income	114.0	110.8	77.7	86.7	n.a.
Total operating expenses	8.9	10.0	10.5	15.0	n.a.
Net profit before tax (US$ million)	105.1	100.8	67.2	71.7	n.a.
Gross assets (US$ million)	3,940	4,320	4,689	6,617	7,886

Source: BoM annual reports for 2003 and 2004 and FSC annual report for 2005 (for employment figures).

The banking sector in Mauritius is divided into the domestic commercial banking sector and the offshore banking sector. Eleven Category 1 (C-1) banks operate in the domestic banking sector. Of these, five are local banks, two are wholly owned subsidiaries of foreign banks that are incorporated locally and four are branches of foreign banks. Twelve banks hold a Category 2 (C-2) license to operate in the offshore banking sector. Of these, seven banks provide only IFS. The remaining five undertake both domestic banking and IFS, but with a dividing wall between these two types of operations.

These two sets of profiles need to be kept in mind in interpreting the responses provided by MCs and banks on their incremental AML/CFT cost burdens and the qualitative responses provided to amplify on the quantitative information provided.

Management companies: analysis of questionnaire responses on costs

Taking into account the three main cost categories that respondents were asked to provide quantitative data for (i.e. costs for developing their internal AML/CFT compliance regime; costs of creating their KYC/DD data bases; and costs of preparing, submitting and responding to queries about STRs) the summary picture for the 30 out of 32 responding management companies that provided quantitative data is portrayed below (table 9.9). Aggregate figures for all 85 management companies are extrapolated using simple averages derived from the returns for each type of MC. Although this approach may not yield the most accurate results for the total costs of the MCs, it nevertheless provides a useful illustrative/indicative figure.

Table 9.9 Incremental AML/CFT costs for management companies 2002–2005 (US$)

Costs incurred by MCs in Mauritius for	Small (20)	Medium (4)	Large (6)	Total (30)
From sample responses received				
1. Establishing internal compliance regime	1,808,400	311,400	3,973,300	6,093,100
2. Developing KYC/DD databases	1,344,580	334,000	3,462,400	5,140,980
3. Reporting STRs & regulatory interaction	419,700	42,300	528,500	990,500
Total incremental AML/CFT costs 2002–2005	3,572,680	687,700	7,964,200	12,224,580
Memo: Average costs per type of MC				
1. Establishing internal compliance regime	90,420	77,850	662,220	203,100
2. Developing KYC/DD databases	67,230	83,500	577,100	171,366
3. Reporting STRs & regulatory interaction	27,980	14,100	105,700	33,016
Incremental AML/CFT costs per MC	185,630	175,450	1,345,020	407,486
Extrapolated totals for ALL MCs	[66]	[9]	[10]	[85]
1. Establishing internal compliance regime	5,967,720	700,650	6,622,200	13,290,570
2. Developing KYC/DD databases	4,437,180	751,500	5,771,000	10,959,680
3. Reporting STRs & regulatory interaction	1,846,680	126,900	1,057,000	3,030,580
Total incremental AML/CFT costs 2002–2005 for all 85 MCs (extrapolated)	12,251,580	1,579,050	13,450,200	27,280,830

[Some of these averages appear different when dividing figures shown by number of MCs because not all companies in each category have reported for all three main categories and sub-categories of cost]

As Table 9.9 shows, the aggregate incremental AML/CFT regulatory cost for **all MCs** for the four-year period 2002–2005 is extrapolated (from sample return averages) to amount to nearly **$27.3 million**. A close scrutiny of individual returns suggests that this figure may be understated for a variety of reasons. **First,** many respondents registered larger amounts for costs for the single year 2005 (for which they had recent data readily to hand) than they did for the four-year period 2002–2005, suggesting that they either read the period as 2002–2004 or did not focus on reconciling their responses. **Second,** many respondents have provided overall estimated figures for each of the three main cost categories without providing breakdowns for the several sub-categories of costs included (e.g. staffing, training, IT costs, audit costs overheads etc.) There is a consistent pattern of understatement when aggregate figures, without breakdowns, are related to totals supported by detailed breakdowns. **Third,** some costs appear obviously understated when **total** costs for many MCs are lower than just **audit** costs reported by other similar sized companies. For these and other reasons, a reasonable guess based on detailed scrutiny suggests a degree of understatement in the range of 30–40 per cent. However, no adjustment has been made for such understatement in the analysis that follows.

The pattern of response across different types of MCs (by size) also suggests some interesting contradictions, characteristics and other anomalies that need to be investigated further (in another study) to determine the accuracy of the returns. This was not possible to do under the time and budget constraints that this study operated under.

For example, total average incremental costs for small MCs were larger than for medium-sized MCs. Average dollar costs for AML/CFT **compliance regime development** were higher for small MCs than for medium-sized MCs, while average costs for **establishing KYC/DD databases** were significantly lower. The average costs of **STRs and regulatory interaction** reported by small MCs were **double** those of medium-sized companies. That is difficult to explain unless it is presumed that smaller MCs may have riskier clients who generate a higher proportion of suspicious transactions. This type of superficial anomaly needs further exploration and clarification.

The ten largest MCs dominate in accounting for 65 per cent of the industry's total AML/CFT costs. That is unsurprising given their 60 per cent share of the total MC market, and their even larger share of gross and net incomes derived from the provision of IFS. Average incremental AML/CFT costs for large MCs was 8–10 times higher than for small and medium MCs.

Interestingly, in the group of MCs classified as 'small', there were in-house affiliates of global groups like ING, Investec and Halifax. An affiliate of Fidelity Trust was classified as 'medium-sized'. On the face of it, these names would suggest classification in the 'large' category, given the likely size of their in-house business. Although small in terms of number of employees, these affiliates may be large in terms of business volume, although the questionnaires circulated (which were modified locally without further reference to the lead consultants) did not explicitly ask that question.

Another pointer to the probable understatement of overall costs was the wide range of variation in the responses of MCs of different sizes. For example, small MCs reported variations in total AML/CFT incremental costs from a low of US$25,000 to a high of US$750,000, with statistical medians being quite different to (and more meaningful than) arithmetic averages. The range of variation for more detailed sub-breakdowns (e.g. staffing costs) was even wider. The variation for medium-sized MCs was much lower, however, ranging from a low of US$86,000 to a high of US$319,000. The variation for large MCs was higher than for medium MCs, but much lower than for smaller MCs, with a low of US$387,000 and a high of US$2.25 million.

Incremental costs for establishing the set-up of their internal corporate AML/CFT compliance machinery and for establishing their KYC/DD databases accounted for the largest proportion of total costs for all three types of MC. This was not surprising given the pressure that MCs were under to substantially refurbish their KYC/DD databases on their 25,750 GBC clients retroactively over the four years to 2006. The largest sub-item of cost for establishing compliance machinery was staffing costs (40 per cent), while the costs of legal and technical assistance for establishing the AML/CFT framework, training costs and IT hardware and software costs accounted for around 16 per cent each, with audit and other costs accounting for the remaining 12 per cent. Incremental expenditures on IT systems for AML/CFT compliance appeared to be low when compared to expenditure patterns for the same purpose in other jurisdictions. The largest cost where the KYC/DD databases were concerned was that of information collection (45 per cent), with the second largest cost being that of verification (26 per cent). Exchanging client information with other parties accounted for 18 per cent of total KYC/DD costs, with safekeeping and other costs amounting to 11 per cent. By comparison, costs for dealing with STRs and interacting with regulatory and investigation agencies were relatively low, accounting for 8.1 per cent for all MCs together (but ranging from 12 per cent for small MCs to 6 per cent for medium MCs and 6.6 per cent for large MCs) and 10.3 per cent for banks.

The low proportion of costs absorbed by STRs and regulatory interaction bears further scrutiny. This finding from questionnaire returns calls into question claims made by the FIU about the urgent and pressing needs for its services. The FIU reported just 65 STRs being filed by financial institutions and MCs in 2004 and 75 in 2005. The filing of STRs with the FIU, investigation by the FIU and ICAC or other law enforcement agencies, and the disclosure of beneficial owners' information to regulators on submission of licence applications creates the most difficulty for MCs with their clients. It puts them in legally untenable conflict-of-interest positions in providing information to regulators, which their clients deem to be a breach of fiduciary trust.

From participant reactions at the seminar, it became clear that banks spend a considerable amount of time and money examining dubious client files. They have recourse to greater internal control and wider checking mechanisms through head-office access, which provides them with global reach in tracking down credit records and other relevant information. However, MCs appear to spend more on: providing information on 'ultimate beneficiary' ownership to the regulator in cases of licence applications; satisfying the criteria established for meeting the 'fit and proper person' test; and responding to requests by the regulator and the FIU for further information. This may be explained by regulatory obligations in the IFS industry requiring disclosure of 'ultimate beneficiary' information to the FSC in respect of GBC-1 licences to strip out corporate veils. MCs have complained loudly that the FSC is much too rigid and bureaucratic in its scrutiny on beneficial owners' information, with demands for supporting information (such as 10-year-old utility bills) that do little to establish the *bona fides* or purity of motives of GBC license applicants.

Overall, incremental AML/CFT costs for MCs were higher (in absolute and relative terms) than for banks (as shown below). The reason probably is that banks have been subject to creeping increases in regulation since 1998. Banks have therefore been able to absorb the incremental burdens of post-2001 AML/CFT legislation/regulation more readily within their overall (already very large) compliance budgets than have management companies, for whom post-2001 AML/CFT regulatory impositions have been particularly demanding and traumatic to adjust to. A second reason (that came out during the seminar) is that the six foreign bank branches/subsidiaries that dominate a significant share of the offshore banking market in Mauritius have most, if not all, of their compliance costs absorbed by head office compliance departments and therefore do not feel the impact of incremental costs on their own budgets or books. This led to a considerable understatement of incremental AML/CFT costs by banks.

Comparing incremental AML/CFT costs to the profitability of MCs and banks highlights another facet (in Table 9.10 below) that explains why MCs have felt more burdened than banks in coping with AML/CFT regulatory demands. It also explains some of the differences in their respective (different) responses to qualitative probing, which are elaborated upon in the next section (9.2). Table 9.10 is illustrative and makes no pretence of total accuracy in presentation. It compares costs for 2005 (obtained from sample data) with profits for 2004/2005 published by the FSC for the MCs and (using extrapolations based on averages) aggregates costs for 2002–2005, while comparing them with profits for 2001/2002–2004/2005. In other words, the profits figures lag costs by between six months and a year. The same is true for banks. The lack of precision in matching periods is the same for MCs and banks.

However, while accuracy has been sacrificed, the illustrative impact is nevertheless revealing and substantive. Even if cost/profit periods were perfectly matched and published profit data were available for 2005/2006, it is doubtful that the resulting cost/profit aggregate ratios would be significantly different. The table explains powerfully why MCs (and particularly the smaller more numerous MCs) feel more aggrieved than banks in resenting and opposing the additional cost burdens of AML/CFT regulations being imposed upon them. These costs are eating more heavily into their rapidly thinning profit margins – particularly in the case of small and medium-sized MCs, whose future existence has to be in doubt if the cost/profit (C/P) ratios in table 9.10 are indicative.

Table 9.10 Incremental AML/CFT costs vs. profits for MCs and banks (US$ million)

	Year	Costs	Profits-BT	C/P-%
Reporting management companies	2004/05	4.28	10.79	**39.7**
	2001/02–04/05	12.22	37.30	**32.8**
10 largest management companies (extrap.)	2001/02–04/05	13.45	33.80	**39.8**
Other 75 management companies (extrap.)	2001/02–04/05	13.83	16.10	**85.9**
Reporting banks	2004/05	2.97	71.70	**4.2**
	2001/02–04/05	6.61	344.80	**1.9**

Sources: BoM Annual Report 2004 for Banks, FSC Annual Report 2005 for MCs: See Tables 9.7 & 9.8, above.

This situation exists because, in providing IFS to GBC licensees, it is the management companies that bear the primary responsibility of establishing complete KYC/DD databases on their 25,750 clients. They share privileged client information in these databases with banks, which then have to duplicate client records and recheck them because – until the seminar – BoM examiners were unwilling to accept information signed off by the FSC without undertaking their own verification and vice versa. After the seminar, the BoM and the FSC agreed to jointly examine ways in which unnecessary duplication of requirements could be minimised, with one regulator accepting what the other has signed off on.

More interestingly, during the seminar it emerged that client information in the same KYC/DD databases had to replicated yet again if the same offshore client (or domestic client investing offshore) happened to avail of insurance or stockbroking facilities from insurance brokers and stockbrokers in Mauritius, resulting in four-fold replication of the same client information – even though insurance and stockbrokers are regulated by the FSC. In this electronic age the duplication of so much paper-based data to meet unduly bureaucratic regulatory/supervisory procedural requirements appears extraordinarily costly and inefficient and ought to be remedied swiftly.

Offshore and other banks: analysis of questionnaire responses on costs

Nine banks returned survey questionnaires before the seminar was held. Further post-seminar intervention and follow-up by the MBA resulted in another six banks completing and returning the questionnaires. Of the total of 15 banks eventually responding, all provided quantitative data on their incremental AML/CFT costs. This was an extraordinarily large sample out of a population of 18 banks, of which 11 are engaged in offshore banking. All 11 of these were included in the group that responded with quantitative data, thus resulting in 100 per cent coverage of the banks engaged in providing IFS. Unlike MCs, there was no sub-categorisation of banks as small, medium or large or even as foreign or domestic. The quantitative cost data obtained from banks is depicted in table 9.11, below.

Table 9.11 Incremental AML-CFT costs for banks (US$)

Costs incurred by Banks in Mauritius for	Year 2005		Total for 2002–05	
	US$	%	US$	%
Establishing internal AML-CFT compliance machinery	2,089,500	70.4	4,588,700	69.4
KYC-DD database	499,100	16.6	1,341,800	20.3
STRs and regulatory/investigative interaction	385,200	13.0	682,700	10.3
Total costs:	2,973,800	100.0	6,613,200	100.0
Cost per bank	198,250		440,880	
Extrapolated costs for all 18 banks	3,568,500		7,934,400	

The incremental cost of adjusting to enhanced AML/CFT regulations was $6.6 million for the 15 reporting banks and is extrapolated (using a simple average) to have been about $8 million for all banks. That is less than a third of the costs incurred by the MCs.

The cost for establishing internal AML/CFT compliance machinery was by far the largest cost incurred by banks (70 per cent compared to 50 per cent for MCs), while costs for establishing the KYC/DD database were much lower (20 per cent compared to 42 per cent for MCs) – suggesting that banks (especially foreign banks) had a great deal of help from the head offices. STR and other costs were slightly higher (10 per cent) than for MCs (8 per cent). However, within each of these three main categories the proportions accounted for by different sub-categories of costs showed a pretty similar pattern as that for MCs indicated above.

Hidden costs

The quantifiable costs incurred by MCs represent only direct visible costs. At the seminar (and in annotated responses to questionnaires) many respondents highlighted hidden costs that were difficult to quantify or identify. MCs repeatedly alluded to the **real** (losing existing clients to other jurisdictions) as well as **opportunity** costs (clients being discouraged from coming to Mauritius) of lost business because of the rigorous regulatory demands of AML/CFT compliance in Mauritius. The most frequent complaint made by MCs concerned the persistent questioning of clients on beneficial ownership details and the submission of excessive documentary particulars.

Opportunity losses are by definition difficult to measure, though they are not any the less real or less painful to bear because of that deficiency. It is practically impossible to ascribe a monetary figure to the lost business volume and profits that might otherwise have come to the country or the firm had AML regulation not been applied in as draconian a fashion. The study makes no attempt to estimate such losses, but acknowledges from evidence presented informally by many MCs that such losses have been accrued. In private, in privileged discussions with some MCs about their long-standing client relationships, many admitted to referring their more valued clients to correspondent firms or affiliates in other, more tolerant and less rigorous, jurisdictions (Dubai, Singapore and London) when they were unwilling to submit ultimate beneficiary ownership information that was insisted upon by Mauritian regulators.

Total AML/CFT costs: their relation to other performance variables

The foregoing analysis suggests that the **total quantifiable incremental cost to Mauritius** (i.e. to regulators and the IFS industry) in the four years 2002–05 of developing and applying the kind of AML/CFT regulatory regime recommended by the FATF and the IFIs **was about US$40 million**.

This figure comprised a total cost of $4.8 million incurred by public agencies, $27.3 million incurred by MCs and a further US$7.9 million incurred by banks. One-third of the total incremental cost accrued by the public sector was of a non-recurrent (capital) nature. Capital costs for MCs and banks were around a fifth of their total AML/CFT costs. As observed, these costs appear to be understated by around 25–30 per cent on the basis of inconsistencies and anomalies in the questionnaires returned. The real quantifiable costs could be in the order of about US$50 million, although that is not the figure adopted for analysis.

These sums are not trivial in the context of Mauritius, which had a 2005 Gross National Income (GNI) of US$6.04 billion. Gross value added in the financial services sector was under 10 per cent of GDP, or US$605 million. Of this amount, offshore banks were estimated to account for about US$85 million – i.e. 14 per cent of value-added by the financial services industry as a whole or about 1.4 per cent of GDP.

Incremental AML/CFT costs of nearly US$8 million incurred by banks between 2002 and 2005 (an annual average of $2 million) in addition to overall compliance costs of $8–10 million annually, have to be seen in the context of profits (after tax) averaging about $63 million annually over the four-year period 2002–2005 for Category 1 (domestic) banks and about US$65 million annually (before tax) for Category 2 (offshore) banks. They also have to be seen against an annual average wage bill of about US$35–40 million for domestic banks and around US$4.5 million for offshore banks.

The costs of MCs of US$27.3 million (or an annual average of US$6.8 million) have to be seen in the context of annual turnover of $37 million and annual profits for the industry averaging US$10 million before tax (US$7 million after tax) over the 2002–2005 period. The MC industry's net profits (after tax) declined sharply in 2004 to an industry total of under $2 million, thanks largely to additional regulatory costs and provisions. The MC industry's annual average AML/CFT costs also have to be seen in the context of an annual average wage bill of around US$5 million over the period in question, and in the context of total license income derived by the FSC averaging US$6 million annually of which 80 per cent ($4.8 million) was assumed to be attributable to annual fees payable by GBC and MC licensees. An illustrative picture of AML/CFT costs relative to these other variables is shown in table 9.12.

9.2 Qualitative assessment of costs and benefits

Qualitative assessment of incremental AML/CFT costs

Apart from the quantitative data on costs provided by the regulators, banks and MCs analysed in the previous section, respondents were also asked to react to qualitative questions and/or statements on which they were asked to express a view along a five-point scale (1–5). The low end of the scale (i.e. rating 1) reflected strong agreement, while the high end (rating 5) reflected total disagreement with the statements being made. Qualitative responses to questions on how the IFS industry in Mauritius saw the incremental costs and benefits of the enhanced anti-money laundering/countering financing of terrorism (AML/CFT) regime are scrutinised in this section. It highlights areas in which these responses support, or are inconsistent with, the quantitative

Table 9.12 AML/CFT costs in perspective

Indicators & variables for comparison (Amounts in US$ million; Ratios in %)	2002	2003	2004	2005 (Est.)	2002–05
Incremental AML/CFT costs: total	**8.0**	**8.3**	**9.5**	**14.2**	**40.0**
Of which: Public sector institutions	1.1	1.5	1.1	1.1	4.8
Banks	1.4	1.3	1.7	3.6	8.0
Management companies	5.5	5.6	6.7	9.5	27.3
Macro-indicators: **GNI at market prices**	*4,910*	*5,415*	*5,723*	*6,038*	
Financial intermediation:					
Gross Value-Added	411	469	555	605	2,040
Net Value-Added (NVA)	173	206	255	308	942
IFS Industry:					
Gross Value-Added	45	56	71	85	257
Net Value-Added (NVA)	28	33	39	43	143
Banking Industry:					
NVA in domestic banks	104	124	163	204	595
NVA in offshore banks	21	25	30	33	109
Ratios:					
AML/CFT Costs/Net VA in FI (%)	4.6	4.0	3.7	4.6	4.3
AML/CFT Costs/Net VA in IFS (%)	28.5	25.2	24.4	33.1	28.0
Banks: Net profits of domestic banks	56	58	66	73	253
Net profits of offshore banks	55	64	69	74	262
Ratios:					
Bank costs/Net VA in all banks (%)	1.1	0.9	0.9	1.5	1.1
Bank costs/Net VA in offshore banks (%)	6.7	5.2	5.6	10.8	7.3
Bank costs/Net profits of all banks (%)	1.3	1.0	1.2	2.5	1.5
Bank costs/Net profits of offshore banks (%)	2.2	2.0	2.4	5.0	3.1
Management Companies: **Turnover (US$ m)**	29.4	33.1	41.2	45.4	149.1
Total expenses	24.0	26.8	39.6	41.5	131.9
Profits (after tax)	5.4	6.3	1.6	3.9	17.2
GBC-MC License Fees collected by FSC:	2.6	6.5	5.1	5.9	20.1
Ratios:					
MC costs/GBC-MC license fees (%)	210.9	85.0	132.7	161.3	135.9
MC costs/MC turnover (%)	18.5	16.8	16.3	21.0	18.3
MC costs/MC expenses (%)	22.7	20.7	17.0	23.0	20.7
MC costs/MC profits (%)	101.0	88.1	420.1	244.9	158.6
Memo: employment in: ALL banks	*4,353*	*4,586*	*4,697*	*5,371*	
Offshore banks	*512*	*562*	*588*	*643*	
MCs	*510*	*600*	*785*	*950*	

Sources: FSC Annual Reports 2002 to 2005; BoM Annual Reports 2002 to 2004; National Accounts 2001 to 2005.

Considering the Consequences

estimates provided to provide a better nuanced picture of reality. How respondents perceived **benefits,** and whether they felt that intangible benefits (such as reputation) were being translated into tangible benefits (by way of increased turnover, profitability, efficiency, business diversification etc.) is also explored in this section. It concludes with an attempt to establish a clearer perspective on whether net benefits and side-benefits have been derived from the strengthening of the AML/CFT regulatory and compliance regimes in Mauritius.

Leaving aside any opportunity costs/losses that might have occurred as a consequence of the new AML/CFT regime, MCs and banks were unambiguously clear that the AML/CFT had imposed significant direct costs. In the view of MCs (and small MCs in particular) these costs were onerous and disproportionate to any benefits derived by individual firms operating in the IFS domain, the IFS industry as a whole or the country at large. The views of the banks were more moderate. A few banks expressed views that reflected the strong MC position, while the response of others was more generous and attenuated. The difference is explained partly by the fact that incremental AML/CFT costs for banks are a relatively insignificant proportion of their turnover and net profits. For MCs, the opposite is the case. Also, banks are more accustomed to demanding compliance regimes, whereas up until 2001 MCs were regulated with a lighter, more flexible (and perhaps more appropriate) touch.

The views of regulators were as to be expected, i.e. that the new AML/CFT regime had imposed extra costs but that these were low, tolerable and had to be absorbed by the IFS industry as an essential cost of doing business. Regulators saw themselves as doing the best they could, under formidable external pressure, to adopt new AML/CFT standards that they felt they were not in a position to question or oppose as that would have resulted in blacklisting by the FATF. They did not perceive their actions as being supine, bureaucratic or as imposing excessive cost burdens on the IFS industry. At the seminar the regulators, who were accustomed to a certain level of IFS industry dissatis-faction and complaint, seemed surprised at the depth and strength of feeling that they had perhaps over-stepped the mark and had damaged the competitiveness and profit-ability of the IFS industry in Mauritius.

The qualitative statements made (and questions asked) about respondents' perceptions of incremental AML/CFT costs were supposed to be modified at the local level by the study for contextual relevance. Given inordinate local delays in sending out question-naires, and the time pressures under which respondents were told to respond, few such modifications were made. In addition, several questions were omitted, ostensibly to avoid respondent overload, while the lead consultant was unable to review and ap-prove the final version of the questionnaire that was sent out. It appears in retrospect that problems may have arisen with the perceived meaning of some statements/ques-tions and with their interpretation by respondents. Nevertheless, despite these difficul-ties, enumerated in each case below, the qualitative parts of the questionnaire yielded responses that are worth in-depth exploration.

There were 12 (amended from the original 20 suggested by the lead consultant) qualitative statements/questions inserted in the questionnaires to amplify and elaborate respondents' views on incremental costs. They were:

1. **Has the new AML/CFT regime imposed reasonable additional costs to ensure the reputation of Mauritius as an International Financial Centre (IFC)?**

   [Note: The problem with this question was that it did not make clear whose costs were being referred to. Were they the costs of the firm asked to respond? Or overall costs for the IFS industry? Or costs incurred by the government and regulators? Or were they all three? In reality respondents might not have known what costs were incurred by anyone other than themselves. Their responses reflect that reality.]

2. **Has the new AML/CFT regime imposed reasonable additional costs on the official regulators of the financial system** (i.e. BoM, the FSC etc.)?

   [Note: The note above also applies in this instance. Unless respondents were aware of costs incurred by regulators, their impressions could only have been speculative.]

3. **Has the new AML/CFT regime imposed excessive additional costs for financial regulation in Mauritius (i.e. disproportionate to any conceivable benefit)?**

   [Note: In addition to the complications noted above, this is a leading question that might have reinforced respondent biases in a particular direction.]

4. **The new AML/CFT regime has imposed disproportionately high costs on our firm compared to any likely benefits that might accrue to us.**

   [Note: This direct statement does not require respondents to make judgements based on information they do not have. Answers were clearer and less confused for that reason. The same is true for the final eight statements/questions.]

5. **The new AML/CFT regime has imposed additional costs that are so high that our firm is considering exiting the IFS business.**

6. **The new AML/CFT regime has made excessive demands on the capabilities of our personnel in meeting new compliance requirements.**

7. **The new AML/CFT regime has required us to increase our staff complement substantially.**

8. **The new AML/CFT regime has required us to retrain front line staff dealing with customers.**

9. **The new AML/CFT regime has required us to retrain back office staff dealing with KYC/DD compliance and with regulators.**

10. **The new AML/CFT regime has required us to invest in additional new IT systems and retraining for staff handling these systems.**

11. **The new AML/CFT regime has required us to spend far more on systems, training and staff than was necessary for regular business growth.**

12. The new AML/CFT regime has diverted our attention from other more important matters concerning the diversification and growth of our IFS business [Note: In the version sent out this statement was garbled.]

Statement-by-statement analysis of respondents' qualitative views on costs

The pattern of responses from management companies and banks to each of these questions is shown in tabular form below and accompanied by a discussion of the responses.

Has the new AML-CFT regime imposed reasonable additional costs to ensure the reputation of Mauritius as an International Financial Centre (IFC)?

Responses from			AS	A	No opinion (%)	D	DS
			1	2	3	4	5
Management companies:	Small	[21]	4.8	42.9	28.6	23.7	0.0
	Medium	[4]	0.0	0.0	75.0	0.0	25.0
	Large	[7]	14.3	28.6	14.3	42.9	0.0
	Total	[32]	6.7	36.7	30.0	23.3	3.3
Banks:		[15]	33.3	33.3	13.3	20.0	0.0

AS 1= Agree Strongly; A 2= Agree; 3= No Clear Opinion; D 4= Disagree; DS 5= Disagree Strongly

Although the question is imprecise, with a caveat that created some confusion, the pattern of responses from MCs clusters between 2 and 4 on the rating scale (i.e. agree, no opinion and disagree), and between 1 and 3 for banks. The percentage of views at either end of the scale is insignificant. A third of all banks **agreed strongly** that the costs imposed had been reasonable to safeguard the reputation of Mauritius. Large and small MCs provided a pattern of answers within the same 2–4 rating cluster; but as many large MCs disagree with the statement as agree, while smaller MCs agree more than disagree. Medium-sized MCs indicate a response pattern skewed by too small a sample size. There was too high a proportion of 'no opinions' for comfort[4]. Discussions at the seminar made it clear that, if the question had not included the caveat ('to ensure the reputation of Mauritius as an IFC'), the proportion of answers for MCs would have shifted to 4–5 on the rating scale (i.e. disagree and strongly disagree that the additional costs were 'reasonable'). However, the proportion would have remained the same for banks. The pattern of responses reflected above does not accord with the quantitative information (and accompanying annotations) provided. These suggest that all MCs, regardless of size, felt that the additional costs were unreasonably high – although that applied to costs incurred by firms, rather than the expenditures made to safeguard the reputation of Mauritius. The above responses do accord with the quantitative information and views provided by banks.

Has the new AML/CFT regime imposed reasonable additional costs on the official regulators of the financial system?

Responses from			AS	A	No Opinion (%)	D	DS	NS (%)
			1	2	3	4	5	6
Management companies:	Small	[21]	9.5	23.8	38.1	19.0	4.8	4.8
	Medium	[4]	25.0	0.0	50.0	0.0	25.0	
	Large	[7]	0.0	28.6	42.9	14.3	14.3	
	Total	[32]	9.3	21.9	40.6	15.6	9.3	3.1
Banks:		[15]	20.0	13.3	53.3	13.3	0.0	

AS 1= Agree Strongly; A 2= Agree; 3= No Clear Opinion; D 4= Disagree; DS 5= Disagree Strongly; NS: Not Specified

The key feature of responses to this question for MCs and banks is the number of 'no opinions', which is perhaps understandable given that respondents were largely unaware of what the costs incurred by regulators were. However, of those who did have an opinion, the number of MCs in agreement with the view that 'costs were reasonable for regulators' marginally outweighed those that disagreed (by 31 per cent to 25 per cent) while, in the case of banks, those that agreed significantly outweighed those that disagreed (43 per cent to 13 per cent). Those opinions tend to support the view of regulators themselves that their costs were reasonable if not low.

Has the new AML/CFT regime imposed excessive additional costs for financial regulation in Mauritius (i.e. disproportionate to any conceivable benefit)?

Responses from			AS	A	No opinion (%)	D	DS
			1	2	3	4	5
Management companies:	Small	[21]	14.3	23.8	33.3	19.0	9.6
	Medium	[4]	50.0	0.0	25.0	25.0	0.0
	Large	[7]	14.3	42.9	14.3	28.6	0.0
	Total	[32]	18.8	25.0	28.1	21.9	6.2
Banks:		[15]	6.7	26.7	13.3	46.7	6.7

AS 1= Agree Strongly; A 2= Agree; 3= No Clear Opinion; D 4= Disagree; DS 5= Disagree Strongly

This was included as a test question to cross-check against responses to the previous question. The pattern of responses was inconsistent in the case of MCs, but consistent in the case of banks. The one revealing inconsistency in the case of both banks and MCs was that the proportion of 'don't knows or no opinions' should have been at least as high as for the previous question, given that respondents did not know what the costs of regulators were. However, they were much lower. Some 44 per cent of MCs agreed that costs for financial regulation were excessive whereas for the previous question just 25 per cent had disagreed with the view that the same costs were reasonable. The two proportions should have been more or less the same. About 28 per cent of MCs disagreed that costs were excessive, which seemed to reconcile with the view expressed by 31 per cent of them for the previous question suggesting that costs were reasonable. The MC view was somewhat reversed for the banks, of which a third agreed that costs were excessive while over 52 per cent disagreed. The inconsistencies revealed in the responses to the above two questions indicate how sensitive a survey of this nature can be to the particular words used to evoke a response.

The new AML/CFT regime has imposed disproportionately high costs on our firm compared to any likely benefits that might accrue to us.

Responses from			AS	A	No opinion (%)	D	DS
			1	2	3	4	5
Management companies:	Small	[21]	23.8	28.6	19.0	19.0	9.6
	Medium	[4]	50.0	0.0	25.0	25.0	0.0
	Large	[7]	0.0	57.1	14.3	28.6	0.0
	Total	[32]	21.9	31.2	18.8	21.9	6.2
Banks:		[15]	6.7	26.7	0.0	53.3	13.3

AS 1 = Agree Strongly; A 2 = Agree; 3 = No Clear Opinion; D 4 = Disagree; DS 5 = Disagree Strongly

The qualitative responses to this particular statement (which is clear and unambiguous) appear to be misaligned with the views expressed by MCs in their quantitative responses and more vociferously during the seminar. It may suggest a problem with statement misinterpretation by junior personnel, who may have been too inexperienced to understand their business, or the meaning of their response. That was clearly not the case for banks, all of which had an opinion with the majority (two-thirds) being clearly of the view that their costs were not disproportionately high. It seems almost inconceivable (especially in view of the seminar discussion on this subject) that nearly a fifth of MCs had no opinion on whether the incremental cost burden imposed by new AML/CFT regulations was disproportionately high or not, when all their other responses suggest strongly that they had. It was odd, in the light of other responses (see below) and the discussions at the seminar, that only 53 per cent of MCs indicated that costs were too high, while 28 per cent disagreed with that view. The reactions of MCs at the seminar suggested a figure closer to 100 per cent believing that costs were too high. That picture can only be reconciled if the respondents who had expressed no opinion (19 per cent) were aligned with the small majority (53 per cent) who thought costs were too high. It is of course possible, but unlikely, that MCs disagreeing with that view were not at the seminar.

The new AML/CFT regime has imposed additional costs that are so high that our firm is considering exiting the IFS business.

Responses from			AS	A	No opinion (%)	D	DS
			1	2	3	4	5
Management companies:	Small	[21]	0.0	4.8	23.8	28.5	42.9
	Medium	[4]	0.0	0.0	0.0	50.0	50.0
	Large	[7]	0.0	0.0	0.0	0.0	100.0
	Total	[32]	0.0	3.1	15.6	25.0	56.3
Banks:		[15]	0.0	0.0	13.3	26.7	60.0

AS 1= Agree Strongly; A 2= Agree; 3= No Clear Opinion; D 4= Disagree; DS 5= Disagree Strongly

This again was a test statement (carrying the previous statement to an extreme) to gauge the degree to which the IFS industry felt overburdened by the incremental cost of the post-2002 AML/CFT regime. The response was unambiguous. Over 81 per cent of MCs (indeed 100 per cent of medium-sized and large MCs) and 87 per cent of banks disagreed that incremental costs were so high as to prompt them to consider exiting the IFS business. Indeed only one small MC agreed with the proposition. Strangely, five small MCs had no opinion on even as extreme a statement, nor did two banks.

Questions/statements relating to staff and staff costs: The following four statements were designed to draw respondents out on the staffing implications and staff costs of coping with the new AML/CFT regime. The responses were as might have been expected, with increasingly strong views being expressed about pressures on staff in reaction to more specific statements relating to training front and back office (including compliance) staff

The new AML/CFT regime has made excessive demands on the capabilities of our personnel in meeting new compliance requirements.

Responses from			AS	A	No opinion (%)	D	DS
			1	2	3	4	5
Management companies:	Small	[21]	19.0	28.6	14.6	28.6	9.5
	Medium	[4]	50.0	0.0	25.0	25.0	0.0
	Large	[7]	42.9	28.6	0.0	14.3	14.3
	Total	[32]	28.1	25.0	12.5	25.0	9.4
Banks:		[15]	6.7	33.3	6.7	46.7	6.7

AS 1= Agree Strongly; A 2= Agree; 3= No Clear Opinion; D 4= Disagree; DS 5= Disagree Strongly

The new regime has required us to increase our staff complement substantially.

Responses from			AS	A	No opinion (%)	D	DS
			1	2	3	4	5
Management companies:	Small	[21]	14.3	57.1	14.3	14.3	0.0
	Medium	[4]	50.0	25.0	0.0	25.0	0.0
	Large	[7]	71.4	14.3	0.0	14.3	0.0
	Total	[32]	31.2	43.8	9.4	15.6	0.0
Banks:		[15]	0.0	46.7	20.0	33.3	0.0

AS 1= Agree Strongly; A 2= Agree; 3= No Clear Opinion; D 4= Disagree; DS 5= Disagree Strongly

The new regime has required us to retrain front line staff dealing with customers.

Responses from			AS	A	No opinion (%)	D	DS
			1	2	3	4	5
Management companies:	Small	[21]	19.0	57.2	9.5	9.5	4.8
	Medium	[4]	75.0	25.0	0.0	0.0	0.0
	Large	[7]	57.1	58.6	0.0	14.3	0.0
	Total	[32]	34.4	46.9	6.3	9.3	3.1
Banks:		[15]	53.3	33.3	0.0	13.3	0.0

AS 1= Agree Strongly; A 2= Agree; 3= No Clear Opinion; D 4= Disagree; DS 5= Disagree Strongly

The new regime has required us to retrain back office staff dealing with KYC/DD compliance and with regulators.

Responses from			AS	A	No opinion (%)	D	DS
			1	2	3	4	5
Management Companies:	Small	[21]	33.3	42.9	23.8	0.0	0.0
	Medium	[4]	75.0	25.0	0.0	0.0	0.0
	Large	[7]	42.9	42.9	0.0	14.3	0.0
	Total	[32]	40.6	40.6	15.6	3.2	0.0
Banks:		[15]	53.3	33.3	0.0	13.3	0.0

AS 1= Agree Strongly; A 2= Agree; 3= No Clear Opinion; D 4= Disagree; DS 5= Disagree Strongly

As can be seen from the above pattern of responses, banks were evenly divided in their views about whether their extant staff resources had been overstretched, or needed to be increased, because of AML/CFT demands when asked about the issue in general terms. However, they reacted more strongly when asked specific questions about front and back office staff having to be retrained (presumably with accompanying costs).

An increasing majority of MCs felt, on the other hand, that their staff resources had been overstretched (53 per cent), had needed to be increased substantially (75 per cent), and had to be retrained (81 per cent for both front and back office staff) because of additional AML/CFT related work. This view was substantiated by their quantitative data on overall costs, in which staff accounted for a significant proportion of total additional costs.

While banks had the same retraining needs (and costs), they did not feel quite as strongly as MCs about the need to increase staff to alleviate overstretching. Only 40 per cent of banks thought their staff had been overstretched by additional AML/CFT demands and just under a half had to increase their staff resources for this purpose. Again, the qualitative view is supported by the quantitative evidence on this particular issue.

The new AML/CFT regime has required us to invest in additional new IT systems and retraining for staff handling these systems.

Responses from			AS	A	No opinion (%)	D	DS
			1	2	3	4	5
Management companies:	Small	[21]	19.0	33.3	19.0	14.3	14.3
	Medium	[4]	50.0	0.0	0.0	50.0	0.0
	Large	[7]	14.3	56.1	14.3	0.0	14.3
	Total	[32]	21.9	34.4	15.6	15.6	12.5
Banks:		[15]	13.3	60.0	13.3	6.7	6.7

AS 1= Agree Strongly; A 2= Agree; 3= No Clear Opinion; D 4= Disagree; DS 5= Disagree Strongly

The new AML/CFT regime has required us to spend far more on systems, training and staff than was necessary for regular business growth.

Responses from			AS	A	No opinion (%)	D	DS
			1	2	3	4	5
Management companies:	Small	[21]	23.8	47.6	14.3	14.3	0.0
	Medium	[4]	50.0	50.0	0.0	0.0	0.0
	Large	[7]	57.1	28.6	0.0	14.3	0.0
	Total	[32]	34.3	43.7	9.4	12.5	0.0
Banks:		[15]	13.3	33.3	6.7	46.7	0.0

AS 1= Agree Strongly; A 2= Agree; 3= No Clear Opinion; D 4= Disagree; DS 5= Disagree Strongly

The above two statements were aimed at drawing out MC/bank views on incremental IT systems expenditures necessitated by the enhanced AML/CFT regime. A majority (56 per cent) of MCs felt that they had been required to make significant additional investments in IT systems as a result of increasingly complicated AML/CFT compliance demands. However, a fairly significant proportion (44 per cent) had either no view or disagreed. Banks were more emphatic about this than MCs, with more than 73 per cent believing that they had to make such investments. However, a higher proportion of MCs (78 per cent) felt they had to spend disproportionately more on such systems than was necessary than banks (46.6 per cent), with the majority of banks (53 per cent) having no opinion or disagreeing.

The quantitative evidence does not fully reflect this divided view. Despite half of all respondents believing that additional investment in IT systems was significant, the quantitative evidence was surprising. It showed how little the IFS industry in Mauritius (relative to jurisdictions elsewhere) has spent on increasing or upgrading IT systems (hardware and software) to meet increased AML/CFT compliance, and to maintain much larger databases of confidential client information that has to be instantly referred to, cross-matched and exchanged. If the qualitative data were to be reconciled with the quantitative data, the only reasonable conclusion might be that respondents had either understated their incremental IT costs or they had not incurred really high IT costs as yet. (Note: This seems to be true of the FSC, the FIU and the BoM, all of which in their most recent annual reports indicate that they will need to make substantial new IT investments in the coming year to cope with substantially increased regulatory/supervision workloads.)

The new AML/CFT regime has *diverted our attention* from other more important matters concerning the diversification and growth of our IFS business

Responses from			AS	A	No opinion (%)	D	DS
			1	2	3	4	5
Management companies:	Small	[21]	38.1	23.8	33.3	4.8	0.0
	Medium	[4]	50.0	0.0	25.0	25.0	0.0
	Large	[7]	28.6	14.2	28.6	0.0	28.6
	Total	[32]	37.5	18.8	31.1	6.3	6.3
Banks:		[15]	6.7	26.7	20.0	26.7	20.0

AS 1= Agree Strongly; A 2= Agree; 3= No Clear Opinion; D 4= Disagree; DS 5= Disagree Strongly

Finally, over 56 per cent of MCs felt that coping with the new AML/CFT regime had diverted their attention from more important matters concerning their growth and diversification. However, only a third of banks concurred. A significant proportion of both groups expressed no opinion. It was clear from the seminar that the difference in views between banks and MCs was because: (a) banks had taken additional AML/CFT demands in their stride partly because they were used to greater compliance demands; but also (b) when it came to providing IFS to licensed GBC clients, it was the MCs that took the brunt of dealing with the additional KYC/DD information load which they later shared with banks.

In an overall sense the qualitative responses broadly supported the quantitative returns provided, albeit with a few inconsistencies and anomalies that suggest the need for further exploration of the issues they raise in a future study.

Qualitative assessment of incremental AML/CFT benefits

A perspective on 'benefits': Before this study was launched in Mauritius, preliminary discussions were held by the lead and local consultants with MCs and banks to determine whether it might be possible to identify any tangible benefits that had been derived from enhancing the AML/CFT regulatory and compliance regime. It was clear from those discussions that it would be difficult to **identify**, and almost impossible to **quantify**, any tangible incremental benefits resulting from the new regime. Regulators and policy-makers felt, however, that one obvious tangible benefit was Mauritius's ability to stay in the offshore financial centre business as a consequence of adopting the new regime. If one takes that as a serious rather than self-justifying proposition, and attempts to put a value to it then, as the estimates in table 9.12 suggest, the benefits are large. Staying in business has resulted in:

- Net value addition by the IFS industry amounting to an aggregate US$143 million between 2002 and 2005 (an average of about US$36 million annually);

- Aggregate net profits of offshore banks amounting to US$262 million (US$63 million pa);

- Aggregate net profits of MCs amounting to US$17.2 million (or US$4.3 million pa);

- GBC-MC license fees aggregating US$20 million (US$5 million pa) – although these might be seen as a benefit to Mauritius, they represent a cost to the IFS industry although there is a positive net balance-of-payments effect when fees are paid by offshore clients; and

- Net employment of about 1,400 people with an annual average wage bill of about US$15 million (again perhaps a benefit to Mauritius, but a cost to the IFS industry and difficult to ascertain how much of this employment can be counted as a net benefit).

That provides an estimate of total benefits amounting to US$457 million over the four-year period, or an average of US$114 million per annum. However, that figure includes some double-counting because an element of net **financial** profits would be captured in net **economic** value addition and in employment figures as well. Discounting that complication for argument's sake, and not trying to net it out, the volume of benefits – seen against aggregate costs of US$40 million for the new AML/CFT regime – make

net benefits amounting to US$417 million look quite substantial, with a cost/benefit ratio of over 1-to-11.

Can the assertion of regulators and policy-makers – i.e. that the main benefit was that the imposed AML/CFT regime allowed Mauritius to stay in the offshore financial centre business – be taken seriously for the purposes of this study? As far as this study is concerned, that would stretch credulity to its limits. Put simplistically, the proposition is tantamount to someone threatening to end your existence if you do not accede to their demands, regardless of cost. You then pay the cost without calculating it in advance (assuming you can afford it) for the 'benefit' of staying alive. Then you count the income you receive from being alive as a benefit without counting the threat itself (only the blackmail part of it) as a cost. However, what if the threat had not arisen in the first place, because you did nothing to arouse it, although some other party might have? It was an artificial threat contrived by other parties determined to deal with perceived threats to themselves in ways that protected **their** perceived interests regardless of the cost to **your** legitimate existential and business interests. Under those circumstances, can succumbing to what is effectively blackmail be considered a legitimate benefit?

Putting it differently, before the new AML/CFT regime was introduced, Mauritius could not, under any circumstances, have been portrayed as being poorly regulated even by the standards of regulation in many **developed** jurisdictions. Arguably, even today, regulation in some of these jurisdictions is more flexible and accommodating than in Mauritius. The case of Mauritius was not that of a poorly-regulated, small OFC jurisdiction, vulnerable to predation by criminal elements openly abusing the financial system. Prior to 1992 Mauritius had a thriving IFS industry whose gross benefits were almost the same as in 2005/6, but with much lower regulatory costs.

Set against those circumstances, the study takes the view that the incremental net benefits of enhanced AML/CFT legislation are virtually zero. They have added almost nothing of value in protecting Mauritius' legitimate interests. Allowing generously that they might have helped in keeping criminality in financial transactions further at bay, it is difficult to see any incremental benefit because even the previous regulatory regime did that quite adequately. If the new regime is 'tighter' it is impossible to assess by how much or even how much such tightening has benefited Mauritius. The new regime certainly is more process driven, requires more documentation – some of which may (as suggested at the seminar) be useless. It does not necessarily enable MCs, banks or regulators to 'know-their-clients' any better, nor to discern their motives more transparently, through due diligence – than they did before.

Those circumstances notwithstanding, and taking into account the view of the IFS industry that any benefits that might have been derived would be intangible (i.e. reputational) and could not be quantified, the questionnaires incorporated 15 questions aimed at eliciting a qualitative 'feel' for what unquantifiable benefits might still have accrued from the new regime. These statements (listed below) and the responses to them are analysed in the paragraphs that follow. The statements to which reactions on 'benefits' were sought were:

Has the new AML/CFT regime:

- Strengthened overall financial system regulation in Mauritius?
- Enhanced the reputation of Mauritius as an international financial centre?
- Increased the competitiveness of Mauritius compared to other offshore centres?

After new KYC/DD compliance requirements were introduced, what has been the impact on:

- Your firm's overall business, i.e. by what percentage has it increased/decreased?
- Your firm's total revenue from IFS activity?
- Your firm's profits from IFS activity?
- Staff efficiency/productivity in your firm?
- Client and source country diversification?
- Access to foreign markets?
- Your firm's product/services diversification
- Increased competitiveness of Mauritius as an IFC?
- Increased competitiveness of your firm in the IFS Industry?
- Improving your firm's technological capacity?
- Improving your firm's overall knowledge base in providing global IFS?
- Increasing the profitability of your firm from improved risk management?

The pattern of responses is portrayed below, along with an analysis of what they imply.

Has the new AML/CFT regime *strengthened financial regulation in Mauritius?*

Responses from			AS	A	No opinion (%)	D	DS
			1	2	3	4	5
Management companies:	Small	[21]	23.8	28.6	38.0	4.8	4.8
	Medium	[4]	50.0	25.0	25.0	0.0	0.0
	Large	[7]	42.9	28.6	28.6	0.0	0.0
	Total	[32]	31.3	28.1	34.4	3.1	3.1
Banks:		[15]	40.0	40.0	20.0	0.0	0.0

AS 1= Agree Strongly; A 2= Agree; 3= No Clear Opinion; D 4= Disagree; DS 5= Disagree Strongly

An overwhelming majority (80 per cent) of banks felt that the new regime had strengthened overall financial system regulation in Mauritius. A slightly lower but clear majority (59 per cent) of MCs felt the same way, although the majority was higher (75 per cent) among the larger and the medium-sized MCs. Oddly, over a third of MCs and a fifth of banks had no opinion on that question, while an insignificant minority of MCs (the smaller ones) but no banks, actually disagreed.

Has the new AML/CFT regime *enhanced the reputation of Mauritius* as an international financial centre?

Responses from			AS	A	No opinion (%)	D	DS
			1	2	3	4	5
Management companies:	Small	[21]	23.8	42.9	14.3	19.0	0.0
	Medium	[4]	25.0	50.0	25.0	0.0	0.0
	Large	[7]	14.3	57.1	28.6	0.0	0.0
	Total	[32]	21.9	46.9	18.9	12.3	0.0
Banks:		[15]	33.3	33.3	26.7	6.7	0.0

AS 1= Agree Strongly; A 2= Agree; 3= No Clear Opinion; D 4= Disagree; DS 5= Disagree Strongly

The pattern of responses to this complementary question supports the views expressed in the previous one. Nearly 69 per cent of MCs and 67 per cent of banks agreed that the reputation of Mauritius had been *enhanced* as a result of introducing the new AML/CFT regime. About 19 per cent of MCs had no view and only 12 per cent disagreed. The respective proportions for the banks were 27 per cent (no view) and 7 per cent (disagreed). The industry response was therefore unambiguous and tallied with that of regulators.

Has the new AML/CFT regime *increased the competitiveness of Mauritius* compared to other offshore financial centres?

Responses from			AS	A	No opinion (%)	D	DS
			1	2	3	4	5
Management Companies:	Small	[21]	0.0	14.3	42.9	28.6	14.3
	Medium	[4]	0.0	0.0	50.0	50.0	0.0
	Large	[7]	14.3	0.0	28.6	42.8	14.3
	Total	[32]	3.1	9.4	40.6	34.4	12.5
Banks:		[15]	6.7	26.6	46.7	0.0	20.0

AS 1= Agree Strongly; A 2= Agree; 3= No Clear Opinion; D 4= Disagree; DS 5= Disagree Strongly

This question was asked to establish more clearly whether enhanced reputation had resulted in a competitive benefit to Mauritius. After all, if regulation was strengthened to make the financial system sounder and safer, and to protect the interests of offshore clients better, it should have: (a) incentivised existing clients to do more business in Mauritius; and (b) prompted more new clients to use the services of Mauritius as an IFC. Yet, the response to this question from both MCs and banks was strangely reserved and ambiguous. Most felt that financial regulation had been strengthened, and Mauritius' reputation enhanced, by the new AML/CFT regime. Whether they presumed this was the case axiomatically (i.e. if regulation is strengthened, reputation must automatically be enhanced), or whether they actually discerned this from surveying their clients, is unknown. However, oddly enough, a sizeable 41 per cent of MCs and 47 per cent of banks had 'no opinion' on whether the competitiveness of Mauritius had been increased as a result, while 47 per cent of MCs and 20 per cent of banks disagreed with this view. That left only a small minority (12.5 per cent) of MCs and a more substantial minority (a third) of banks actually agreeing that competitiveness had been increased.

When this view was tested at the seminar, the above finding was altered resoundingly. During the seminar respondents stepped off the fence and expressed a virtually unanimous view that Mauritius' competitiveness had definitely been **diminished** as a consequence of the new AML/CFT regime. Most discussants who spoke cited anecdotal evidence of losing extant clients (a real loss) as well as losing potential business they thought they 'had in the bag' (an opportunity cost). They were adamant that this was because of a view among offshore clients that regulation in Mauritius had become so demanding, bureaucratic and mindless, that they would rather shift their business elsewhere; not just to new jurisdictions like Dubai, but also to supposedly more stringent jurisdictions like Singapore and London, which clients felt were actually more flexible and reasonable in their disclosure information demands than regulators in Mauritius.

Thus, respondents who participated in the seminar made it abundantly clear that, while the reputation of Mauritius as an IFC may in theory have been enhanced, that did little or nothing in practice in terms of enhancing its competitiveness from a business viewpoint. Indeed, it may even have had the opposite effect: the IFS industry in Mauritius felt that its image and prospects had been damaged rather than assisted by the way in which AML/CFT regulation had actually been introduced and implemented.

With this important issue articulated and put to rest, the rest of this section focuses on respondents' views about the specific benefits derived by their firms (rather than by Mauritius generally) along a variety of parameters and dimensions.

What has been the impact of new KYC/DD compliance requirements on *your firm's overall business*; i.e. by what percentage has it increased or decreased?

Responses from		NS	Business **decreased** by:			Business **increased** by:		
			0–15%	>15–30%	>30%	0–15%	>15–30%	>30%
Management:	Small	[21]	4.8	19.0	4.8	19.0	28.6	9.5	14.3
companies	Medium	[4]	0.0	55.0	0.0	0.0	25.0	25.0	0.0
	Large	[7]	0.0	14.3	0.0	0.0	46.7	33.3	6.7
	Total	[32]	3.1	21.9	3.1	12.5	25.0	15.6	18.8
Banks:		[15]	0.0	13.3	0.0	0.0	46.7	33.3	6.7

NS: Not Specified

As is evident from the table above, the revenues of a majority of respondents, MCs (over 59%) and banks (87 per cent) saw an overall increase in their turnover between 2002 and 2005. Most of these witnessed an increase of 0–15 per cent, which is to be expected as normal or average under typical business circumstances. Over 40 per cent of MCs (and over 45 per cent of small and medium MCs) saw a *decline* in their revenues. Most of these saw a decrease in the 0–15 per cent range, although four small MCs suffered a decline of more than 30 per cent. The question asked specifically whether the increase/decrease was due to the impact of new KYC/DD compliance requirements. However, private discussions with respondents during the seminar revealed that the responses reflected actual increases/decreases in revenues without specific attribution to increased KYC/DD requirements when revenues increased, yet definitely ascribing the decline to KYC/DD demands when revenues decreased. That asymmetry suggests that the results above need to be interpreted with caution. The pattern of responses reflects what has happened to MCs and banks in terms of their business volume (gross revenues) over the last four years. However, it invalidates the purpose of the question with the responses not being properly attributable to any particular reason. Another problem with the question is that it did not specify whether the decline was in *annual* (i.e. annually for each of the four years) or *aggregate* terms (i.e. overall increase/decrease over the four year period as a whole). The result was a mixed response. Some respondents indicated annual performance, while others answered for the aggregate over the period.

The overall picture that emerges is therefore confusing in that the qualitative responses do not fully reflect the several opinions expressed about lost business. However, the fact that over 40 per cent of small and medium MCs saw their revenues fall does partially support that picture and is disconcerting. The fact that two (out of 15) banks saw revenues fall by 0–15 per cent contrasts with the picture for MCs. These banks did not attribute KYC/DD specifically as being responsible for their revenue declines. The general picture that emerges is that the new AML/CFT regime did not result in an overall revenue loss for the IFS industry. Instead, at least three (out of the seven reporting) large MCs and the overwhelming majority of banks (13 out of 15 responding) saw increased revenues (40 per cent of them by more than 15 per cent), while many small and medium MCs lost revenues in the post-2002 regulatory environment.

That finding has implications for increasing concentration of market power among MCs in the IFS industry (a fact borne out also by the large market share – 60 per cent of large MCs and their even larger share – 75 per cent – of the industry's net profits) which should cause policy-makers and regulators some concern. If additional regulation has the net effect of increasing the concentration of a larger market share among fewer companies then it is probably discouraging competition of the kind needed to have a thriving IFS industry by making the costs of regulation unbearable for small firms.

What has been the impact of new KYC/DD compliance requirements on *your firm's total revenue* from IFS activity?

Responses from			Nil	Low	Moderate	High	NS
				(%)			
			1	2	3	4	5
Management:	**Small**	[21]	23.8	38.1	33.3	0.0	4.8
companies	**Medium**	[4]	25.0	50.0	25.0	0.0	0.0
	Large	[7]	0.0	28.6	71.4	14.3	0.0
	Total	[32]	9.3	21.9	40.6	15.6	9.3
Banks:		[15]	20.0	13.4	53.2	13.4	0.0

Although this question seeks almost the same information about revenues, but without specifying percentages, it elicits a supportive pattern of responses thus confirming by a cross-check the validity of responses on how revenues have been affected by the new AML/CFT regime. Nearly 41 per cent of MCs and over 53 per cent of the banks saw the impact on revenues as being moderate (which compares with the 41 per cent of MCs that saw increases in revenues of 0–30 per cent and 47 per cent of banks that saw an increase of 0–15 per cent; obviously the MCs and banks interpreted the word 'moderate' differently).

By the same token, nearly 16 per cent of MCs saw the (negative) revenue impact of new KYC/DD requirements as being high (compared to the 16 per cent whose revenues declined by over 15 per cent) while 13.3 per cent of banks saw the revenue impact as high. This again corresponds exactly with the 13.3 per cent of banks that registered a revenue decline in answering the previous question. This pattern of responses confirms the finding that, while MCs and banks were quick to link additional KYC/DD requirements with **declines** in revenue, they were less ready to associate **increases** in revenue to the same KYC/DD requirements, as that would have seemed counterintuitive.

What has been the impact of new KYC/DD compliance requirements on *your firm's incremental profits* from IFS activity?

Responses from			Nil	Low	Moderate	High	NS
				(%)			
			1	2	3	4	5
Management:	Small	[21]	33.3	28.6	33.3	0.0	4.8
companies	Medium	[4]	75.0	0.0	25.0	0.0	0.0
	Large	[7]	14.3	57.1	28.6	0.0	0.0
	Total	[32]	34.3	31.3	31.3	0.0	3.1
Banks:		[13]	7.7	69.2	23.1	0.0	0.0

Contrary to the picture presented on revenues, the situation with regard to MC and bank profits is more subdued. No MC or bank recorded the impact on profits as being high. A significant minority (31 per cent of MCs and 23 per cent of banks) recorded it as moderate. The majority of MCs (66 per cent) and banks (77 per cent) felt that the impact on profits was nil or low. Profits-wise, MCs have been having a poor time. Annual profits averaged US$5.5 million for the MC industry in 2001–03. However, they fell to US$1.6 million in 2004 and are estimated to have recovered to just under US$4 million in 2005.

The profit performance of MCs is surprising. Turnover had not declined in 2001–2005, although it levelled off in 2002–2003. However, expenses (mainly the costs of regulation) took a quantum leap in 2004 and have stayed on a higher plateau since. Discussions with a number of MCs suggest that the loss of profitability of individual firms reflects the loss of competitiveness of Mauritius as an IFC; nonetheless, differences in the profit performance of small and large MCs also suggest that economies of scale are a factor in determining competitiveness at the level of the individual firm.

What has been the impact of your firm's response to the new AML/CFT compliance regime on *increased staff efficiency and productivity*?

Responses from			Nil	Low	Moderate	High	NS
				(%)			
			1	2	3	4	5
Management:	Small	[21]	19.0	28.6	33.3	14.3	4.8
companies	Medium	[4]	50.0	25.0	25.0	0.0	0.0
	Large	[7]	14.3	28.6	42.9	14.3	0.0
	Total	[32]	21.9	28.1	34.4	12.5	3.1
Banks:		[13]	0.0	53.8	46.2	0.0	0.0

Responses on this question were evenly divided. Half of the MCs and just over half the banks (54 per cent) responding indicated that the impact on staff efficiency/productivity had been nil/low while just under a half in each case (i.e. MCs and banks) reported that it had been moderate/high, although those MCs reporting 'high' were in a minority and represented just one large firm along with three small firms. Clearly the industry has not attempted to cope with increased compliance costs by squeezing more efficiency/productivity out of staff. MCs and banks have just increased staff numbers. Perhaps staff efficiency/productivity were already high, compliance machinery and systems were close to perfect, and higher efficiency could not be squeezed out through greater reliance on better IT systems. Whatever the reason, it is clear that in Mauritius the introduction of a new AML/CFT regime did not have any benefit by way of improved systemic efficiency in the IFS industry's compliance-response.

What has been the impact of your firm's response to the new AML/CFT compliance regime on *increased client base and client source diversification?*

Responses from			Nil	Low	Moderate	High	NS
					(%)		
			1	2	3	4	5
Management:	**Small**	[21]	28.6	38.1	23.8	4.8	4.8
companies	Medium	[4]	50.0	50.0	0.0	0.0	0.0
	Large	[7]	14.3	42.9	28.6	14.3	0.0
	Total	[32]	28.1	40.6	21.9	3.1	3.1
Banks:		[13]	15.4	61.6	15.4	7.7	0.0

At present, measured in terms of inward investments or sources of funds (a better indicator than the origin of supposedly beneficial owners, since these are categorised by the nationality of the shell corporations and trusts set up to own offshore assets rather than by the nationality of the real eventual beneficial owner), almost three-quarters of Mauritian IFS business is heavily dependent on a continuing flow of inward investments by clients from **India** (54 per cent) and **Indonesia** (18 per cent). Clients of **Chinese** origin (from China, Singapore and Hong Kong collectively) account for another 13 per cent. **African** clients account for 5 per cent (of which two-thirds are from South Africa), and clients from all other countries/regions account for a collective 10 per cent. These clients have invested mainly in the (equity and debt) of companies and trusts of in countries such as the USA (27 per cent), Singapore and Hong Kong (24 per cent), other OFCs (20 per cent), the UK (9 per cent) and other countries (including Indonesia, India etc.) – 17 per cent. Thus the Mauritian IFS industry (MCs and banks) is exposed to a high concentration risk.

A key observation made by the First Deputy Governor of the BoM at the seminar was that Mauritian MCs and banks had not done enough to diversify either their geographic market base or to widen and deepen the range of products/services they offered. They were still too dependent for their business on the Indian and Indonesian tax treaties. Conditions in both countries could change easily; e.g. India might soon go for full convertibility of the Indian rupee (Rs) and drop all the NRI investment preferences it presently provides. This might result in a sudden loss of business as a consequence. There is much substantive merit in this observation, which the industry would do well to take up as a strategic challenge and heed.

If the new AML/CFT regime has indeed enhanced the reputation of Mauritius as a well-regulated IFC, it is not implausible to suggest that, as a result, Mauritian MCs and banks (with marketing effort in other countries and regions) should attract a larger number of clients from a wider number of places. This question was asked to test that assumption.

A significant majority of respondents (69 per cent of MCs and 77 per cent of banks) felt that the new AML/CFT regime had done little or nothing to assist either client type or source diversification. In other words, the supposed positive **reputation effect** had not translated itself into a tangible benefit by way of either increased or more diversified business. A small minority of MCs (22 per cent) and banks (15 per cent) felt that the new regime had resulted in a moderate impact, while only one large MC and one bank felt that the impact had been high. How much this outcome has to do with the inherent conservatism and complacency of MCs in the Mauritian IFS industry, and how much it has to do with the effects of the AML/CFT regime, is difficult to discern or attribute. However, it is an issue worthy of further exploration by the IFS industry and government. An answer to that question is crucial in determining the future viability, growth and direction of Mauritius as an IFC.

What has been the impact of the new AML/CFT compliance regime on *increased access to foreign markets?*

Responses from			Nil	Low	Moderate	High	NS
					(%)		
			1	2	3	4	5
Management:	**Small**	[21]	19.0	52.4	14.3	9.5	4.8
companies	**Medium**	[4]	75.0	0.0	25.0	0.0	0.0
	Large	[7]	14.3	57.1	14.3	14.3	0.0
	Total	[32]	25.0	46.9	15.6	9.3	3.1
Banks:		[13]	7.7	46.2	38.4	7.7	0.0

As an extension of the previous question, the response rate is similar though not identical. Nearly 72 per cent of MCs and 54 per cent of banks indicated that the new AML/CFT regime had either no impact or a low impact on the geographic diversification of clientele. Again, however, it is debatable whether it was the additional burden of regulation, or the general complacency of the industry, that is responsible for that outcome. More banks (38 per cent) than MCs (16 per cent) felt there was a moderate impact while only 9 per cent of MCs and 8 per cent of banks though the impact on increased access to foreign markets was high. Again, the responses to this question underlined the fact that even if enhanced AML/CFT regulation had improved the reputation of Mauritius, it had not done much in attracting a wider geographical client base.

What has been the impact of the new AML/CFT compliance regime on *increased product and service diversification by your firm?*

Responses from			Nil	Low (%)	Moderate	High	NS
			1	2	3	4	5
Management:	Small	[21]	33.3	38.1	19.0	4.8	4.8
companies	Medium	[4]	75.0	0.0	25.0	0.0	0.0
	Large	[7]	28.6	42.9	28.6	0.0	0.0
	Total	[32]	37.5	34.4	31.9	3.1	3.1
Banks:		[13]	23.1	46.2	23.1	7.7	0.0

The table above provides support for the criticism that the IFS industry is complacent. In the face of the increased challenge posed by the toughening of the AML/CFT regime, one might have expected the IFS industry to exert active efforts to both diversify its client base and diversify its range of products and services. The previous two tables showed that the industry had failed to diversify geographically. This table supports the view that the IFS industry has failed to diversify functionally as well. Nearly 72 per cent of MCs and over 69 per cent of banks reported that the functional diversification impact of enhanced AML/CFT regulation was either nil or low. Only 35 per cent of MCs and 31 per cent of banks reported a moderate or high impact on product/service diversification.

One explanation might be that tougher AML/CFT regulation has dampened rather than increased the ability of MCs to look beyond their extant geographical client base and offer more products and services to attract new business from existing as well as potential clients. A second reason might be that the additional resources expended by MCs on strengthening compliance regimes have diverted resources away from strategic marketing and business development pursuits. There is some support for this explanation from responses to the question on whether the new regime had diverted attention from more important business priorities. However, the response leaves unanswered the question of whether the IFS industry is picking up the gauntlet and addressing the challenge of survival and growth in the face of enhanced regulation, with its supposedly concomitant reputation-enhancing effects.

What has the impact of the new AML/CFT regime been on *increasing the competitiveness of Mauritius as an IFC?*

Responses from			Nil	Low (%)	Moderate	High	NS
			1	2	3	4	5
Management:	Small	[21]	33.3	23.8	33.3	4.8	4.8
companies	Medium	[4]	50.0	25.0	25.0	0.0	0.0
	Large	[7]	0.0	57.1	42.9	0.0	0.0
	Total	[32]	28.1	31.3	34.4	3.1	3.1
Banks:		[13]	15.3	30.8	30.8	23.1	0.0

This again was a test question aimed to cross-check a previously elicited opinions, but in a slightly different context. However, the pattern of responses this time was different from previous responses to almost the same question. Previously, the largest proportion of MCs and banks (41 per cent and 47 per cent respectively) had expressed no opinion on whether the competitiveness of Mauritius had increased or not as a result of the new AML/CFT regime; almost 47 per cent of MCs and 21 per cent of banks thought that Mauritius had not become more competitive while 12 per cent of MCs and 32 per cent of banks thought it had. This time, however, 59 per cent of MCs and 46 per cent of banks thought that the new AML/CFT regime had little or no impact on increasing the competitiveness of Mauritius, while 38 per cent of MCs and 54 per cent of banks thought that the impact on **increasing** competitiveness was moderate or high.

This inconsistency is difficult to explain other than as a possible misunderstanding of the statement on the part of respondents (i.e. misinterpreting 'increased competitiveness' for 'decreased competitiveness'). The inconsistency might also be explained if the respondents who had previously expressed 'no opinion' (in private discussions some indicated that they had taken a neutral position in responding to the questionnaires in order to avert any prospect of regulatory retaliation) were evenly divided between those that thought competitiveness had increased and those who felt it had not. Equally difficult to explain was the inconsistency between these findings and the almost unanimous sense expressed by discussants at the seminar that Mauritius had definitely become **less** competitive as an IFC as a consequence of the new AML/CFT regime.

What has the impact of the new AML/CFT regime been on *increasing the competitiveness of your firm* in the Mauritian IFC sector?

Responses from			Nil	Low	Moderate	High	NS
				(%)			
			1	2	3	4	5
Management:	Small	[21]	28.6	42.9	23.8	0.0	4.8
Companies	Medium	[4]	25.0	50.0	25.0	0.0	0.0
	Large	[7]	0.0	28.6	42.9	28.6	0.0
	Total	[32]	28.1	31.3	34.4	3.1	3.1
Banks:		[13]	23.1	30.8	30.8	15.3	0.0

In responding to this question, over 59 per cent of all MCs indicated low or no impact of the new AML/CFT regime on increasing the competitiveness of their firm within the IFS industry. However, the difference between small and large MCs was sharp and reflected their profitability numbers. While nearly 72 per cent of small and medium-sized MCs felt that the impact on their increased competitiveness had been nil/low, 72 per cent of the large MCs felt that the impact on their competitiveness had been moderate/high. Clearly, this finding confirms the generally held view that increased regulation has strengthened the position of large firms in the Mauritian MC space. That may lead to further consolidation as economies of scale dominate. Smaller firms will become less profitable and less able to afford the recurrent costs of a much more demanding regulatory/compliance regime. That may mean less competition in the industry, with a 'weeding out' of small firms that cannot afford to remain in the business. Among banks, opinion was more evenly divided; 54 per cent thought that their competitiveness had not increased significantly while 46 per cent thought it had.

Improved knowledge: The next three questions were aimed at determining whether a change in the regulatory regime with higher compliance demands had any impact on firms deriving potential benefits from improving their technical capacity, knowledge base and risk management capabilities. Thus, these three questions revolve around the same premise – i.e. to what extent have firms in the IFS industry used the increased knowledge they have acquired to respond to more demanding compliance requirements to their advantage? However, the questions yield different patterns of answers in each case. The responses suggest that such benefits, to the extent that they were perceived to have accrued, were probably marginal.

What impact has the new AML/CFT regime had on *improving the technological capacity* of your firm?

| Responses from | | | Nil | Low | Moderate | High | NS |
| | | | | | (%) | | |
			1	2	3	4	5
Management:	Small	[21]	9.5	28.6	52.4	0.0	4.8
companies	Medium	[4]	50.0	25.0	25.0	0.0	0.0
	Large	[7]	0.0	42.9	57.1	0.0	0.0
	Total	[32]	12.5	31.3	50.0	0.0	6.3
Banks:		[13]	7.7	38.5	46.2	7.7	0.0

What impact has the new AML/CFT regime had on *improving the knowledge base* of your firm?

| Responses from | | | Nil | Low | Moderate | High | NS |
| | | | | | (%) | | |
			1	2	3	4	5
Management:	Small	[21]	4.8	28.6	42.9	19.0	4.8
companies	Medium	[4]	25.0	50.0	0.0	25.0	0.0
	Large	[7]	0.0	42.9	42.9	14.3	0.0
	Total	[32]	6.3	34.4	37.5	18.7	3.1
Banks:		[13]	0.0	30.8	61.5	7.7	0.0

What impact has the new AML/CFT regime had on *increasing profitability from improved risk management* in your firm?

Responses from			Nil	Low	Moderate	High	NS
				(%)			
			1	2	3	4	5
Management:	Small	[21]	23.8	23.8	38.1	9.6	4.8
companies	Medium	[4]	50.0	25.0	25.0	0.0	0.0
	Large	[7]	14.3	42.9	42.9	0.0	0.0
	Total	[32]	28.1	28.1	37.5	6.2	3.1
Banks:		[13]	0.0	61.5	30.8	7.7	0.0

Where almost all (except four MCs and one bank) respondents agree is that there has been some positive impact of the new AML/CFT regime in improving technological capacity and knowledge base. A significant minority of MCs (31 per cent in the case of **technological capacity,** 34 per cent in the case of **improved knowledge base** and 28 per cent in the case of **better risk management**) thought that the beneficial impact was low. Meanwhile, 28 per cent of MCs thought that there was no impact at all as far as increasing profitability from improved risk management was concerned. Half of all MCs thought that the impact on improving their technological capacity was moderate, while 56 per cent thought that the impact on improving their knowledge base was moderate/high. When it came to risk management, however, fewer than 44 per cent of MCs thought that its positive impact on their profitability was moderate/high.

The pattern for banks was different and more evenly divided. Over 46 per cent of banks thought that the impact on improved technological capacity was nil/low while 54 per cent thought it was moderate/high. When it came to an improved knowledge base, however, over 69 per cent of banks thought that the impact was moderate/high, but only 39 per cent thought they had derived any benefit in terms of profitability from better risk management

Though it is difficult to come up with a definitive overall conclusion from the pattern of responses for these three 'knowledge-based' questions, the general sense that can be derived is that the tangible benefits of improved knowledge were generally perceived to be marginal and intangible – i.e. not translated into greater efficiency, lower costs, higher revenues or higher profitability. However, as indicated before, the absence of a translation effect from intangible to tangible benefit does not concern the AML/CFT regime alone. It also concerns the intrinsic ability of firms and banks to undertake the effort to enable such translation.

9.3 Overall conclusions from the analysis of survey findings for Mauritius

Drawing firm conclusions about costs and benefits of the enhanced AML/CFT regime

What conclusions can be drawn from the analysis of survey responses outlined in the previous two sections when, on many issues, the responses are ambiguous or opinions evenly divided? To the extent possible, the substance of discussions at the seminar has been relied upon to make clearer issues on which survey responses were confused. Clearly, definitive conclusions, extruded from the survey and seminar, are vulnerable to argument about what was said, what was meant, how it should be interpreted and whether a counter-conclusion might not be equally valid. Allowing for that uncertainty, and leaving itself open to amendment, this chapter takes the risk of drawing out some qualified conclusions (for which the lead consultant takes full responsibility) from what has been learnt about: (a) the manner in which enhanced AML/CFT regulation was introduced and implemented in Mauritius and the reasoning of regulators to justify doing what they did; and (b) its overall impact on the IFS industry by way of costs and benefits.

Recognising that many differences of opinion exist between regulators and the IFS industry, as well as within the IFS industry itself (i.e. between MCs and banks, and between large and small or medium MCs) what are the areas in which the survey findings reflected some degree of broad agreement across the board? Simply put, these areas include the following:

- Enhanced AML/CFT legislation and regulation had to be introduced in Mauritius, and the IFS industry was obliged to comply with it. However, the pressures for such enhancement did not emanate from within. They were exerted by external interlocutors (i.e. the Financial Action Task Force [FATF] and international financial institutions) who demanded (excessive?) enhancements regardless of the quality of the extant regulatory regime.

- Such pressures had to be accommodated by Mauritian policy-makers and regulators in order to avoid the threat of being blacklisted by the FATF and risking the IFS industry being put out of business. [That presumes that blacklisting would have put the IFS industry out of business. However, would it? Of course in the US, the Patriot Act cuts off blacklisted jurisdictions and their foreign banks from doing business in America, which makes it difficult for any bank that transacts in US dollars to operate.]

- Enhanced AML/CFT regulation has bolstered the reputation of Mauritius as an IFC. It is now regarded as a well-regulated financial jurisdiction that has the good housekeeping seal of approval of the IFIs. However, the conclusion about 'bolstered reputation' is based on axiomatic presumption rather than definitive objective knowledge acquired by surveying offshore clientele. Whether Mauritius' reputation is regarded by offshore clients as being better than it was before, or better than that of other IFCs/OFCs at the time of writing, is unknown.

- The bolstering of its reputation as a well-regulated financial jurisdiction has not resulted in any discernible tangible benefits accruing to Mauritius by way of enhanced competitiveness resulting in additional business. On the other hand, enhanced AML/CFT legislation has not led to a loss of gross turnover (revenue) on the part of the IFS industry, despite anecdotal evidence of lost business.

- While the reputational benefit of the enhanced AML/CFT regime has not yielded tangible returns, it has resulted in definite and large costs (direct, indirect and opportunity) that appear to have affected the profitability of the management companies, but not that of the offshore banks.

The above are the principal areas of agreement across all the parties concerned. The remaining conclusions of the study, outlined below, are contentious, reflecting in part the views of an oft-quoted, anonymous government bureaucrat who opined that: 'where he stood on an issue depended on where he was sitting at the time'. Taking this into account, the other conclusions the study arrives at, and the questions that they raise, include the following:

- Acknowledging that Mauritius was under intense external pressure to strengthen its AML/CFT regulatory and compliance regime in accord with new international standards set by the FATF and monitored by the IFIs, a conclusion of the study is that Mauritian policy-makers and regulators were perhaps too quick and over-anxious in making commitments to OECD and FATF. They did not take fully into account the impact of these commitments on the IFS industry. Nor were these commitments based on any prior consultation with the IFS industry aimed at arriving at a common position.

- Mauritian policy-makers and regulators simply presumed that they knew what was in the best interests of Mauritius and of the IFS industry. By attempting to be 'front-runners' in meeting new international standards and over-pleasing their interlocutors, Mauritian policy-makers gambled on gaining a competitive advantage for the IFS industry, which has not materialised. In fact, the industry (i.e. MCs) believes that it has become uncompetitive as a result. The experience may even have shown that Mauritius will succumb much too easily to international pressure, even when such pressure might militate against its national interests.

- From quantitative submissions made by regulatory agencies, and a large sample of MCs and banks from which industry totals have been extrapolated, the incremental costs of introducing/implementing the new AML/CFT regime are estimated to have been just over **US$40 million** over the four years 2002–05. In general, both regulators and the IFS industry have responded to new challenges by adding staff resources rather than by investments in IT systems. The proportion of new investment in IT systems to meet the additional demands of AML/CFT regulation has been lower than in other jurisdictions (although there is some evidence that it may have been under-reported). In the case of foreign bank subsidiaries/branches, it is a cost that appears to have been absorbed by head offices rather than at the local level.

- Inconsistencies in the qualitative and quantitative data provided, gaps in detailed breakdowns and estimates provided by regulators in apportioning part of their total regulatory/supervisory costs to the AML/CFT regime using arbitrary percentages, caused the lead consultant to believe that the total incremental cost may be under-stated by 25–30 per cent. The actual costs may therefore be around US$50 million rather than US$40 million, although it is the latter figure that is used here for analytical purposes.

- This figure (US$40 million) does not include the costs of implementing the new AML/CFT regime, and its associated KYC/DD requirements, for the **insurance** and **securities** industries. Using estimates provided by these other groups during the seminar, the total incremental cost of applying the new AML/CFT regime to all financial services (domestic and offshore) in Mauritius may be closer to US$60 million over the four years. In proportional terms that would be equivalent to the UK or France incurring a cost of US$30 billion, the US incurring a cost of US$150 billion, India incurring a cost of US$8 billion and Singapore incurring a cost of US$1.5 billion for the same purpose over the same period.

- Of the total incremental cost incurred by regulators and the IFS industry, about 12 per cent has been borne by the government and regulators, 20 per cent by banks and the remaining 68 per cent by management companies. That asymmetry is particularly onerous. The cost to the public sector (less than US$5 million) has been absorbed as a small fraction of the national budget, while offshore banks have been 15 times more profitable than MCs over the four-year period. Aggregate after-tax profits for offshore banks in 2002–05 were US$262 million (compared to incre-mental costs of around US$8 million) while those for MCs were just over US$17 million (compared to industry-wide incremental costs of over US$27 million). The brunt of the additional cost burden has thus been borne by those institutions least capable of bearing it. This is particularly true in the case of the 66 small MCs, which together account for less than 25 per cent of the IFS market and less than 20 per cent of the MC industry's profits.

- A possible consequence of the above may be a trend toward consolidation and concentration in the structure of the MC industry. Whether that would, in an overall sense, be a good thing (because small weak MCs vulnerable to risk would be weeded out or would merge to achieve better economies of scale) or a bad thing (because it would lead to greater market power on the part of a few large firms which already dominate a large proportion of market share) needs to be looked into further.

- The incremental costs of the new AML/CFT regime are regarded by regulators as being low and acceptable as a cost of doing business. That view is supported by half the banks involved in offshore banking. However, it is opposed by the MC industry, which has borne most of the cost. Judging by comparisons with other jurisdictions of various sizes (see above) the incremental costs of adopting the new AML/CFT regime in Mauritius have been disproportionately high relative to the size of its financial sector and its IFS industry. The consultants are of the view that those costs (in relative and absolute terms) have hurt the MC industry and made it less competitive and profitable.

- The **total** benefits – allowing for an element of double-counting – derived from the IFS industry (in terms of value addition, export earnings, employment and profitability) were estimated to be just over US$450 million over the period 2002–05. Those benefits have to be judged against total regulatory costs, rather than just the incremental regulatory costs for AML/CFT. With incremental costs being estimated at US$40 million and assuming, reasonably generously, that the **incremental** costs were about 25 per cent of **total** regulatory costs (the FSC's incremental AML/CFT cost calculations work out to being less than 7.5 per cent of its total regulatory cost, while for the BoM they work out at 2.6 per cent of its total regulatory cost) that would yield a figure of total regulatory costs of US$160 million, yielding an overall cost-benefit ratio of 1:3 – i.e. a very low proportion.

- If the FSC's ratio was used, total regulatory costs would amount to over US$530 million, which is an obviously ludicrous estimate. The BoM's ratio would yield a total regulatory cost of US$1.6 billion, which is even worse! Using these ratios, there would be negative net benefits from the operations of the IFS sector. This illustration, resulting from applying imputed ratios, underlines the point that the FSC's and the BoM's calculations of their own incremental costs of AML/CFT are probably too low. Their incremental costs for applying the new AML/CFT regime since 2002 have probably been in the range of 15–25 per cent of their total regulatory and supervision costs. Using those more realistic ratios, the total cost to the public sector would increase from US$4.8 million to over US$7 million.

- The argument of regulators in Mauritius is that adopting the new AML/CFT regime has enabled the IFS industry to survive. Had the new regime not been implemented, Mauritius would have been blacklisted. The damage to its reputation would have meant a certain loss of business. Thus the net benefits associated with implementing the new regime are equivalent to the benefits presently being generated by the IFS industry. That would effectively mean counting the entire benefit of US$450 million from IFS operations calculated earlier as an **incremental** benefit for the purposes of deriving the incremental cost-benefit ratio. Using the estimate of US$40 million as the cost incurred, the incremental cost-benefit ratio would be around 1:11. However, this argument needs to be looked at more closely.

- **First,** is it certain that Mauritius would have been blacklisted on the basis of its previous record and performance? Russia, Indonesia, Israel and China have not been blacklisted, although their regulatory environments are much less stringent than that of Mauritius. Their stance vis-à-vis the FATF can hardly be characterised as being 'co-operative'. Or was the threat of blacklisting a convenient argument for domestic regulators and policy-makers to use in persuading the industry that they had no choice but to do what they did? Admittedly the regulatory juggernaut launched by the FTAF (or the regulatory *tsunami* as it has colloquially been referred to in *The Economist*) and which has been rolling unstoppably downhill since 2001, did run the risk of Mauritius being run over and injured had it stood in the way of the FATF and its implementing agencies, the IFIs. However, unlike many other OFCs, Mauritius had a reasonably good regulation prior to 2001. Did its policy-makers do enough to explain that environment to the IFIs and the FATF and make the case that only marginal adjustments were necessary to bring it into line with new standards? Or did they accept every recommendation of the FSAP mission, because that was the path of least resistance? Did policy-makers make the 'risk-based' case that, when it came to AML and CFT, Mauritius simply did not confront the same risks as say Colombia, Pakistan, a Middle-Eastern OFC, or Jamaica in the Caribbean or even, for that matter, the US and EU with their very large underground economies creating much greater scope for money laundering activities and attracting a far greater amount of terrorist financing; so that imposing a draconian AML/CFT regime would add cost, but yield little benefit?

- The evidence is too thin and the study could not go into the detailed history of negotiations with the OECD, IFIs and the FATF (nor was it mandated to) to reach any definitive conclusions on this politically sensitive issue. The view of the IFS industry is that Mauritian policy-makers did not fight their corner hard enough, although that may well be unfair. Nor did policy-makers consult with the industry before making commitments that damaged the industry's interests. The study does note that most offshore clients of the Mauritian IFS industry are Indian, Indonesian, Chinese or African. India had not started discussions with the FATF until late 2005; China had not done so at the time of writing. The other clientele come from countries that have problems meeting FATF demands. So, it would have been odd if these clients suddenly abandoned Mauritius because of blacklisting by FATF, assuming that had occurred.

- **Second**, the argument that, since new AML/CFT regulatory requirements enabled Mauritius to continue operating its IFS industry, all the ensuing benefits must be seen as incremental holds no water. It discounts the fact that almost the same magnitude of benefits were flowing before 2001. Most of them would have continued to flow regardless. The IFS industry could not have been switched off that easily, whatever the FATF decided to do within the bounds of legality. For these and other reasons, the study aligns itself with the IFS industry in concluding that incremental benefits flowing from the tighter AML/CFT regime are difficult enough to identify, leave alone quantify. It goes a step further in believing, on the basis of evidence available, that there were almost no **incremental** benefits accruing from the tightened regulatory regime.

- The inability of an enhanced reputation to translate into tangible business benefits raises three critical questions. **First**, do the clients of Mauritius' IFS industry see it as having an enhanced reputation as a result of tightened AML/CFT regulation? Or is that merely an axiomatic assumption being made by regulators (and, to an extent, by the IFS industry) that is unsupported by evidence? Do offshore clients see Mauritius as having its reputation enhanced, or do they see its new regulatory regime as having become insufferably inflexible, rigidly bureaucratic, too demanding of information requirements that are of questionable value, and too intractable to deal with? **Second**, assuming reputation has been enhanced, why is Mauritius finding it so difficult to attract new business from potential clients and more business from existing clients? **Third**, is it the complacency and lack of aggressiveness of the IFS industry (three or four large firms being the exceptions) that has prevented the intangible benefit of reputation being translated into the more tangible benefit of increased business and revenues?

- The study concludes that the answer to the **first** question is in the affirmative: i.e. although it is assumed by its regulators that Mauritius' reputation has definitely been enhanced, that enhancement may be in their own eyes and those of the country's official international interlocutors only; it is also a view shared by some players in the IFS industry. However, the fact that reputation has not been translated into business may suggest that it is not a view shared widely by MCs or by clients of its offshore financial industry. It is their views that matter if business is to be derived.

- The **second** question is more difficult to answer definitively. However, several indicative strands are visible. To begin with, there are now many more OFCs/IFCs for clients from source countries important to Mauritius to choose from. These OFCs/IFCs are generally easier to do business in and include Bahrain, Dubai, Muscat, Doha, Labuan (Malaysia), Singapore, Hong Kong, Switzerland and London. Moreover, Mauritius has not yet opened up entry to its IFS industry to offshore players, whom their own clients may be more comfortable dealing with. Mauritius may also be too remote geographically and 'off the beaten path'. However, these are more speculations rather than explanations backed by evidence.

- The **third** question also has an indicative answer in the findings of the survey. When asked whether players in the IFS industry had undertaken or witnessed either geographical diversification of their client base or functional diversification of the products/services they offered, the responses were tilted toward the negative. Also, the findings of the study indicate that the IFS industry derived few side-benefits from its improved technological capacity, expanded knowledge base, and improved risk-management capacity that resulted from complying with enhanced regulatory demands. That makes the IFS industry, which is quick to blame regulatory burdens for its travails, vulnerable to the counter-accusation levelled by some regulators that the industry is itself too complacent, conservative (perhaps too protected in its domestic business space) and diffident to make the strategic and tactical effort that is necessary in a much more competitive world; i.e. to really go out and compete with more aggressive players from elsewhere.

- Where incremental benefits and costs of AML/CFT regulation and compliance are concerned, most governments/regulators confront a trade-off between: (a) the reputational benefit of adhering to international standards of regulation/compliance for AML/CFT; and (b) the public + private financial costs that are borne by the IFS industry, along with wider social costs incurred as a result of regulation-induced inefficiencies, which are borne by domestic and external consumers of IFS. Has Mauritius made the correct trade-off? In the view of the authors of this study, it has not. Being overly anxious to please its external interlocutors, Mauritian policy-makers and regulators have traded-off the interests of the IFS industry, its offshore clientele and its own national interest. That trade-off has favoured costs over benefits. As a consequence, the actions of policy-makers have imposed too high a cost burden on the IFS industry in making commitments they perhaps did not fully appreciate the consequences of. That they did so without any prior consultation with the IFS industry beggars belief.

- Two other questions, concerning the actions of policy-makers and regulators, arise in introducing and implementing the FATF/IFI recommended AML/CFT regime. The **first** is whether regulators were over-zealous in applying the new international standards to the detriment of the IFS industry and its clientele? The **second** is whether introduction of the new AML/CFT regime provided an opportunity for indulgence in classic bureaucratic behaviour concerning the capturing of larger budgets, building of empires, protection of turf, and the exercise of personal vested interests (i.e. career, travel, etc.). The study did not look into these issues specifically. However, its findings do touch upon *prima facie* evidence of whether this happened.

- Again, the answer to the first question is 'perhaps'. The study did not go into examining in minute detail all the supporting information that is now required by regulators from MCs and banks to satisfy KYC and DD requirements, although the consultants are fully aware of what such requirements are. However, the anecdotal evidence, and the IFS industry's reactions, both suggest that Mauritian regulators may have gone overboard in requiring unduly extensive (and perhaps even irrelevant) documentation for KYC purposes. They may also have gone overboard in reviewing and interpreting such evidence in ways quite different from other jurisdictions. However, the study cannot be definitive about this. It can only raise the issue as a concern that needs further exploration. What the study can be definitive about (from the seminar discussions) is that regulators have unnecessarily added to MC and client costs by not co-ordinating better among themselves and requiring the same information on KYC/DD to be replicated at least twice in MCs and banks (and occasionally four times when insurance companies and securities brokerages get involved) simply because they are regulated by different institutions, which do not accept one another's findings on verification.

- As for the empire-building argument that has been levelled by many in the IFS industry, the ***prima facie* evidence** creates a degree of discomfort that this may well have happened. It has **not** happened at the BoM where, despite a considerable additional regulatory/supervisory burden, there has been almost no increase in total staffing and no extraordinary increase in the operating budget of the Bank. There has been only a small reallocation of staff to regulation and supervision functions from other functions. In private conversations, senior management of the BoM indicated that the Bank had perhaps overstretched its existing staff resources to meet incremental regulatory burdens and that this approach had now reached its limits. On the other hand, the staff and budget of the FSC has doubled since its inception, while the FIU seems distinctly over-staffed and over-resourced. However, these impressions and indicators are superficial. They need to be confirmed through more detailed analysis. With a new CEO, the FSC appears to be entering a phase of consolidation with a changed approach to regulation. It does have a large mandate and considerable ground to cover, so that a large part of the increase in staffing and budget may well be justified. However, that is not quite as obviously apparent in the case of the FIU.

- Finally, the findings of the study indirectly call into question the way in which external pressures are applied by organisations like the OECD, FSF and the FATF, through the agency of IFIs, on small jurisdictions offering international financial services. They raise uncomfortable issues about the quality of analysis undertaken by these institutions in the first place. For example, there was no justification for the FSF's listing Mauritius as a Category III jurisdiction in assessing the quality of its supervision regime. Such organisations also exercise arbitrary and asymmetrical power in international relations. There is a fundamental inequity in the behavioural duality of international institutions bullying those they can (like small island states with insufficient countervailing power) while side-stepping or treating very carefully those they can't (like Russia, China and India). That duality raises equally fundamental concerns about 'level playing fields'. It also raises questions about: the proportionality of the response to AML and CFT concerns (especially after the events of 9 September 2001); what the FATF and IFIs recommend in the context of particular jurisdictions; and whether their 'one-size-fits-all' approach in matters of financial system regulation and the setting up of financial intelligence units from the same mould in all cases is at all appropriate or sound.

- The findings of the study should give the FATF and IFIs pause to reconsider what they have been doing over the last four years and reach more temperate judgements about whether their ministrations might be unfair and inimical to the legitimate interests of small financial jurisdictions providing IFS and whether they are contributing to strengthening or weakening global financial regulation.

These conclusions represent, reasonably exhaustively, the findings of the study in Mauritius. While it is tempting to leap from arriving at defensible (if contentious) conclusions to making specific recommendations for policy-makers, regulators and the IFS industry, the study desists from doing so for a number of reasons. First, it has no mandate to do so. Second, the analysis undertaken was more from the research viewpoint rather than for prescriptive purposes. Third, in order to make recommendations the study would need to confirm its *prima facie* impressions with more detailed analysis undertaken in a consulting frame of mind.

For the astute regulator, policy-maker and MC/bank manager, the study is replete with a number of findings and observations that lead to some rather obvious conclusions about what might be done to remedy situations that are clearly not satisfactory. However, those are left for readers to draw out and act upon. Should the Government of Mauritius seek, through the good offices of the Commonwealth Secretariat, to have specific recommendations made by the lead consultants based on the findings of the study, that request could readily be acted upon with a modicum of further work being done to confirm the judgements arrived at.

Finally, the findings of the study for Mauritius certainly reinforce the quote ascribed to Graham Dillon of KPMG by *The Economist* in its Special Report on Financing Terrorism (October 22 2005) when speaking about the impact on the global economy of the additional costs imposed by the FATF requirements on countering financing of terrorism (the quote applies with equal force to anti-money laundering measures as well):

> *'The cost (of these measures) to our global economy is so large they've (i.e. terrorists) already had the effect they wanted. The increasing costs of compliance and technology are a form of terrorism. We're damaging ourselves'.*

Notes

1. OECD (1998).
2. Financial Services Commission (2003, 2004, 2005).
3. This followed discussions with incoming FSC staff who were less biased than former staff (who were anxious to downplay the cost impact on the FSC of new AML-CFT regulations, which they had adopted and applied unquestioningly and perhaps even unthinkingly). Each line item was re-assessed and FSC staff gave opinions of what proportion of each line item might be apportioned to AML-CFT.
4. Following discussions at the seminar it became clear that the scale had not suggested to respondents that a rating of '3' reflected 'no opinion'. Many respondents thought they were providing a safe middle-of-the-road answer by ticking '3' without quite realising what that score conveyed.

10

The International Financial Services (IFS) Sector in Vanuatu

10.1 Introduction

Vanuatu or New Hebrides (when it was a British-French Condominium prior to 1980) is a small developing Pacific island country located about 800 kilometres west of Nadi, Fiji Islands and about 2,500 kilometres northeast of Sydney, Australia.

The island nation is made up of a chain of 83 islands and has a population of 205,754. The capital city is Port Vila, which is located on the island of Efate and has a population of about 30,000. The island has a dualistic economy, with a large subsistence agricultural sector, which is supplemented by the financial and tourism sectors.

Vanuatu has a 52-member parliament, which is based on the British system and is headed by a Prime Minister. The head of state is the President, who is elected by Members of Parliament and the Presidents of Provincial Councils. The legal system is also based on the British law model and the judiciary is headed by the Chief Justice. The Court of Appeal is the highest appellate court, followed by the Supreme Court and the Magistrate Court. In addition, there is a National Council of Chiefs, which advises the government on culture and language and looks after the interests of the chiefs.

Vanuatu's international financial centre started in 1969 when it was still a Condominium on the advice of the British government. By 1970 and early 1971 a full offshore regime was legislated.

10.2 Origins and developments of the IFS sector in Vanuatu

An international finance centre (IFC) is a jurisdiction that levies no, or very low, direct corporate and personal income taxes. Such a jurisdiction may also be known as an offshore finance centre (OFC) 'that hosts financial activities that are separated from major regulating units (states) by geography and/or by legislation'[1]. Most IFCs are based on English common law. Countries and territories that host IFC facilities offer a legal system that provides for the formation of international companies and trusts that can be used in the management of tax neutral portfolios and worldwide assets.

The country's international finance centre has had an important effect on the history of Vanuatu (formerly known as the New Hebrides). From 1970, it greatly boosted the revenues of the pro-independence British administration and reduced the relative importance of the French. The IFC brought lawyers, trustees and bankers to Port Vila, particularly from Australia and New Zealand[2].

The initial legislation upon which the offshore sector was founded are the:

- Banking Act [Cap 63] (repealed and replaced by the Banking Act of 2002)

- Trust Companies Act [Cap 69]

- Prevention of Fraud (Investment) Act [Cap 70]

- Insurance Act [CAP 82]

Later, after independence, the Vanuatu government introduced further legislation to compliment the existing IFS framework. The additional governing laws of the IFC are:

- Companies Act [CAP 191]

- Serious Offences (Confiscation of Proceeds) Act No. 50 of 1989

- Casino Control Act No. 6 of 1993

- Financial Institution Act No. 2 of 1999

- International Companies Act No. 32 of 1992

- Financial Transactions Reporting Act No. 33 of 2000

- International Banking Act No. 4 of 2002

- Proceeds of Crime Act No. 13 of 2002

- Mutual Assistance in Criminal Matters Act No. 14 of 2002

- Betting (Control) Act No.37 of 2003

- Insurance Act of 2005[3]

The international finance centre of Vanuatu provides the four most important general products: international business companies (IBCs), or international companies as they are known locally, offshore banks, exempted insurers and offshore trusts. These products are governed by the International Companies Act No. 32 of 1992 (last amended in 2000), the International Banking Act No. 4 of 2002, the Insurance Act of 2005 and the Trust Companies Act of 1971 (last amended in 1988) respectively. Offshore financial products are usually used for the purposes of minimising tax and/or to protect assets.

In 1970 the banks and banking regulation legislation and the company regulation legislation were introduced, and in the same year ANZ opened its first branch in Port Vila. The Trust Company Act was introduced in 1971, and by 1973 other banks including the Bank of New South Wales, National Australia Bank, Barclays, Commonwealth Bank and HSBC were all licensed in the New Hebrides (as Vanuatu then was). Ten trust companies were in operation and the Insurance Act was also introduced[4]. Both population and land prices in Port Vila experienced very rapid growth as Vanuatu attracted business fleeing perceived political instability in IFCs like the Bahamas and Bermuda.

By 1976, the IFC was truly established. At independence in 1980, the first Prime Minister, Father Walter Lini, and all prominent Vanuatu politicians expressed support for the IFC. The Reserve Bank of Vanuatu (RBV) was created and all stakeholders felt the IFC was 'here to stay'. In 1989, the first anti-money laundering (AML) laws, the Mutual Assistance in Criminal Matters and Serious Offences (Confiscation of Proceeds) Act were introduced.

Then in 1993, Vanuatu introduced its first dedicated international company legislation (International Companies Act 1992) to restore competitiveness with other IFCs in this area. The legislation was based on the IBC law of the British Virgin Islands as well as New Zealand company law. Previously, foreign investors had made use of the provision for exempt status in the normal company legislation. Vanuatu's international company legislation restricts the ability of such companies to conduct business in the country under a ring-fencing provision.

International companies are commonly used to provide secrecy for their owners in a number of ways. To guarantee such privacy, company registries are not open for public inspection[5]. If this secrecy provision is breached, the perpetrator(s) face criminal prosecution and jail. International companies do not have to pay any local taxes and duties and are subject to low reporting requirements. Vanuatu does not have offshore trust legislation, but trusts are commonly used in the IFS sector.

The Vanuatu Financial Services Commission (VFSC) was established in 1993, and in 1994 a promotions committee with the Finance Centre Association was set up to advertise the IFC in Australia, New Caledonia, Hong Kong and Eastern Europe. In 1995, the Banking Act [Cap 63] was amended and supervision of offshore banks was transferred from the Minister of Finance to the VFSC, which set up a Bank Supervision Unit. At this time the fee for an offshore bank licence was increased to $5,000.

In December 1999, a group of United States banks decided to suspend electronic banking links with Vanuatu, Nauru and Palau following Congressional testimony alleging links between these centres and money laundering. In January 2000, a joint government/private sector mission from Vanuatu went to Washington and New York to meet with officials. The ban was lifted for the country's domestic licensed banks.

In 2000, there was a joint assessment visit by the Asia-Pacific Group on Money Laundering (APG) and the Offshore Group of Banking Supervisors (OGBS). In addition, in the same year Vanuatu was reviewed by the Financial Action Task Force (FATF) as part of the Non-Cooperative Countries and Territories (NCCT) exercise. The Financial Transactions Report Act was introduced in September 2000 to avoid Vanuatu's being placed on the NCCT list. In May and June 2000, Vanuatu was placed on the lowest tier of the Financial Stability Forum's (FSF) three-tier categorisation of the perceived quality of IFC supervision, and included in the OECD's Tax Havens list with 34 other jurisdictions as part of the Harmful Tax Competition initiative.

The International Monetary Fund (IMF) performed a Module 2 Assessment of Vanuatu's offshore and domestic financial sectors in 2002. The resulting report (published in

2003) made major recommendations to transfer regulatory responsibilities from the VFSC to the RBV, dilute secrecy provisions, overhaul the offshore legal structure and conduct a cost-benefit analysis of the IFS industry. This report also estimated the gross contribution of the offshore sector to government revenues at US$1 million. At this time, the VFSC had 13 staff (two in banking supervision) and the RBV had 53 staff, four in (domestic) banking supervision. The OECD 'Unco-operative Tax Havens' list, published in April of 2002, included Vanuatu along with six other jurisdictions.

In response to the IMF report, in 2003 the International Banking Act was introduced, the major innovation being that offshore banks were required to have a permanent office with the bank's records and at least one full-time employee in Port Vila. As a direct result, the number of exempted (offshore) banks dropped from 35 to nine in the subsequent 12 months. Offshore bank supervision was moved from the VFSC to the RBV, and the licence fee was increased to US$8,000.

Before 2002, offshore banks were accorded more privacy and greater flexibility in operation, as they were not required to have any physical presence (office/staff) in Vanuatu. Also, they were not required to disclose company records to the public, were free from all forms of inspection and did not have to comply with strict capital adequacy requirements. Since 2002, however, offshore banks must maintain an office in Vanuatu, must have a resident manager/full-time employee based in the country and are subject to compliance inspections by the Reserve Bank of Vanuatu[6]. Offshore banks are still forbidden from accepting deposits from the public in Vanuatu, and from soliciting business locally, and in this regard these banks can still be distinguished from local banks.

In May 2003, Vanuatu reversed its earlier decision and agreed to commit to the principles of tax information exchange and transparency required by the OECD, and as a result Vanuatu was removed from the 'Unco-operative Tax Haven' list.

In 2005, a new Insurance Act was passed, and the Australian government made a formal request to enter into negotiations concerning a bilateral Tax Information Exchange Agreement (TIEA) with Vanuatu.

At the time of writing (2006) it was planned that the VFSC would move to immobilise bearer shares according to British Virgin Island model of custodianship, and would register corporate and trust service providers in line with the Isle of Man model. The supervision of insurance companies and trust providers may also be transferred from the VFSC to the RBV. Despite this transfer of responsibility, however, there are no plans to reduce staffing at the VFSC. There are plans to legislate for the provision of new products, such as protected cell companies, based on the Guernsey model, unit trusts and mutual funds. For this, the State Law Office will need expert advice from draftpersons and funding to be able to secure such services. Also, if these laws were passed then regulators would need to recruit at least two more staff per office to carry out the additional supervisory work[7].

The private sector industry, i.e. the banks, insurance companies, accountants, trust companies, lawyers and other service providers, has an organisation called the Vanuatu

List of legislation under which the IFC operates and their amendments

No. Act	Amendments
1. Banking Act [Cap 63] (repealed in 2002)	Banking Regulation (Amendment) Act No.4 of 1989, commenced on 29 December 1989 Banking (Amendment) Act No.7 of 1995, commenced on 28 August 1995 Banking (Repeal) Act No.18 of 2002, commenced on 01 January 2003
2. Trust Companies Act [Cap 69]	Amended by the QR 6 of 1971 Amended by the QR 3 of 1973 Amended by the QR 16 of 1973 Amended by the QR 5 of 1978 Amended by the QR 6 of 1978 Amended by Act No. 18 of 1984 Amended by Act No.10 of 1988
3. Prevention of Fraud (Investment) Act [Cap 70]	Amended by the QR 9 of 1971 Amended by the QR 3 of 1978 Amended by Act No.10 of 1988
4. Insurance Act [Cap 82]	Amended by the QR 18 of 1973 Amended by the QR 11 of 1974 Amended by the QR 2 of 1975 Amended by the QR 7 of 1978 Amended by Act No. 10 of 1988
5. Companies Act No. 12 of 1986	
6. Serious Offences (Confiscation of Proceeds) Act No.50 of 1989	Repealed in February 2003
7. Betting Control Act 1 of 1993	Repealed and replaced by the Betting (Control) (Repeal) Act No. 37 of 2003
8. Casino Control Act No.6 of 1993	Casino Control (Amendment) Act No.7 of 1996 Casino Control (Amendment) Act No.25 of 1998 Casino Control (Amendment) Act No.4 of 2001 Casino Control (Amendment) Act No.6 of 2005
9. Financial Institution Act No.2 of 1999	Financial Institution (Amendment) Act No.20 of 2002
10. International Companies Act No.32 of 1992	International Companies (Amendment) Act No.26 of 1993 International Companies (Amendment) Act No.9 of 1994 International Companies (E-Commerce) (Amendment) Act No.26 of 2000
11. Financial Transactions Reporting Act No.33 of 2000	Financial Transactions Reporting (Amendment) Act No.20 of 2002 Financial Transactions Reporting (Terrorism) (Amendment) Act No.2 of 2002
12. International Banking Act No. 4 of 2002	
13. Proceeds of Crime Act No. 13 of 2002	
14. Mutual Assistance in Criminal Matters Act No. 14 of 2002	
15. Insurance Act of 2005	

Financial Centre Association (VFCA). The VFCA is governed by a constitution and has membership requirements, sanctions and a code of conduct for members. Members of the VFCA meet once a month and liaise between the private sector and government.

10.3 The importance of IFS to the Vanuatu economy

Vanuatu has a domestic financial sector and an international financial sector. The domestic sector consists of banks, insurance, accountants, lawyers and other financial institutions. ANZ, Westpac and the National Bank of Vanuatu (which is government owned) operate within Vanuatu as local banks and operate in the international sector as well. European Bank is registered as a domestic bank, but mainly operates in the international sector. There are currently seven offshore banks registered (with four applications pending for registration) and five local insurance companies operating in Vanuatu. There are eight accounting firms, of which five correspond with international firms.

The Vanuatu National Provident Fund is a statutory fund established by the government in 1987 to function as a compulsory superannuation scheme. It controls the retirement savings (8 per cent of wages and salary) of all employees. Vanuatu also has modern telecommunication and Internet services provided by Telecom Vanuatu Limited, which is important for the international financial services (IFS) sector for trading reasons.

The international sector comprises offshore banks, offshore insurance companies, shipping, trust and company service providers. Currently the most important product is international companies, the number of which is stable at around 4,500. These have had the advantage of enhanced privacy and confidentiality guaranteed under the International Companies Act of 1992; however, since 2000 this privilege has been diluted to some extent by the new anti-money laundering/countering financing of terrorism (AML/CFT) regulatory requirements.

Contribution to the economy/GDP

It is difficult to assess accurately the financial contribution of the offshore centre to the economy of Vanuatu. This is mainly because of the integration between the domestic and offshore sector. However, through government statistics and information from the private and public sector, some degree of assessment is possible.

The main difficulty relating to the private sector is in identifying the proportion of revenue generated by the various accounting and law firms undertaking offshore activities (in terms of their acting as company officers and administering international companies, for example), but which also maintain their own professional practices. The public sector regulatory bodies also have dual responsibilities in regulating both the offshore and domestic sectors[8].

According to an earlier cost-benefit analysis carried out in 2004, the best way to define the two sectors is through determining the residential status of the clients or customers to separate residents from non-residents. If this classification is used, then shipping and Internet gambling would be part of the offshore industry. However, even this approach involves problems, as some 'offshore' clients invest directly in the country and/or become residents of the country over time[9].

The income tax-free regime in Vanuatu that applies to both resident and non-resident owned operations also creates a problem, as it often makes it difficult to distinguish between what is offshore and what is domestic activity. Shipping, the E-commerce industry and Internet gambling are administered by the government separately to other offshore operations. Even though they are not formally part of the private offshore sector, however, these activities involve many of the same operators, and in the case of shipping, directly involve the use of international companies registered through the IFC[10].

Identifying the gross revenue of the offshore sector assists in determining the contribution of the IFS industry to the general economy. One of the main sources of government revenue derived from the offshore sector is the annual fees charged by the VFSC. There is a set annual fee for each type of company registration, which varies by the authorised capital for local companies. According to the Commissioner of the VFSC, the fees charged by the Vanuatu registry are highly competitive compared to other IFCs.

In general, the Government of Vanuatu derives its revenues from various registration and license fees, stamp and customs duties and consumer taxes such as the VAT (12.5 per cent). This is mainly collected from the domestic sector rather than IFS.

Local industry representatives claim the offshore sector contributes upwards of 12 per cent of GDP[11]. Most recent IMF figures put the direct contribution of the IFC (excluding the shipping registry) at 3 per cent of GDP and 1.5–2 per cent of government revenue[12]. However, a recent cost-benefit assessment funded by the Pacific Islands Forum Secretariat at the request of the government of Vanuatu estimated that in mid-2004 the entire 'offshore industry' represented 9.7 per cent of GDP and 5.1 per cent of government revenues. The Reserve Bank of Vanuatu (RBV), meanwhile, estimates that the figures are currently 9 per cent and 5.5 per cent respectively[13].

Much of this discrepancy between the IMF and other figures results from disagreement about how to measure the indirect 'spin-off' benefits of the IFS industry for the general economy. The Ministry of Finance has previously estimated the multiplier effect[14] as being 2.5, which (when including the shipping registry) would largely resolve the conflicting figures on the contribution of the IFS sector as a proportion of GDP.

Offshore (exempt) banks

Offshore banks operate in a closed environment, and generally do not form part of the local industry in Vanuatu. As the name suggests, these banks are allowed to operate overseas as exempt companies through the IFC. The offshore banking sector had a healthy growth rate until 1993, at which time its numbers peaked at 120 licensed banks. After 1993, offshore banks experienced a decline to 92 in 1995. This pattern of decline began to take place even before the recent regulatory changes. By 2000, the number of banks had reduced steeply to 59, with only seven remaining by 2005[15]. The offshore banking sector was previously dominated by shell operations. With the enactment of the International Banking Act of 2002, which required a physical presence through an office and staff to be located in Vanuatu, a majority of the remaining licensees withdrew from the IFC.

At the time of writing (2006), only seven offshore banking licenses and one general banking license were issued to offshore banking operations in Vanuatu[16]. Only three of the offshore banks have significant physical presence in Vanuatu, employing between five and seven staff each. However, the remaining banks are in the process of establishing business operations as required by the new International Banking Act of 2002. Overall, approximately 20 people are employed locally by the offshore banks[17].

The operating offshore banks are not associated with any international banking or financial service institutions. They are held by private interests and generally operate in niche markets and products. Offshore bank assets amounted to US$202.3 million at the end of 2005, a significant drop since March 2003 when such assets were recorded at US$1,442 million. The offshore banking sector generates around 14 million vatu (Vt)[18] per year (US$127,680 at the inter-bank rate), which is about 0.4 per cent of the overall GDP[19].

The RBV believes that, following the International Banking Act of 2002, there are now greater prospects for the development for the offshore banking industry. An indication of the potential growth in this area is that there are currently four pending applications for new offshore bank licenses[20].

Trusts

At the time of writing, 11 trust company licenses had been issued, of which three operate independently in the offshore sector and the rest operate in conjunction with legal and accounting firms[21]. Vanuatu has no trust legislation such as that in the Cook Islands and other IFCs.

International companies

Offshore company registration is the main offshore activity in Vanuatu. The bulk of clients are from Australia, New Zealand and Asia.

These international companies are awarded enhanced privacy rights and confidentiality. They are not required to file annual accounts or reports similar to Australia, New Zealand and the USA and their records are not open to the public unless special permission is acquired from the company director[22]. The number of offshore companies peaked during the 1990s, but has remained stable or slightly in decline since 2000. The 2004 cost-benefit analysis attributes this to 'increased competition through developed technology and aggressive pricing from other jurisdictions such as the British Virgin Islands and Samoa'[23].

Vanuatu has a tiny share of the IBC market by international standards, with 4,664 international companies currently registered through its IFC[24]. This is compared to other IFCs such as Samoa, which has over 20,000 such companies, and the British Virgin Islands with over 400,000[25].

Offshore insurance

The number of offshore insurance firms has significantly increased in recent years, with the number of offshore insurers increasing from 15 at the end of 2002 to 26 at the

Table 10.1 International company registrations[26]

Year of registration	1980	1986	1992	1995	1999	2000	2001	2002	2003	2004	2005
Cumulative total	505	666	1,018	1,419	2,911	4,015	4,330	4,690	4,462	4,561	4,786
Net increase	–	150	184	401	1492	1104	315	360	(228)	99	225

Table 10.2 Offshore client entities by registration/establishment as at January 2006[27]

Entity	International companies	Exempt companies	Offshore insurers	Offshore banks	Trust companies	Ships	Total
Number registered	4,664	122	23	7	11	600	5,427
% of total	85.94	2.25	0.42	0.13	0.20	11.06	

Table 10.3 Total companies registrations[28]

Type of company	Local company	Overseas company	Exempt company	International company	Charitable organisations	Trade unions	Credit unions	Business names
Total	1,364	27	122	4,664	65	3	1	830

Table 10.4 Specialised licenses[29]

Type of company Total	Trust license 12	Insurance license 40	Security dealers 4
		(Local – 5	
		External – 3	
		Exempt – 23	
		Brokers – 4	
		Agents – 5)	

end of 2005[30]. This is in comparison to the five domestic insurance companies operating within Vanuatu.

Offshore insurers have only a minimal presence in Vanuatu compared with the offshore banks, and are almost exclusively managed by the local trust companies. They provide for 'mainly captive insurance business primarily sourced out of North America, with some finance-based insurance products marketed into Australia'[31]. The offshore insurance sector is still small by most standards and is in a development stage. A new Insurance Act was passed in late 2005, but its impact on offshore insurance is yet to be seen. The private sector is, however, concerned that the stricter requirements imposed by new Act will mean that offshore and captive insurance companies will exit Vanuatu.

Shipping

In the late 1980s, Vanuatu became popular as an international shipping registry; since that time the country has seen a steady growth, with about 600 international ships now registered[32].

Even though the shipping industry is not directly dependent on the rest of the offshore sector, it relies largely on the generally tax-free operating environment in Vanuatu. It contributes significantly to offshore revenues by making up 10 per cent of the total revenue generated by the offshore sector and about 28 per cent of the overall offshore contribution to government revenues[33].

The administration of the shipping registry has been under private contract since 1981, when the international shipping registry commenced, producing gross returns of approximately Vt100 million (US$912,000) per annum for that period. The shipping registry is operationally administered in New York and there is a central registry (kept at Vanuatu Maritime Authority [VMA]) in Port Vila, Vanuatu[34].

Securities/managed funds/E-commerce

The E-commerce sector offers services such as Internet gaming, Internet pharmaceutical operations and credit card processing. It is relatively small and still developing as an industry in Vanuatu. The E-commerce sector works through the offshore industry, yet it relies just as much on the domestic environment. The services provided and infrastructure of Vanuatu, zero or low domestic tax rates and low general operating costs, are important to the future growth of these offshore industries[35].

Moreover, the local banks also earn some revenue for the government through the funds invested by offshore entities. At the end of the financial year in 2005, one of the country's domestic banks held Vt32,522 million (US$298,500,00 as at 31 March 2005) out of which approximately 80 per cent was held in offshore accounts in foreign deposits. The offshore sector overall had Vt415.7 million (US$3,904,000 as at 31 March 2005) in net foreign exchange earnings at the end of the first quarter in March 2005[36].

Table 10.5 Registration and annual fees charged by the VFSC[37]

Company type	Local companies					
Authorised capital (in vatu)	35 million (m) or less	>35m<50m	>50m<100m	>100m<200m	>200m<300m	>300m
Registration fee (Vt)	30,000	50,000	100,000	150,000	200,000	250,000
Annual fee (Vt)	30,000	50,000	100,000	150,000	200,000	250,000

Company type	Exempt companies				
Authorised capital (in vatu)	<50 million	>50m<100m	>100m<200m	>200m<300m	>300m
Registration fee (Vt)	50,000	75,000	100,000	200,000	250,000
Annual fee (Vt)	50,000	75,000	100,000	200,000	250,000

Company type	Overseas companies
Authorised capital (in vatu)	n/a
Registration fee (Vt)	30,000
Annual fee (Vt)	30,000

Company type	International companies
Authorised capital (in vatu)	n/a
Registration fee (US$)	150
Annual fee (US$)	300

Employment

The integrated working environment of the domestic and offshore sector makes it difficult to calculate the number of employees working exclusively in the offshore sector. Although the RBV provides employment figures for the financial sector as a whole (600 in March 2005, 531 ni-Vanuatu and 69 expatriates), these do not distinguish between those involved in IFS and those employed in the domestic financial sector. It is probable that over half of this 600 employee figure represents the domestic sector, particularly domestic banking.

The commercial banks employ about 300 staff and offshore banks employ 27. There are a total of 115 employees working in accounting firms, out of which 26 could be said to be doing IFC work. Insurance and trust companies employ 153 staff, out of which

53 work in the area of the IFC. Out of the legal firms, five persons work within the IFC[38].

Notes

1. Hampton, M. (1996), p.4.

2. Van Fossen, Anthony B. (2002), pp.38–62 .

3. Note that this Act had yet to be gazetted at the time of writing.

4. G. Rawlings (2004), pp.325–341.

5. See International Companies Act 1992 s 65, which provides that only members of the company or authorised persons can inspect the company records.

6. International Banking Act No.4 of 2002 s14 and s20.

7. Estimate provided by the Commissioner of the VFSC.

8. Weenink, B.G. (2004).

9. Ibid.

10. Ibid.

11. Lindsey Barrett, BDO Accountants.

12. IMF (2005), p.24.

13. Information provided by the research and statistics officer, Mark Mera, at RBV on 20 February 2006.

14. The multiplier effect: that is, the value of the indirect economic benefits from the IFS industry. If the IMF estimates the figure at 4 per cent and the government says more like 10 per cent, then it could be that the IMF was counting only the direct benefits, while the government was adding on the indirect benefits as well.

15. Data provided by the Vanuatu Financial Services Commission (VFSC) and the RBV.

16. Data provided by the RBV.

17. Estimate provided by the deputy governor of RBV, Mr. Peter Tari, during an interview on 6 December 2005.

18. In general, unless specified otherwise currency values for Vanuatu are taken from 1 February 2006.

19. Information provided by the research and statistics officer, Mark Mera, at the RBV on 20 February 2006.

20. Information provided by the banking supervision officer, Nelson Shem, at the RBV on 10 February 2006.

21. Data provided by the VFSC.

22. See International Companies Act 1992 s65.

23. Weenink, B.G. (2004), p9.

24. Statistics at 30 September 2005, as provided by the Vanuatu Financial Services Commission (VFSC).

25. *Offshore Investment* Company Formation Survey March 2006. Available at http://www.offshoreinvestment.com [accessed 15 February 2008]

26. Statistics at 30 September 2005, as provided by the Vanuatu Financial Services Commission (VFSC).

27. Ibid.

28. Ibid.

29. Ibid.

30. Statistics at 31 December 2005, as provided by the Vanuatu Financial Services Commission (VFSC).

31. Weenink, B.G. (2004), p11.

32. Statistics at end of December 2005, as provided by the Vanuatu Maritime Authority (VMA).

33. Weenink, B.G. (2004).

34. Information provided by Mr. Tom Bayer, 7 March 2006.

35. Weenink, B.G. (2004).

36. Reserve Bank of Vanuatu Quarterly Review, March 2005.

37. Statistics at 20 February 2006, as provided by the Vanuatu Financial Services Commission (VFSC).

38. Information provided by research and statistics officer, Mark Mera, at the RBV on 20 February 2006.

11

Regulation and Supervision of the IFS Sector in Vanuatu

11.1 Structure of IFS regulation and supervision

Two separate regulatory bodies have the responsibility of regulating the offshore sector in Vanuatu. These are the Reserve Bank (RBV) and the Vanuatu Financial Services Commission (VFSC). Both are supported by the Financial Intelligence Unit (FIU), which is established within the State Law Office (SLO). The SLO, though not a regulator, provides important drafting and technical legal assistance. In addition, although the Vanuatu Investment Promotion Authority (VIPA) is not an IFS regulator as such, it does have the authority to approve investments, assist investors and set down requirements to regulate investment.

Reserve Bank of Vanuatu (RBV)

The RBV is the central bank of Vanuatu. It was enacted and operates through the Reserve Bank of Vanuatu Act 1980, the Financial Institutions Act 1999 and the International Banking Act 2002.

As the bankers' bank, the RBV is generally responsible for the banking and financial system of the country. By statute, it is responsible for granting licenses to and supervising/regulating both the domestic and offshore banks. It currently has 60 staff, out which 52 are professionals and eight support staff. At the time of writing, seven staff were involved in the supervision and regulation of offshore activities.

Since 2003, the RBV has taken over responsibility from the VFSC for issuing licenses and regulating offshore banks. It has become quite efficient at revoking the licenses of offshore banks that do not follow the new regulatory requirements. The RBV may in the future acquire responsibility for regulating the insurance industry from the VFSC.

Vanuatu Financial Services Commission (VFSC)

The VFSC is a statutory body set up under the Vanuatu Financial Services Commission Act 1993. It comprises a commissioner (who also serves as registrar of companies) and a government-appointed board, consisting of the governor of the RBV or his/her nominee, a person with legal background and experience, and four people appointed by the Minister of Finance, at least two of whom must have a financial background and experience (Vanuatu Financial Services Commission Act)[1]. The Commission currently has 20 staff, out of which 17 are professionals[2]. The VFSC is a regulator in both the domestic and offshore financial sectors. Domestically, it is responsible for the registration of local companies, licensing of local insurers, collection of stamp duties, charities, and recording trademarks and patents. It charges penalties for breaches of licensing requirements and the late payment of annual fees. In relation to the offshore sector, it is responsible for the licensing of offshore insurers, trust companies and the registration of international and exempt companies. It also collects the registration and annual fees of these companies.

In addition, the VFSC is responsible for the promotion and development of the offshore sector. There has been a move to make the VFSC responsible for licensing corporate service providers, a prerogative that in the past rested directly with the Minister of Finance[3].

To meet the international standards of regulation required under the OECD and FATF initiatives, the VFSC had to establish a new supervision unit with four officers. This increased salary costs to the Commission by Vt6,750,000 per year. Its operating costs also increased by Vt2 million and Vt4,250,000 was spent on training new or existing staff. Hence the VFSC faced an overall increase in its costs of Vt13 million to set up and run the new supervision unit[4].

In addition, several draftpersons were required to perform a legislative overhaul in 2005. This was funded by the IMF. The estimated costs were as follows: Vt3 million for drafting, Vt10 million technical advice (IMF advisor), Vt3 million for consultation and Vt3 million for translation[5].

Financial Intelligence Unit (FIU)

A Financial Intelligence Unit was established in Vanuatu by the Financial Transactions Reporting Act 2000 (FTRA). Situated at and administered by the State Law Office, its main function is to monitor and control Vanuatu's anti-money laundering regime. It is responsible for monitoring accounting and law firms, company service providers and fund managers. Any transaction of Vt1 million or more suspected of being connected with money laundering must be reported to the FIU. The FIU provides training and guidelines to financial institutions to assist them in identifying such transactions, and performs an information gathering and compliance role under the financial institutional structure.

At the time of writing, there was one full-time staff member and one part-time staff member at the FIU. There are plans to employ two more full-time staff. The FIU works closely with the Reserve Bank and to some extent with the VFSC. At present the FIU is co-funded by the VFSC and the RBV, but there is some uncertainty as to whether this arrangement will continue.

If a suspicious transaction is reported by a financial institution, then the FIU disseminates the report and conducts investigations to ensure compliance with the FTRA. The FIU is not mandated to analyse suspicious transaction reports (STRs), and the determination of any possible money-laundering activities is carried out by the police and public prosecutor's office[6].

Vanuatu Investment Promotion Authority (VIPA)

The main role of the VIPA is to promote foreign investment in Vanuatu. Once the VIPA approves applications for investments in Vanuatu, it has the added responsibility of assisting investors facilitate implementation of their approved projects in the country. The office of the VIPA has not had to employ any extra staff to accommodate the new regulatory requirements, as the private sector is responsible for complying with the requirements by the time investment applications are filed. As such, the VIPA did not experience any extra costs as a result of the new regulatory requirements, though it hopes that the reputational benefits of compliance will lead to increased foreign investment in the country.

11.2 Emergence/evolution of the post-2000 regulatory regime for IFS

Since 2000, multilateral organisations such as the OECD and the FATF have put considerable pressure on IFCs to introduce new and stricter regulatory requirements. In June 2000, the FATF produced a blacklist of Non-Cooperative Countries and Territories (NCCT)[7]. In the same month, the OECD published a blacklist of international financial centres accused of practicing 'harmful tax competition'[8]. Vanuatu was included on this OECD blacklist, and on the subsequent 'unco-operative tax havens' list of April 2002.

Since Vanuatu has committed itself to the conditions of the OECD initiative in return for being struck off the blacklist, it will need to continue to introduce laws that will promote transparency. According to the Ministry of Finance, even though Vanuatu has not yet signed any tax information exchange deal with any country, legislation relating to this can still be passed in the absence of such an agreement[9].

Vanuatu has not been blacklisted on the NCCT list, which would have a significant adverse effect on Vanuatu's reputation as an IFC. In order to stay off this list, more stringent laws have been introduced. The Financial Transactions Reporting Act was introduced in 2000, and according to the public sector there may be additional laws passed to further strengthen regulatory requirements.

Vanuatu has been through many assessments in recent years, including this study. In 2000, the Financial Stability Forum (FSF) surveyed its members concerning the perceived quality and standard of supervision and co-operation offered by international finance centres and produced a three-part catergorisation. Vanuatu was placed in Group III along with other IFCs that were considered to have inferior standards when compared with Groups I and II[10].

Also in 2000, a joint mutual assessment of Vanuatu was performed by the Asia Pacific Group on Money Laundering (APG) and the Offshore Group of Banking Supervisors (OGBS). That assessment provided a number of recommendations to strengthen the

AML system. Vanuatu acted on the recommendations, with the Financial Transactions Reporting Act was introduced in September 2000[11]. Another joint APG/OGBS visit took place February-March 2006.

In 2002, the IMF conducted a Module 2 Assessment of the Supervision and Regulation of the Financial Sector of Vanuatu, as part of its Offshore Audit Program. In response to one IMF recommendation, in 2004 a cost-benefit analysis of the IFS sector in Vanuatu was conducted on behalf of the Vanuatuan government and the Pacific Islands Forum Secretariat.

At the time of writing, it was planned that the VFSC would soon be licensing trust and company service providers under a proposed bill modelled on Isle of Man legislation. The powers awarded to the VFSC will be along the same lines as the Insurance Act of 2005. Insurance and trust regulation may be moved from the VFSC to the RBV, however the private sector is totally against such a transfer of responsibility. The private sector claims that the RBV has no expertise in these areas.

The main differences between the old Insurance Act (see list of legislation, above) and the new one (of 2005) are that: the licensing powers given to the VFSC previously rested with the Minister of Finance; previously the VFSC had no powers to supervise, inspect or regulate insurers, but those powers now exist under the new Act; and the VFSC can also approve or remove principals of insurers and obtain and exchange information. Under the new Act there is a set minimum capital requirement and the fees have increased.

Notes

1. See s3 of the VFSC Act of 1993; note that the VFSC (Amendment) Act of 2002 has amended the VFSC Act, taking away the requirement that one member of the Commission had to be a member of the Finance Centre Association.
2. Statistics given by senior staff of the VFSC on 20 January 2006; there is a plan to recruit a further two senior persons to supervisory roles.
3. Information provided by the Commissioner of the VFSC, November 2005.
4. Information provided by the Commissioner of the VFSC on 20 February 2006.
5. Ibid.
6. IMF (2003b).
7. FATF (2000, 2001, 2002).
8. OECD (1998, 2000a).
9. Comments from the Finance Department 27 February 2006.
10. Financial Stability Forum (FSF) (2000).
11. Weenink, B.G., (2004).

12

Incremental Costs and Benefits of Enhancing the IFS Regulatory Regime in Vanuatu

12.1 Incremental costs of adopting new international regulatory standards

The public sector in Vanuatu has had to recruit new staff and retrain existing staff to meet the new international regulatory standards. The private sector has also had to recruit new staff and retrain existing staff to fulfil the new due diligence and suspicious transactions reporting requirements. Where new staff members have been recruited, new office space has had to be allocated and additional hardware and software systems have had to be bought or licensed. Some offices have also bought new IT systems such as 'World Check' in order to be able to satisfy the new international regulatory standards. Overall administrative overheads have increased for both the private and public sectors in Vanuatu.

Vanuatu Financial Services Commission

The country's regulatory bodies have also borne increased compliance costs in accommodating the external demands for enhanced regulation. The Vanuatu Financial Services Commission (VFSC) has had to take on new responsibilities, and in doing so has had to create a new section conducting supervision and compliance with four new staff. To accommodate the growing number of staff and resources needed to house them, the VFSC has had to move into a bigger building, which cost Vt5 (US$43,163 as at 1 July 2004) million in 2004 and Vt7 million (US$60,428 as at 1 July 2004) in 2005. The overall renovation and extension to the building cost Vt47 million (US$405,732 as at 1 July 2004), which was funded from the Commission's reserves. In 2003, it cost the VFSC Vt4 million to hire more officers to regulate the area of money laundering, which increased to Vt5 million in 2004 and Vt7 million in 2005. It spent Vt1 million in both 2004 and 2005 on training new staff in the area of news systems installed for anti-money laundering (AML) and countering the finance of terrorism (CFT) transactions. Moreover, staff were sent to special conferences on AML and CFT, which cost Vt1.5 million in 2003, Vt2 million in 2004 and Vt3 million in 2005.

The VFSC has had to rely on aid from other countries, both in the form of financial and technical assistance. For example, in 2003 Vt6 million was provided by the Asian

Development Bank (ADB) and the IMF for technical assistance and advisers; this increased to Vt12 million in 2004 and Vt18 million in 2005. A further Vt3 million was provided in 2003 for foreign legal advisers; this increased to Vt6 million in 2004 and Vt8 million in 2005.

In 2005 the VFSC installed an additional hardware system to meet suspicious transaction reporting (STR) and know your customer (KYC) requirements, which cost Vt3 million. It spent an additional Vt750,000 in 2003, Vt1.5 million in 2004 and Vt3 million in 2005 to recruit draftpersons to draft legislation to comply with AML/CFT requirements. The cost of additional internal audit requirements for the new STR/KYC was Vt1 million in 2003 and increased to Vt3 million in 2004 and Vt5 million in 2005. The cost of additional external audit requirements for the new STR/KYC was Vt500,000 in 2004 and increased to Vt1 million in 2005[1]. The VFSC contributed Vt1 million in both 2004 and 2005 towards the budget of the Financial Intelligence Unit (FIU); however, the government has now taken over the funding of the FIU.

The Reserve Bank of Vanuatu

The Reserve Bank of Vanuatu (RBV) has also had to take on demanding new duties as a result of the multilateral initiatives. The government has had to increase the RBV's budget to cope with the increased costs of regulation. For example, the RBV has spent Vt400,000 per year since 2000 to train four staff working in the area of STR/KYC in relation to banks. It also sent staff overseas for training in these areas, although the costs for this were covered by AusAID (the Australian government's overseas aid programme). For other external trainings, the RBV has spent about Vt1 million per year since 2003. It received technical assistance for the purposes of AML/CFT, which was funded by the IMF. The RBV recruited seven persons in 2002 to act as domestic regulators, which cost approximately Vt7 million. It also planned to recruit a further five persons for this purpose in 2006. New equipment for these staff cost Vt600,000 in 2002, and Vt300,000 each year from 2003 to 2005. The Reserve Bank also contributes towards the operations of the FIU and provided Vt2 million in both 2004 and 2005 in this regard[2]. In order to house the bigger banking supervision department, office space has had to be renovated, which cost Vt500,000 and was borne by the RBV.

Financial Intelligence Unit

The FIU has received assistance from the VFSC and the RBV budgets, but has also had to rely on international aid to help meet the new regulatory demands. From 2000 to 2003, there were two persons from the State Law Office (SLO) working part-time for the FIU, which cost about Vt1 million. AusAID initially provided the equipment to set up the FIU department. In 2004, a dedicated FIU office was set up and a full-time employee recruited, costing about Vt1 million per annum. At this stage, more equipment was needed by the FIU to be able to provide training for private financial institutions in the area of AML/CFT. The French government and the United Nations Office for Drugs and Crime (UNODC) provided for and funded seven computers for this purpose. In 2005, the British High Commission donated a laptop, scanner, desktop computer and printer to the FIU. Early in 2006, AusAID provided another computer for the FIU database.

In 2005, another full-time employee was recruited, increasing staff costs to Vt2 million. To accommodate the two staff members of the FIU, new office space had to be created, costing Vt1.5 million for the extension to the building and an increase in the rent of Vt540,000 per year. Between 2000 to 2003 the staff of the FIU attended special conferences on AML/CFT, which cost about Vt400,000; this cost Vt1 million each year in 2004 and 2005. In 2005, AusAID funded one officer of the FIU to receive specialist training in Singapore and to become the specialist enforcement officer for AML/CFT for Vanuatu. About Vt800,000 was spent between 2000 to 2003 to train the staff on new hardware and software systems for AML/CFT; a further Vt500,000 was spent on this between 2004 and 2005. External technical advisers were also needed to help with setting up the office and assisting in AML/CFT matters, these positions being funded by the IMF. The IMF also funded the cost of additional external audit requirements for the new STR/KYC regime, which have been approximately Vt4 million since 2004[3]. In 2006, further offers of assistance were made by the ADB, FIRST and the EU. FIRST has proposed to complete the Trust and Company Service Providers and Trust bills, while the EU has proposed to look at the issue of governance in the areas of finance, tax and the judiciary.

Table 12.1 One-off costs for the public sector

	RBV	VFSC	FIU
New building/extension to building	Vt500,000	Vt47m	Vt1.5m
Additional computer hardware/software for STR/KYC		Vt3m	
New equipment (laptop, desktop, scanner, printer)			Vt400,000

Table 12.2 External technical assistance awarded to the public sector

	2000	2001	2002	2003	2004	2005
VFSC				Vt6m – technical assistance/ advisers; VT3m – foreign legal advisers	Vt12m – technical assistance/ advisers VT6m – foreign legal advisers	Vt18m – technical assistance/advisers VT8m – foreign legal advisers
RBV	Vt2m for external adviser	Vt2m for technical adviser	Vt13m for resident technical advisers	Vt13m for resident technical advisers	Vt13m for resident technical advisers VT1.8m for database expert	Vt1.5m for foreign technical advisers
FIU					Vt1.8m for setting up office, assistance in AML/CFT matters VT1.8m for drafting purposes	Vt1.8m for drafting purposes

Table 12.3 Recurring costs (VFSC)

	2000	2001	2002	2003	2004	2005
Recruit new staff				Vt4m	Vt5m	Vt7m
Train staff in AML/CFT					Vt1m	Vt1m
Special conferences on AML/CFT				Vt1.5m	Vt2m	Vt3m
Recruit draftpersons to draft AML/CFT laws				Vt750,000	Vt1.5m	Vt3m
Internal audit requirements for STR/KYC				Vt1m	Vt3m	Vt5m
External audit requirements for STR/KYC					Vt500,000	Vt1m
Contribution towards FIU budget					Vt1m	Vt1m

Table 12.4 Recurring costs (RBV)

	2000	2001	2002	2003	2004	2005
Recruit new staff (salary)				Vt7m	Vt7m	Vt7m
Train staff in STR/KYC	Vt400,000	Vt400,000	Vt400,000	Vt400,000	Vt400,000	Vt400,000
External trainings on AML/CFT				Vt1m	Vt1m	Vt1m
New equipment			Vt600,000	Vt300,000	Vt300,000	Vt300,000
Contribution towards FIU budget					Vt2m	Vt2m

Table 12.5 Recurring costs (FIU)

	2000	2001	2002	2003	2004	2005
Recruit new staff (salary)	Vt1m	Vt1m	Vt1m	Vt1m	Vt1m	Vt2m
Train staff in STR/KYC					Vt400,000	Vt1m
Specialist trainings on AML/CFT						Vt1m
Train staff on new software/hardware for AML/CFT	Vt800,000	Vt500,000				
Contribution towards FIU budget					Vt2m	Vt2m

IFS service providers

International financial services providers, too, have had to shoulder added costs due to the new regulatory requirements. Banks, accounting and law firms, and those providing corporate and trust services have faced an increase in operating costs. This has been due to the added requirements of the KYC regime and STR checks.

The commercial banks reported that they did not experience any significant new incremental costs as a direct result of the new regulatory requirements. This was because two of the banks are associated with larger foreign banks (ANZ and Westpac, both based in Australia) and have had to implement international KYC requirements before Vanuatu was required to do so. For example, these banks had already introduced new IT system hardware or software to better regulate client information by 2000. The third bank, Vanuatu National Bank, maintains a very small number of clients in the offshore sector and the costs associated with the changes in recent years have not been significant enough to cause concern to this particular bank[4].

The offshore banks surveyed reported that they faced an increase in costs due to the new regulatory requirements, but no specific figures were provided. However, they also pointed out that these are costs that it is necessary to bear if they wish to continue operating in competition with other IFCs[5]. If the country had not introduced recent reforms (expensive as they are) it might be that foreign customers onshore would be progressively restricted from access to Vanuatu's IFS.

The accounting firms that operate within Vanuatu's IFC experienced a significant increase in operating costs. One particular firm had to retrain (in-house) its existing staff in the areas of STR, which cost about Vt863,652 (US$7,525), as well as spending Vt12,954,786 (US$112,876) on enhanced KYC procedures between 2003 and 2005. As well as these direct monetary costs, there were additional indirect costs in terms of staff spending time away from their other responsibilities. Another firm had to appoint a person to carry out STR/KYC requirements on a half-day basis, which cost Vt1 million in 2004. In relation to extra space needed to house new staff, only one firm faced this problem: it spent Vt240,000 in increased rental costs.

Most of the firms surveyed reported that they sent staff to specialised conferences on AML/CFT, which cost Vt9 million from 2000 to 2005. Some of the firms invested in new systems of hardware and software for AML/CFT which cost about Vt400,000. All firms surveyed reported that they experienced additional costs of compliance relating to AML/CFT. While this figure was as low as VT2 million for some, it was more than Vt6 million per year since 2000 for some others. One firm in particular experienced a significant increase in this area in 2004 (Vt13 million) and 2005 (Vt18 million). While most firms did not face any extra costs due to additional internal/external audit requirements, one firm experienced an increase of Vt1 million and Vt500,000 respectively for 2004 and 2005[6].

The law firms that operate within the IFC experienced a significant increase in operating costs too. These firms reported that from 2000 to 2005 they spent between 20 and 50 additional hours each year on fulfilling the new STR/KYC requirements, which added about an extra Vt1 million each year to their operating costs. However, the law firms did not recruit any new staff to perform this work, either retraining existing staff or, in the majority of cases, the senior partners performing these duties personally. About Vt120,000 was spent by some firms on attending special conferences on AML/CFT[7].

In some instances, the incremental costs were passed on from the regulators to the IFS providers and from the IFS providers to the clients. This was mainly by way of higher fees and other charges. For example, the fee for registering an offshore bank in Vanuatu was increased from $US5,000 (the fee under the old banking act) to $US8,000 (fee under the new banking act)[8]. Other non-pecuniary costs clients had to cope with were the loss of privacy and confidentiality, and delays in remittance transaction periods due to the new more detailed due diligence/KYC requirements. Overall this increased the time that is usually taken to clear documentation and do business, which frustrated some clients and drove them to other destinations. This led to lost business opportunities for the offshore sector in Vanuatu.

Because most forms of regulatory requirement lead to employment opportunities for local workers in the country, however, some of these costs may also have provided employment benefits.

Table 12.6 Cost of regulating offshore sector 2000–2005 (Vt, millions)

	2000	2001	2002	2003	2004	2005
RBV	2.4	2.4	14	21.7	25.5	12.2
VFSC	10	10	10	16.35	32	47
FIU	1	1.8	1.8	1	7.5	7.8
TOTAL	13.4	14.2	25.8	39.05	65	67

Table 12.7 Revenue from offshore sector 2000–2005 (Vt, millions) (as estimated by RBV)

	2000	2001	2002	2003	2004	2005
(International) Shipping & Companies fees	357	309	281	253	218	202
Offshore banks	64.9	42.9	38.5	37.4	12.32	12.32
Total estimated revenue	421.9	351.9	319.5	290.4	230.32	214.32

Table 12.8 Cost of regulation versus revenue from offshore sector 2000–2005 (Vt, millions)

	2000	2001	2002	2003	2004	2005
Cost	13.4	14.2	25.8	39.05	65	67
Revenue	421.9	351.9	319.5	290.4	230.32	214.32
Ratio (%)	3.2	4.0	8.1	13.5	28.2	31.3

12.2 Incremental benefits of enhanced IFS regulation and supervision

It is difficult to identify incremental benefits to the offshore centre in Vanuatu due to the enhanced IFS regulation and supervision, and impossible to quantify any such benefits. One qualitative benefit identified by public sector regulators and some (though by no means all) private sector respondents is that the enhanced regulation and supervision requirements are said to have improved Vanuatu's reputation as an IFC. It has also possibly enhanced Vanuatu's competitiveness with other IFC jurisdictions, though this assessment is supported only by some of the public sector and by a minority in the private sector, who believe that such benefits may only be seen over a period of time. Other sceptics think that, due to its remoteness, Vanuatu is not in competition with other geographically better placed IFCs like the British Virgin Islands and the Cayman Islands.

By complying with the FATF initiatives, Vanuatu avoided being placed on the NCCT list and so avoided the associated negative publicity, which would tend to have discouraged offshore clients and international aid. Since committing to the OECD Harmful Tax Practices initiative in May 2003, Vanuatu has been removed from the 'Uncooperative Tax Haven' list[9]. Given the serious reputational and material damage inflicted by blacklisting on other Pacific IFCs since 2000, these are significant achievements. Public sector regulators and those offshore bankers that remain identify the major benefit of adopting reforms as the sector's continued ability to enjoy access to the global market for IFS.

According to the RBV and the VFSC, the number of registrations of international companies and offshore banks have declined due to the new regulatory requirements since 2000. However, both regulators were positive that with time the numbers would increase and the offshore centre will attract more business. It is anticipated that the new international regulations will increase growth and in turn will bring a more diverse IFS client base. However, there has not been any significant positive growth since 2000[10].

In general, a large majority of the participants in the workshop for this case study agreed that it was difficult to identify any direct 'reputational dividend' accruing to Vanuatu as a result of its compliance with new regulations. The general feeling among workshop participants was that both the public and private sector had spent a great deal of effort meeting new regulatory standards with very little to show for it in terms of increased revenue, and with little thanks from the outsiders that have driven these regulatory changes, in particular by the threat of blacklisting.

A significant negative change has been noted in the collection of the offshore sector's revenues due to the new international regulations. A private sector source claimed that the loss of offshore banks has cost the public and private sector in Vanuatu a total of US$1 million.

12.3 Overall assessment of net benefits accruing to Vanuatu from adoption of new international regulatory standards and strengthened regulatory regime

The overall net impact on the Vanuatu economy in adopting the new international regulatory standards has been generally negative to date. Complicating this assessment, however, is the improved reputation Vanuatu may have gained in the international business arena. The new regulatory standards may result in reputational gains, which would result in foreign authorities removing barriers to the marketing of financial services from the IFC. Private investors may also be more likely to invest in a jurisdiction that has met international standards and is not on any blacklist. However, there is as yet little or no firm evidence to support this optimistic scenario.

The government and the public sector regulators, under international pressure, have had to adopt new international regulatory requirements. This has cost the public sector far more to implement the new standards than has been received in any quantitative benefits to date. In most instances, new staff members have had to be employed or existing staff retrained to take on the new responsibilities. In some instances, new office space has had to be rented to accommodate the new staff. Where new staff have been recruited, new equipment has had to be bought, which has increased the cost of operations for public sector regulators.

Private sector IFS providers have also had to implement the new international standards, particularly in the form of stricter due diligence/know your customer requirements. As a result, a substantial volume of business has been lost, as the IFC's international clientele have found the new regulatory requirements excessively intrusive[11]. In particular, some private sector respondents emphasised in interviews and workshops that a significant amount of business had been lost to less strictly regulated onshore jurisdictions, like Delaware or London, or to IFCs like Hong Kong and Singapore that have so far not been targeted by the OECD or the FATF.

In order to be able to comply with the new regulatory requirements, the private sector has often had to retrain existing staff. For some operators, senior partners have had to perform the compliance work themselves due to the lack of experience of existing staff in this area. A few operators bought new IT software to comply with new regulatory requirements, while others indicated that they were already using such software before 2000. As with the public sector, for the private sector the overall net quantitative benefits in adopting new international regulatory standards have been negative to date. However, some private sector operators believed that there was a net qualitative benefit from Vanuatu's compliance with the new international regulatory standards, again through the country's enhanced reputation internationally.

The costs borne overall by Vanuatu's international finance centre (i.e. by both the public and private sectors) are far greater than any apparent benefits to date. The public sector is generally hopeful that the benefits from adopting the new standards will become more obvious in the near future with an increase in business.

For Vanuatu's offshore industry to grow and become more profitable, however, the implementation of new regulatory standards is not sufficient. Even though its name has been cleared from the OECD's blacklist, there is significant concern in the public sector that Vanuatu is still labelled by many banks as a 'blacklisted country'. Vanuatu is now explicitly marked out for unfavourable treatment in national tax blacklists maintained by Argentina, Brazil, Colombia, France, Italy, Latvia, Mexico, Peru, Portugal, Spain and Venezuela[12]. There have also been difficulties processing transactions from foreign banks, particularly in the United States. Some of these problems date from 1999, but the FSF's and OECD's blacklists have been an important contributing factor. The private sector believes that because banks in OECD states still treat Vanuatu as a non-compliant country, it is very difficult for private service providers to establish new banking contacts or maintain existing ones. Major international banks such as HSBC, Deutsche Bank and the Bank of New York, to name but a few, still refuse to carry out any transactions involving Vanuatu.

Some in the private sector believe that due to the small size of the Vanuatu's IFC operations, its success in meeting new international regulatory standards may not make any difference to the amount of business that comes its way, certainly not enough to compensate for the costs of implementing these standards.

12.4 Conclusions and future implications of current international regulatory initiatives for Vanuatu

According to some industry members, the imposition of new standards by a number of diverse sources is not an appropriate response to the underlying problems that are being addressed. The substantial volume of regulatory requirements imposed on Vanuatu in the recent years is said to be excessive considering the small scale of operations and the country's remoteness with reference to transactions relating to money laundering and the financing of terrorism. Private sector sources believe that this is particularly true, because in order to get to Vanuatu's offshore providers such transactions would have to go through other larger countries that should be already picking up on any illegal activity. The new regulatory requirements are said to be going in the wrong direction by requiring over-regulation of the IFS sector for AML/CFT concerns, when the possibility of such incidents occurring in Vanuatu is remote.

The FATF has been very active in ensuring that Vanuatu adheres to new AML/CFT international regulatory standards. Some sceptics have characterised its behaviour towards Vanuatu as oppressive, and believe that other larger financial centres have not had to implement such requirements, a suspicion confirmed in relation to Delaware, Nevada and Wyoming by recent US government reports[13]. The industry generally believes that new and more rigorous standards are being developed at a frenetic pace, not because there is an actual need for them in accomplishing desired objectives, but because an industry with vested interests has now emerged within the OECD and the international financial institutions (the World Bank and the IMF) for generating standards to give the impression of 'something' being done.

Vanuatu has made some conditional commitment to international tax information exchange (ITIE) with the OECD. In May 2003, the Minister of Finance wrote a letter to the OECD Secretary General agreeing to implement the reforms requested[14]. The commitment letter noted, however, that the reforms desired by the OECD would have 'significant adverse cost and revenue implications' for Vanuatu, and asked for donor countries to keep this sacrifice in mind when allocating development aid. In the commitment letter, the government of Vanuatu agreed to:

- Exchange tax information with other countries relating to criminal matters from 31 December 2003 and on civil tax matters from 31 December 2005. The fact that particular acts may not constitute crimes in Vanuatu or that Vanuatu has no fiscal interest in the case are not sufficient grounds to refused information exchange.

- Establish beneficial ownership of companies, banks, partnerships and other corporate vehicles and the settlors, trustees and beneficiaries of trusts, make this information available to regulators, and exchange this information with foreign tax authorities. Authorities will have access to and exchange bank information on a similar basis.

- Ensure that companies and other corporate vehicles will submit regular accounts in line with standards to be drawn up by the Joint Ad Hoc Group on Accounts.

Vanuatu's commitment letter was made conditional on the 'level playing field' being achieved in that all countries would meet the OECD standards on information exchange, and any countries failing to meet those standards being subject to 'co-ordinated defensive measures'. Although the OECD has refused in principle to accept 'conditional commitments', the status of Vanuatu's commitment and the specific measures is now unclear. Four OECD members have so far refused to abide by new rules on international tax information exchange (Austria, Belgium, Luxembourg and Switzerland), while the remaining five jurisdictions on the 'Unco-operative Tax Havens' list (Nauru having committed in December 2003) have not been subject to any co-ordinated defensive measures.

Representatives from Vanuatu attended the November 2005 OECD Global Tax Forum, at which it was agreed that information exchange should take place on a bilateral, voluntary basis according to the principle of mutual benefit. Australia is particularly keen to conclude a Tax Information Exchange Agreement (TIEA) with Vanuatu.

Vanuatu does not have any tax treaties with any country to date, though it may negotiate a bilateral tax information exchange agreement with Australia. Therefore, no information was available or collected from the country relating to the cost of international tax information exchange. Sceptics from the private and public sector are of the opinion that Vanuatu will have nothing to gain from such an agreement since it is a tax haven, hence any other country's tax information will be of no use to it. There were suggestions that if Vanuatu were made to release such information relating to its investors, then the body or country interested in this information should pay the price for it by way of some compensatory benefit to the country. Concerns were raised about the domestic privacy laws of countries like Australia and New Zealand, which may result in a one-way traffic flow from Vanuatu with nothing in return because under domestic law these countries would not be able to provide any tax/confidential information.

The other 'participating partner' governments in the OECD process are now in the situation of deciding whether the direct and indirect costs of concluding TIEAs are worth the benefits OECD countries are offering. Thus far, the TIEA between the Isle of Man and the Netherlands, concluded in late 2005, is regarded as being the most successful model of an arrangement conferring substantial mutual benefits.

Potential future costs from the OECD's initiative arise in several forms. There are the direct costs of implementing the specified reforms, particularly establishing beneficial ownership. Because the measures required by the OECD are largely the same as those in the FATF's 40 Recommendations[15] (and those called for in the 2003 IMF report[16]), it is artificial to attribute the costs of implementing such reforms to the OECD initiative alone.

However, there is also the impact to consider in terms of the reforms reducing Vanuatu's attractiveness as an IFC in the eyes of foreign investors. These costs can be expected to be significant. In both promotional material and in interviews, local corporate service providers tend to emphasise the importance of secrecy and confidentiality for clients forming international companies and trusts, either separately or in combination. To the extent that the identities of beneficial owners and directors of companies and the identity of trust beneficiaries must be disclosed to the authorities and thence passed on to foreign governments, the attractiveness of these vehicles can be expected to decline. Even for discretionary trusts it is expected that beneficiaries must be identified as soon as they receive income or assets from the trust. Similarly, increased reporting requirements for international and insurance companies may be expected to reduce their appeal to prospective clients.

Finally, both the public and private sectors agree a priority for the future is to improve the marketing of Vanuatu's international financial centre. For example, the VFSC is seeking to introduce online services and a marketing plan with the assistance of the ADB, which may cost approximately $US500,000. Despite the consensus on the need for enhanced marketing, there is no consensus as to who should take the lead and bear the costs: the private sector regards the government as having primary responsibility, while regulatory bodies see marketing as being incompatible with their role.

Table 12.9 Quantitative survey findings of the public sector – costs

Type of incremental cost incurred for AML/CFT	2000	2003	2004	2005	Total 2000–05
Additional person-hours for suspicious transactions reporting (STR)	1 person full time			2 persons full time	2 persons
Additional person-hours for know your customer requirements (KYCR)	1 person full time		4 persons full time	4 persons	
Number of money laundering reporting officers hired by your firm	1 person full time		2 persons full time	2 persons	
Cost of additional person-hours/ people hired for above (in Vt, millions)	1m	4m		7m	12m
Cost of additional space that needed to be rented/bought for this purpose (in Vt, millions)			5m	7m	12m
Regular in-house training on AML/ CFT (STR/KYC) (hrs/Vt, millions)	0 hrs/Vt		Vt1m	Vt1m	Vt2m
Cost of attendance by staff at special conferences on AML/CFT (in Vt, millions)			1m	3m	4m
Cost of training on new systems (hardware and software) for AML/ CFT (in Vt, millions)	0		1m	2m	3m
Costs to firm of external technical assistance obtained for AML/CFT:					
• from OECD, IMF, World Bank and other IFIs (in Vt, millions)	6m	12m from ADB	18m from ADB	36m from ADB	from ADB
• from foreign legal advisers (in Vt, millions)	3m	6m	8m	17m	
Costs of investment in additional systems for STR/KYC: hardware/ software (in Vt, millions)	0			3m	3m
Costs of additional internal audit requirements for new STR/KYC rules (in Vt, millions)	0	1m	3m	5m	9m
Costs of additional external audit requirements for new STR/KYC rules (in Vt, millions)		1m		5m	6m

Table 12.10 Quantitative survey findings of the public sector – benefits

	2000	2001	2002	2003	2004	2005	2000–05
Incremental business revenue from increased IFS activity				(14,655m)	35,322m	(23,777m)	
Incremental profit from increased IFS activity							
Increased staff efficiency/ productivity				7m	7m	7m	
Increased client base and client source diversification (numbers)							
Increased product/service diversification				0	0	3m	
Increased competitiveness of Vanuatu as an IFC				0	0	3m	
Increased competitiveness of your firm in the Vanuatu IFC sector							
Improved technological capacity				0	0	3m	
Improved knowledge base in providing global IFS				1m	1m	2m	
Increased profitability from improved risk management				1m	1m	2m	

Table 12.11 Quantitative survey findings of the private sector – costs

Type of incremental cost incurred for AML/CFT	2000	2003	2004	2005	Total 2000–05
Additional person-hours for suspicious transactions reporting (STR)	50hrs	50hrs	100hrs	100hrs	300hrs
Additional person-hours for know your customer requirements (KYCR)	50hrs	50hrs	100hrs	100hrs	300hrs
Number of money laundering reporting officers hired by your firm	0	0	0	0	
Cost of additional person-hours/people hired for above (Vt)	1m	1m	1m	1m	4m
Cost of additional space that needed to be rented/bought for this purpose (Vt)	240,000	240,000	240,000	240,000	960,000
Regular in-house training on AML/CFT (STR/KYC) (hrs/Vt)	100hrs	200hrs	300hrs	300hrs	900hrs/Vt5m
Cost of attendance by staff at special conferences on AML/CFT (Vt)	30hrs	40hrs	40hrs	80hrs	190hrs/Vt9m
Training on New Systems (Hardware and Software) for AML/CFT	0	20hrs	20hrs	40hrs	80hrs/VT 400,000
Costs to firm of external technical assistance obtained for AML/CFT:	0	0	0		0
• from OECD, IMF, World Bank and other IFIs		0	0	0	0
• from foreign legal advisers		0	0	0	0
Costs of investment in additional systems for STR/KYC: hardware/software (Vt)	0	680,000	680,000	680,000	2m
Costs of additional internal audit requirements for new STR/KYC rules (Vt)	0	1m	1m	1m	3m
Costs of additional external audit requirements for rew STR/KYC rules		500,000	500,000	500,000	1.5m

Notes

1. Information provided by the Commissioner of the VFSC during an interview on 13 December 2005.

2. Information provided by Mr. Peter Tari, deputy governor, Reserve Bank of Vanuatu, during an interview on 6 December 2005.

3. Information provided by Mr. Mackenzie Obed, FIU officer, during an interview on 15 December 2005.

4. Information collected by the author from interviews.

5. Ibid.

6. Ibid.

7. Ibid.

8. Information provided by the Reserve Bank of Vanuatu.

9. Note that being removed from the OECD blacklist was not the only reason why Vanuatu committed to the OECD Harmful Tax Initiative. There were eight other conditions listed in Vanuatu's commitment letter to the OECD, in addition to the removal from the 'OCED list of Unco-operative Tax Havens' – information provided by Vanuatu's Finance Department on 27 February 2006.

10. Indication by the private sector.

11. Statement made by a private sector operator, who believes that international clientele jealously guard their privacy when dealing with offshore centres and that any additional requirements to provide personal information are treated as being intrusive.

12. See J.C. Sharman and G. Rawlings (2005).

13. See US Government Accounting Office (2006); US Treasury (2005).

14. See http://www.oecd.org/dataoecd/61/28/2634587.pdf [accessed 21 February 2008]

15. Available at: http://www.fatf-gafi.org/document/28/0,3343,en_32250379_32236930_33658140_1_1_1_1,00.html [accessed 21 February 2008].

16. IMF (2003c).

13

Case Study Synthesis, Conclusions and Future Directions

....

This final chapter presents a synthesis of the results from the preceding case study reports from Barbados, Mauritius and Vanuatu. It broadly considers the costs and benefits of enhancing the regulatory regime for international financial services in the public and private sectors for these three countries, and draws out some general implications for the international financial centres under consideration. The authors end by forming a number of overall conclusions and ask readers to consider the importance of further research to assess the developmental impact of recent international tax and AML/CFT initiatives to the much larger number of IFCs worldwide.

13.1 Costs and benefits to the public sector in Barbados, Mauritius and Vanuatu

Direct costs and benefits to the public sector

The most obvious direct cost to the public sector in all three countries was that of expanding existing regulatory agencies, or creating new regulatory agencies either from scratch, or rationalising and consolidating a number of fragmented regulatory authorities under a single umbrella (as was the case with the Financial Services Commission (FSC) in Mauritius). All three jurisdictions studied have set up Financial Intelligence Units (FIUs). In Barbados, the Anti-Money Laundering Authority and Financial Intelligence Unit was established in 2000, the Mauritius Financial Intelligence Unit was created in 2002 (succeeding the Economic Crimes Office set up in 2000) and the Vanuatu Financial Intelligence Unit was set up as part of the State Law Office from 2000. Expenditure on FIUs is relatively large and looks likely to grow. A joint Offshore Group of Banking Supervisors/Asia-Pacific Group on Money Laundering assessment mission to Vanuatu in March 2006 judged the one-person FIU (recommended by the IMF after a 2003 assessment) inadequate and in need of at least two more full-time staff. The Barbadian FIU is also under considerable pressure to fulfil its responsibilities with existing staff levels. In contrast, the Mauritius FIU appears to be over-staffed and over-resourced with 27 full-time staff handling an annual average of 70 suspicious transactions reports in 2004 and 2005.

Existing regulatory agencies (especially central banks) have also taken on increased supervisory responsibilities since 2000. In line with these burdens, regulatory agencies either took on more staff (the most common solution, as for example in the Reserve

Bank of Vanuatu and the Vanuatu Financial Services Commission, the FSC in Mauritius and the Central Bank of Barbados), or else stretched existing staff resources by increasing overtime and reallocating staff from other tasks to compliance (as for example in the Bank of Mauritius and the Ministry of Industry and International Business in Barbados). Of course these responses are not mutually exclusive. Some agencies have taken on more staff and sacrificed other important priorities in order to implement internationally-mandated reforms.

In general, regulators proved less likely than private firms (especially CSPs/MCs) to identify high costs resulting from the new regulatory initiatives in their responses to the questionnaires. They were more forthcoming in private interviews. There was a tendency to understate costs on the part of these agencies, for example by not attempting to assess the opportunity costs incurred when staff were switched from one priority to another (for instance, switching staff from bank capital adequacy and risk management supervision to examining whether banks were complying with upgraded AML/CFT standards). Regulators were also more likely than operators in the IFS industry to assert the existence of benefits springing from the initiatives. These were primarily said to be reputational (of which more below), but also included in some cases modest gains in IFS *industry* productivity, as well as improved *regulatory* efficiency and productivity, although no evidence was provided to support this assertion in either instance.

The impact on government revenue

In keeping with the diversity of IFCs in general, the three governments in the jurisdictions studied in this project aimed to derive different benefits from their IFS industries. Aside from general commitments to IFS as a pathway to increasing national development and prosperity, governments also gain direct revenue benefits from hosting IFCs. This revenue may be generated either directly, in terms of incorporation fees and offshore banking licences, or indirectly through general tax revenue derived from the IFS sector.

Vanuatu does not have any corporate or income tax. Although the offshore sector does contribute some Value Added Tax (VAT) and import duties, its main contribution to government revenue has been fee revenue. In early 2006, this contribution was estimated by the Reserve Bank of Vanuatu to be 5.5 per cent of total government revenue. In contrast, Barbados derives approximately 60 per cent of its corporate tax revenue from the IFS sector, despite the very low tax rates applied (between 1 and 2.5 per cent for international business companies [IBCs]). Together with the associated personal income tax and fees, the IFS industry contributes over 10 per cent of the Barbadian government's total revenue. In Mauritius, license fees paid by offshore licensees, MCs and offshore banks account for less than 1 per cent of total public revenues. However, direct corporate tax and indirect taxes (VAT) paid by MCs, global business licensees and banks providing offshore banking services (as well as direct and indirect taxes paid by their employees) were estimated to average about 5 per cent of total public revenue for Mauritius between 2000 and 2005.

What can be said about the impact of the new internationally-mandated regulations on the revenue of the small Commonwealth IFCs under comparison? After a dip in 2000–2001 in Barbados and Mauritius (attributable in the main to the direct and indirect effects of blacklisting), government revenue derived from IFS has continued to grow, albeit at a slower rate than pre-2000. In Mauritius this has been a product of an increase in the number of IBCs ('global business companies' in Mauritian parlance), but at a much slower rate in 2002–05 than was the case between 1995 and 2002. In Barbados, even though the number of active entities (primarily IBCs) has fallen from the late 1990s, the total tax take from the IFS sector has increased. Workshop participants interpreted this as extant clients (predominantly from Canada) moving more of their business to Barbados, thus generating more tax from existing firms.

Vanuatu provides a contrast in that fee revenue from IBCs (international business companies) has stayed static, while revenue from banking licences has collapsed in line with the sharp fall in the overall number of banks. Revenue from offshore banking licences declined by 91 per cent between 2000 and 2005, although the licence fee increased from US$5,000 to US$8,000. The suddenness of the decline in bank numbers in the six months after changes in legislation governing offshore banks makes the inference that this drop was caused by (rather than just coinciding with) regulatory changes relatively robust. This interpretation was confirmed by both public and private sector representatives at the workshop.

If in Vanuatu the core of offshore banks pre-2002 was 35–40, compared with only seven banks remaining in 2003, this represents a loss of approximately US$1 million in fee revenue for the period 2003–2006 (given the offshore banking licence fee of US$8,000 plus the US$750 exempt company fee). Judging by standard international rates, this imputes a loss of as much as an additional US$3–4 million in management fees and associated services for corporate service providers (CSPs) over the same four-year period. As there has not been any compensating gain in any other area of the IFS industry, overall fee revenue has declined every year after 2000, and by half in total in 2005 compared with the base year 2000 level. This represents a major economic sacrifice, given Vanuatu's development challenges and steadily escalating regulatory costs. It may be the case that Vanuatu constitutes an outlier in this sample (i.e. compared with Barbados and Mauritius) with regard to revenue. However, it may be more typical of the broader experience of other smaller Caribbean and Pacific IFCs. Once again, however, this speculative hypothesis can only be substantiated through further research.

The impact of international technical assistance (TA)

International agencies have played a substantial, but uneven, role in defraying partially the costs associated with upgrading regulatory standards. Bodies such as the IMF, World Bank, the FIRST Initiative, United Nations Office on Drugs and Crime and the Commonwealth, as well as regional bodies such as the European Union and Pacific Islands Forum Secretariat, have taken the lead in this area. Technical assistance (TA) has been of greatest significance in Vanuatu, though bodies such as FIRST and the Caribbean

Technical Assistance Centre have also been important in Mauritius and Barbados respectively.

TA has been disproportionately directed at legislative drafting and public sector training in AML/CFT and, to a lesser extent, at financing increased information technology (IT) costs for regulators. This kind of support has been much less evident in meeting the increasing recurrent (staff salaries and office overheads) costs associated with the steady expansion of regulatory agencies, leaving the countries in question to pay a substantially increased annual bill in this respect.

Net assessment of costs and benefits for the public sector

In all three countries, public sector regulators identified the new regulatory regime as making a significant and positive net contribution to the health and global image of the IFC. This belief is most clearly expressed in the sentiment that new, more stringent standards have strengthened the overall financial system and enhanced the reputation of the jurisdiction in the outside world, both with reference to multilateral standard-setting bodies and foreign investors.

This positive conclusion belies the fact that the direct and opportunity costs (hiring new staff and the relevant other costs or diverting existing staff from other duties) of the new regulatory regime have been rising much faster than any associated tax or fee revenue gain, or the overall growth in IFS business. Indeed, in Vanuatu sharply rising regulatory costs have co-existed with a precipitous decline in government revenue from the IFC, though local regulators hope that this trend will be reversed in the future.

The quantifiable benefits from implementing new regulations have been modest, with some small increases in productivity. Instead, regulators' judgment about the net benefits derived from conforming to new standards of regulation in the IFS industry rests on two crucial assumptions. The first is that meeting these standards is a *sine qua non* for competing in the global IFS market. Failing to meet these standards is not an option, being tantamount to making an exit from that market. In this sense, regulators in all three jurisdictions observed that their IFCs had no choice but to pay whatever costs were necessary for full regulatory compliance with international demands. According to this logic then, *all* the benefits derived from the IFCs have to be ascribed to the new regulatory regime, because in the absence of this regime there would be no IFC.

The second crucial point is that increased regulation has provided commensurate benefits by improving the reputation of the IFC, as evidenced in the regulators' questionnaire responses in all three countries. In turn, reputation is seen as one of the most, and probably *the* most, important single factor in determining the competitiveness and viability of the IFC. The question of reputation is examined in further detail below. However, it is worth noting the anomaly that despite respondents in the public sector being confident about the increased standing of their IFC generated by increased regulation, they were generally unable to identify any tangible benefits accruing to the competitiveness or growth of the IFC.

This result is puzzling. If reputation is so important for competitiveness (as respondents in both the public and private sector claim), and reputation has indeed been boosted, then the ensuing competitiveness benefits should be clearly identifiable. The dearth of evidence supporting this presumed relationship in any of the countries surveyed indicates that either: reputation is less important for attracting business than generally assumed and axiomatically asserted; or that countries' reputations have not received the boost commonly assumed; or that there have been invisible competitiveness benefits that have escaped the notice of regulators and the IFS industry. The results gained from the questionnaires, workshops and interviews do not enable a definitive conclusion to be drawn from these three possibilities, although the last seems remote.

There are two other factors that have a possible bearing on this puzzle. The first is the methodological point that it may well make more sense to assess the reputation of an IFC by asking its actual or potential foreign customers than representatives from the public and private sector. Thus in discussing the question of reputation one participant suggested that consultants should catch a plane to Toronto and ask about Barbados' reputation among Canadian consumers of Barbadian IFS. After all, a jurisdiction's reputation is the standing in which it is held by outsiders, not the opinions of locals about themselves. This same point was also made at the seminar in Mauritius.

Referring to various international assessments of the three IFCs provides only a partial corrective to this bias. The IFCs singled out for unfavourable attention from the Financial Stability Forum in 2000[1] (Barbados being placed in Group 2, and Mauritius and Vanuatu in Group 3) are fiercely critical of what they see to be the arbitrary way in which this ranking was generated. Similarly Barbados and Vanuatu took a strongly negative position in response to being labelled as 'tax havens' by the OECD in June 2000, and in Vanuatu's case as an 'unco-operative tax haven' in April 2002. On the other hand, Barbados and Mauritius are more likely to endorse the positive conclusions reached by the IMF in the context of its Financial Sector Assessment Programs (Vanuatu received a far more ambivalent assessment from the IMF's 2002 module 2 assessment).

Further questioning in the regional workshops, which related to this lack of an observable 'reputation dividend' of complying with new regulatory standards, also threw up the issue of a benefit being equivalent to an 'avoided cost' i.e. whether IFCs had benefited from a positive boost to their reputation, or had merely avoided the damage of being blacklisted for non-compliance. IFC anxieties have centred particularly on the FATF's Non-Cooperative Countries and Territories (NCCT) list. In the Vanuatu workshop, most of those who had indicated on the questionnaire that the IFC had had its reputation enhanced by complying with AML/CFT standards and the like, subsequently modified their view to argue that Vanuatu had instead avoided the reputational damage associated with non-compliance and blacklisting. In the Mauritius case, those MCs and banks that had responded affirmatively when asked about whether Mauritius' reputation had been enhanced by adoption of the new regulatory standards for AML/CFT, confirmed simultaneously that its competitiveness as an IFC had been concomitantly eroded. This combination of 'reputation-enhancement' with 'competitiveness-erosion' is a troubling one that needs to be explored.

As a final point on the net impact of reforms on the public sector, it was interesting to note that regulators rarely if ever mentioned any local benefits of regulatory reform. In the main, the standards propounded by the OECD, FATF, FSF and others are aimed at reducing financial instability, fighting financial crime and countering tax evasion and avoidance. Other potential benefits that could conceivably arise from instituting strict AML/CFT and KYC/DD procedures might be the strengthening of the domestic financial system, the reduction of local money-laundering activities, seizure of criminal assets or reducing local corruption. Yet no such benefits were seen or claimed.

Even those most enthusiastic about the financial sector reforms since 2000 saw the pay-off in terms of positive recognition (or the avoidance of sanctions) from 'outsiders'. Perhaps it is not surprising that those involved in IFCs have such a strong external orientation. On the other hand, there is also a very clear understanding – even among favourably disposed regulators – that the reforms are driven by outside rather than local priorities. In regulatory and IFI jargon, there is almost no local regulatory or industry 'ownership' of the reforms in the affected IFCs. Moreover the 'outsiders' in question, are seen as being the international, standard-setting organisations. Offshore clientele are not even given secondary importance in this regard by IFC regulators, although they are of primary importance to the IFS industry.

This lack of concern about the views of 'external clientele' on the part of all three IFC regulators seems odd, if not negligent. The IFCs do not make a living from their official external interlocutors, but from their offshore clients. This tendency to view the picture (about external perceptions of the jurisdiction concerned) so asymmetrically suggests a degree of compartmentalised institutional 'incestuousness' that IFC regulators need to guard against. There is a danger that regulators' horizons and frames of reference may be confined and blinkered to what other international regulators think of them, while their IFS industries are (correctly) much more concerned about what their clients think.

13.2 Costs and benefits to the private sector in Barbados, Mauritius and Vanuatu

All three countries saw a slowdown in the growth of their IFS sectors in 2000–2002 with the release of the OECD 'tax havens' list, the Financial Stability Forum's three-tiered assessment of Offshore Financial Centres and the FATF's Non-Cooperative Countries and Territories list. In all three cases, the IFS sectors have grown much more slowly since 2002 than they did through the 1990s. In Vanuatu the offshore banking industry has virtually collapsed, whereas in Barbados and Mauritius it has consolidated after earlier rapid growth. Data from the questionnaires and qualitative evidence gathered in the regional workshops identify both the direct effect of the blacklists, and general uncertainty about the provision of IFS from small states as being behind the pronounced drop-off or slowdown in offshore business. Growth has since resumed in Barbados and Mauritius, albeit at a much slower rate than pre-2000, while the IFS sector in Vanuatu has yet to recover from its longer and steeper decline.

Of course, country-specific developments have also had an impact on each country's IFS sector. Barbados lost all of its US foreign sales corporations (FSCs), which numbered 2,975 in 2001, after they were ruled to be illegal by the World Trade Organization. The IFS sector in both Barbados and Mauritius suffered from uncertainties concerning key bilateral treaty relationships. Some doubts were expressed about the Canadian-Barbadian tax treaty, while the interpretation of the double tax treaty between India and Mauritius was (unsuccessfully) challenged in the Indian courts. Indonesia unilaterally (it is unknown whether this was at the behest of the IFIs) abrogated its double tax avoidance treaty with Mauritius on 1 July 2005 without providing the Mauritian authorities with any advance warning as the treaty provisions required. In addition, there were a multitude of other factors affecting the IFS industries in all IFCs, from the shock of the terrorist attacks on 11 September 2001 to changes in competitors' products and marketing. Nevertheless, despite these intervening developments, both the survey data and interview material gathered from the countries indicates that the activities of multilateral agencies and the associated impact of new regulations have been key determinants of the fortunes of the IFS sectors since 2000.

Employment trends in the industry since 2000 are difficult to assess since national statistical offices in Barbados and Vanuatu do not make a distinction between domestic and international financial services. In Vanuatu it is, however, possible to estimate that there has been modest growth in the number of people employed in the IFS industry. The increase in income tax revenue derived from the IFS in Barbados also seems to suggest that the total payroll for the IFS sector has also increased. In Mauritius, employment and payrolls in the IFS industry have increased slowly since 2002 (while the unemployment rate in the economy more generally has increased dramatically). However, as emerged during the seminar, almost all of that increase is explained by the need of MCs and offshore banks to hire more staff to cope with increased compliance demands rather than promote business expansion. The Mauritian experience suggests strongly that, while employment may have increased in the IFS sector in each country (although the evidence in Barbados and Vanuatu is incomplete), the increase was driven by the extra staff needed for compliance work outweighing those exiting the industry. Thus, while new regulations might be seen as benefiting the macroeconomy in general, they have been implemented at the expense of a significant meso-cost to the IFS industry and micro-costs to individual corporate service providers/management companies.

From the qualitative questionnaires, 75 per cent of Mauritian MCs and 47 per cent of banks had to substantially increase their staff to handle new compliance requirements, while in Barbados the figure was 44 per cent of private sector respondents in total. In Vanuatu, however, only 17 per cent of private sector respondents had to substantially increase compliance staff, though a majority of CSPs did have to retrain front line and back office staff (54 and 58 per cent, respectively).

Variations in the impact of new regulations among different sections of the IFS industry

The new regulations have, unsurprisingly, had different effects on different parts of the IFS industry in all three countries. Banks in Barbados and Mauritius have suffered less from the new state of affairs than CSPs, whose business comes from company and trust formation and related services. The relative ease with which banks have adapted to the new regulatory regime seems to stem from their exposure to much greater prudential regulation dating back well before 2000, and their earlier exposure to much tighter regulation concerning the money laundering regime. This is in contrast to CSPs (including legal and accounting firms), which until recently had a lighter regulatory burden and were not subject to any licensing system in Barbados and Vanuatu (this is currently still the case in most OECD countries); there was, however, such a licensing system in Mauritius. In Barbados and Mauritius, subsidiaries of international banks have often been able to pass on much of the cost of more stringent KYC/DD requirements to their head offices, with the increased costs of compliance being absorbed by headquarters compliance budgets.

In the context of this uneven impact between the two types of businesses, the highest costs for banks were generally new and more demanding KYC/DD requirements, while for CSPs it was the cost of establishing the beneficial ownership of corporate vehicles (primarily IBCs) for both new and existing customers.

The massive decline in Vanuatu's offshore banking sector marks it as exceptional, both in the magnitude of the decline directly attributed to the new regulations adopted in 2002 (much greater than in any other sector in any country, excluding Barbadian Foreign Sales Corporations), and in the distribution of costs, with banks being more heavily impacted than CSPs. What explains this anomalous result, particularly when Vanuatu and Barbados had a roughly similar number of banks in 2000, and both instituted equivalent changes to banking supervision and regulation?

The population of offshore banks in Vanuatu had been in decline before the launch of the FATF, OECD and related initiatives, but had stabilised at a core of 35–40 banks. The requirement of having effective 'mind and management' within the country – interpreted to mean an office with at least one full-time employee and the records of all customers – is regarded as having been crucial in the drop in bank numbers from 36 in 2002 to seven in 2003. This *mind and management* requirement was imposed even on the subsidiaries of major foreign banks, such as BNP Paribas, which subsequently withdrew from Vanuatu as a result. Unlike the situation in Barbados and Mauritius, however, far fewer offshore banks were subsidiaries of major foreign banks in Vanuatu. They were smaller independent entities established for treasury and intra-group transfer operations, often for private family companies (the two exceptions, both subsidiaries of Australian banks, gave survey responses very similar to their Barbadian and Mauritian counterparts).

Vanuatu's experience with the collapse of its offshore banking industry seems to have more in common with other East Caribbean and South Pacific IFCs (such as Antigua

& Barbuda, Dominica, Grenada, the Cook Islands or Niue) than either Barbados or Mauritius. However, further research in some of these other jurisdictions would be needed to confirm this speculation.

This exception notwithstanding, there are some common patterns evident across the three jurisdictions. Large firms have generally found it easier to bear the costs of new regulatory requirements than small firms, leading to increased pressure on small firms to exit the market. International firms have often had to meet higher standards earlier to fit in with group-wide practices and/or have been able to pass on compliance costs to the head office, whereas local firms have had to make a more rapid and wrenching adjustment.

Small CSPs have been especially hard hit by new requirements relating to establishing the true identity of those associated with offshore companies and trusts. In seeking to explain the very high proportion (27.3 per cent) of those considering exiting the IFS market in Barbados, workshop participants hypothesised that these were disproportionately small CSP firms. By contrast, the proportion of CSPs/MCs in Vanuatu and Mauritius that felt that they might need to exit the IFS business was insignificantly small, confined to one firm and two or three small MCs respectively. Questionnaire responses from Mauritius and Vanuatu confirm that CSPs were most likely to identify significant costs imposed by new requirements and least likely to identify any significant benefits. In Vanuatu, 80 per cent of CSPs adjudged the costs associated with AML/CFT to be excessive and disproportionate to any benefits. In Mauritius, 85 per cent of MCs agreed that AML/CFT compliance had required far more spending on systems, training and staff than was necessary for business purposes (in Vanuatu the figure was 66 per cent for CSPs).

To the extent that CSPs in Vanuatu have gained any new business as a result of the multilateral initiatives, this has been through picking up clients from sole practitioners and small firms that have withdrawn from the market. As a methodological (though obvious) point it is worth noting that those firms which had withdrawn from the IFS market prior to the administration of the questionnaires in late 2005 and the regional workshops March-April 2006 do not show up in either the country studies or this report, which might therefore understate substantially the magnitude of the negative impact on CSPs in general of the multilateral initiatives.

Further commonalities include the tendency to regard many new regulations as not only burdensome, but having limited relevance to fighting financial crime. In Barbados and Vanuatu, very low thresholds for suspicious transaction reporting (10,000 Barbados dollars [Bds$] and 1 million vatu [VT], or approximately US$5,000 and US$9,000 respectively) were seen as being more an exercise in creating paper work than a credible AML/CFT measure. Similarly, the requirement of establishing beneficial ownership of firms was seen as unnecessarily time-consuming, when there was a rigid insistence on, for example, old utility bills. As many participants at the Mauritius seminar put it, the new requirements did not enable them to 'know their customers' any better than they did before, nor did the 'due diligence' required enable them to discern client motives any more clearly. The net result was to irritate clients to an unnecessary degree, which many MCs had to counteract with higher expenditures on maintaining client relations.

Competitiveness effects

By and large business respondents could not identify any competitiveness benefits resulting from the new regulations. In Barbados, Mauritius and Vanuatu a majority of firms thought that the reforms had made the IFC *less* competitive than before. In the workshops and interviews this seemed to reflect the belief that there had been substantial indirect costs in terms of business that would, but for the presence of demanding new regulatory hurdles, have been attracted. Obviously as with any counter-factual condition, assessing the magnitude and distribution of these costs poses particular difficulties.

Thus among private sector respondents only 17 per cent thought that the reforms had made Vanuatu more competitive as an IFC (with the percentage disagreeing rising to 58), and in Barbados only 30 per cent saw competitiveness advantages (while 44 per cent disagreed). In Mauritius, while a third of banks agreed that there had been competitiveness benefits (with none disagreeing and the remainder unable to say), amongst MCs only 12 per cent agreed compared with 47 per cent disagreeing.

It became apparent in the workshops and interviews that firms in all three countries were particularly concerned about losing business as a result of regulatory arbitrage, as clients sought out locations that, for example, did not subject them to the delays and inconvenience associated with strict KYC/DD procedures. Competing jurisdictions came in three types. The first involve competition from more lightly regulated onshore jurisdictions, with products such as Delaware Limited Liability Companies, Swiss private banking or New Zealand offshore trusts. The second are IFCs outside the OECD that have so far escaped being targeted by multilateral standard-setting bodies, despite their generally having less well developed AML/CFT and tax information exchange procedures. Prominent amongst such competing jurisdictions are Singapore, Hong Kong and Dubai. Finally there are those IFCs that have been targeted by international standard-setting bodies, but have either refused to comply with new standards or have adopted a more flexible attitude towards compliance, such as the Marshall Islands.

Benefits to the private sector

Perhaps unsurprisingly, the IFS industry was less convinced of the benefits of tightening up regulation than the regulators were. Nevertheless, there were many in the industry in Barbados, Mauritius and Vanuatu (in descending order of support) that saw the new regulatory regime as having generated net benefits for their IFC, if less so for their firm as such. As indicated earlier, those favourably disposed towards the recent changes saw the first (and main) benefit as being reputational, rather than in the form of tangible business advantage.

In Vanuatu, 31 per cent of private sector respondents agreed and 46 per cent disagreed with the contention that the regulatory initiatives had improved the IFC's reputation; the comparable figures from Barbados were 64 per cent agreeing and 36 per cent disagreeing (the different wording of the question in Mauritius prevents a direct quantitative comparison).

This poses the puzzle, referred to above, concerning the failure of 'reputation-enhancement' to produce any tangible effect on business as such. It raises questions about whether there was actually a positive reputational effect generated by compliance in the eyes of offshore clientele, or whether it was axiomatically assumed that because regulations had been tightened reputation had automatically been enhanced without that presumption being confirmed by customer-surveys. Alternatively, the benefit could have been seen merely as the avoidance of costs, which might have been incurred in the form of blacklisting-related reputational damage for non-compliance.

Like most regulators, some private sector participants in the workshops, especially banks, indicated that there was no alternative to meeting the new standards. Non-cooperation and non-compliance would simply have brought about the end of the IFC. The second benefit was that this outcome (the end of the IFC) was avoided. Again this poses the conceptual problem identified earlier of attributing all the benefits of the whole IFC to regulatory reforms, based on the counter-factual reasoning that if the reforms had not been undertaken, then the IFC would have failed.

These two diffuse 'benefits' aside, few other specific benefits were identified. One exception was that over 90 per cent of private sector respondents to the questionnaire in Barbados said that the KYC/DD procedure had produced useful information about their clients' needs, and this was potentially helpful for future marketing campaigns. This finding was not replicated in Mauritius or Vanuatu.

Net assessment of private sector impact

With the exception concerning the uncertainty over reputation benefits noted above, the predominant view of the private sector is that the new regulatory regime has created a net negative impact, leaving the IFS industry in each jurisdiction worse off than before. Any reputation benefits that may have accrued have yet to flow through in the tangible form of increased business activity. Variations within this picture are that CSPs/MCs in Barbados and Mauritius have been more severely affected by new regulations than banks. In Vanuatu that situation is reversed, with offshore banks suffering a major decline directly attributable to the imposition of the 'mind and management' requirement.

A final point is that for all the changes in the period 2000–2005, Barbados and Mauritius remain heavily dependent on just one key bilateral relationship each (with Canada and India respectively); this leaves the IFS sector in both extremely vulnerable in the event of problems with the relevant tax treaties. Both IFCs thus continue to be exposed to highly concentrated 'client geography risk'.

13.3 General implications for the international financial centres

Quantifying the overall net impact for the IFCs

The ideal result from a cost-benefit exercise such as this, is one global figure for each country representing in an exact dollar figure the net impact of the regulatory reforms. Arriving at such a figure is beset with threats to validity and reliability, especially given the partial questionnaire responses, the sometimes primitive state of statistical knowledge about the IFS sectors, and the reliance on counter-factual reasoning. These caveats should be kept in mind when examining the following results. In each case, however, the report has adopted conservative estimations, and has simply (but unrealistically) assumed that costs not easily measured are counted as zero.

The report can come closest to a headline figure for Mauritius. This is thanks to both the more complete questionnaire responses and the more detailed statistics collected by national authorities for the IFS sector as a whole, which allowed for more confidence in extrapolating from partial data. The global figure is that the AML/CFT reforms have cost the Mauritian public and private sector a combined total of **US$40 million** in the four-year period 2002–2005. This includes $4.8m in recurrent and non-recurrent costs for the public sector, $27.3m incurred by the MCs and $7.9m by banks. These totals represent only *direct* costs to the public and private sector; there is no allowance for business or government revenue foregone. For a variety of reasons, explained fully in the Mauritius country report, the authors believe the $40 million figure to be an underestimate, but have used it nevertheless for analytical purposes.

For Vanuatu the main challenges to coming up with a global figure were the sometimes conflicting data on public agencies and incomplete quantitative questionnaire responses from the private sector. Judging from the questionnaire responses, the total direct cost of regulatory reform to the public sector in the period 2002–2005 is about US$1.4 million, including both recurrent and non-recurrent costs. Total direct costs to the private sector, based on extrapolations from incomplete data from quantitative questionnaires, come to approximately US$1.1m in direct private sector costs, including both direct costs and extra time spent on compliance tasks. The sharp drop in offshore bank numbers from 2003 also allows for the calculation of indirect costs, specifically private sector and government revenue forgone 2002–2005. For the government the net loss of 30 offshore banks for the last three years of this period meant the loss of US$0.75m in fee revenue. Allowing for the standard prices charged for maintaining offshore banks by CSPs, this suggests a loss in business of approximately US$3m over the same period. If all these simplifications, extrapolations and assumptions are correct, this would lead to a total of **US$6.25 million** in net direct and indirect costs for the public and private sectors in Vanuatu 2002–2005.

Barbados presents an even tougher case, and no quantitative estimate of the net impact to the public sector is possible, either in terms of direct or indirect costs. Even estimating private sector direct costs relies on extrapolation from partial data, without the aid of the national statistical data that was present in Mauritius. Based on incomplete quantitative questionnaire data, the country study suggests that the minimum average annual net loss for a single firm, taking into account only wages and salaries, is US$10,000. However, added to this are the average annual figures for in-house training (US$8,000), external technical assistance (US$11,000), IT (US$16,000) and new licensing procedures (US$50,000). Setting the costs of conferences, internal and external auditors at zero, this would give a figure of about US$95,000 per firm annually, or US$380,000 in total for a firm for the 2002–2005 period. Given the 120+ private firms in the IFS industry (including offshore banks, registered agents, trust companies, offshore insurance companies etc.), this would give an industry-wide figure of **US$45.6 million** in direct costs to the private sector in the period 2002–2005. This figure is obviously the crudest estimation of the three. However, it may represent the lower limit of net costs because: (a) it focuses on the *minimum* level of net direct costs to the private sector; (b) it disregards all indirect costs associated with business lost; and (c) it ignores all the evidence of public sector costs by assuming these to be zero. If this figure is the right order of magnitude it would represent a similar result to Mauritius, intuitively plausible since the two countries applied the same regulatory standards to their IFCs of roughly equivalent size.

Taking into account the wide disparities in economic size (Barbados GDP: US$4.84 billion in 2005 measured at purchasing power parity; Mauritius GDP: US$16.28 billion; and Vanuatu at US$0.58 billion), this would indicate that the net negative developmental impact of recent tax and AML/CFT initiatives has been proportionately heaviest on Vanuatu (per capita by far the poorest), followed by Barbados and then Mauritius. It bears emphasizing, however, that because the figures for each country include different costs, they are not strictly comparable.

Level playing field concerns

The generally negative impact of the new regulations on the IFS industries of Barbados, Mauritius and Vanuatu is particularly significant in light of 'level playing field' concerns. This principle, explicitly endorsed by the OECD in the context of its work on Harmful Tax Practices, means that all jurisdictions should commit to the same standards on the same timetable with the same consequences for non-compliance. The level playing field is particularly significant in light of the increased mobility of capital and the degree of competition between OECD and non-OECD IFCs for IFS business. Together, these factors mean that disparities may lead to unwanted regulatory arbitrage and the tendency of money launderers and financiers of terrorism to exploit the 'weakest link in the chain' in entering the legitimate financial system.

Yet at present the three developing countries under consideration actually exceed the standards of financial regulation in many OECD country IFCs. For example, in line with outside requests, all three countries have instituted licensing regimes for CSPs. Yet, major OECD countries like the United Kingdom and the United States do not have any such licensing regime in place. All three countries have either abolished or immobilised bearer shares in light of the AML/CFT risks these instruments pose.

However, in major OECD economies like Germany and the Netherlands bearer shares are still issued and mobile. In all three countries it is mandatory to establish the beneficial ownership of all companies and partnerships, yet this requirement does not apply in certain states of the US such as Delaware, Nevada and Wyoming.

Both the public and the private sector in Barbados, Mauritius and Vanuatu are keenly aware of these disparities, which are a source of some considerable resentment. As noted earlier, in Mauritius and Vanuatu in particular (and in Barbados to a lesser extent), local respondents are of the opinion that they are losing business to less onerously regulated OECD financial centres, or other IFCs like Hong Kong, Singapore and Dubai, which have neither met new standards nor been pressured to do so. The continued existence of such disparities runs counter to the effective combating of global financial crime as well as being incompatible with basic norms of fairness.

The impact of blacklisting

Even among regulators generally well disposed to the changes that have occurred since 2000 there is a general feeling in these three small island states that their IFCs had no choice but to comply with regulatory campaigns, because otherwise they would be subject to blacklisting which would in turn deal a fatal blow to the IFS sector. This view concerning the inevitability of regulatory compliance, compared with the non-option of 'death-by-blacklisting', is also shared among significant sections of the IFS industry, particularly offshore banks. As one senior regulator put it in one of the regional workshops with respect to the NCCT list, IFCs have had 'a gun to their head' in instituting a comprehensive AML/CFT system. In these quarters it is taken as almost axiomatic that no matter how poorly suited international standards are to local conditions, it is always better to comply rather than be blacklisted and thus excluded from the IFS market. Jurisdictions that have bucked this trend and refused to comply are seen as providing a cautionary tale of the fate awaiting the obdurate.

Mauritius is the clearest example of this desire to avoid blacklists above all else, making an advance commitment to the OECD in the context of the Harmful Tax Competition campaign even though the vast majority of its offshore clients were not of OECD origin. The Mauritian government agreed to remove the ring-fenced provisions of its IFS laws, put in place procedures to establish beneficial ownership of corporate vehicles and participate in a programme of exchanging criminal and civil tax information. Mauritius made these concessions just before the release of the June 2000 'tax haven' list, when only five of 41 other targeted jurisdictions had made such a commitment (the other five being Bermuda, the Cayman Islands, Cyprus, Malta and San Marino).

Barbados is an intermediate case. Like Mauritius it ensured that it avoided the FATF's list, but (uniquely) managed to face down the OECD in demanding successfully that it be removed from the 'tax havens' list without making a commitment to the slate of OECD demands. Vanuatu refused the OECD demands both in advance of the June 2000 'tax haven' and the April 2002 'unco-operative tax haven' list, before reversing its decision and complying the following year. Vanuatu was, however, quick to strengthen

AML laws and relax secrecy provisions in order to avoid being included in the FATF's first NCCT list in 2000.

The conventional wisdom notwithstanding, the short- and long-term effect of black-lists on IFCs has not been studied in a systematic manner (an area that would repay further investigation). Many non-OECD jurisdictions with IFCs (e.g. in the Middle East) have ignored FATF ministrations and representations, and yet have not seen their offshore business decline or disappear. In fact such business appears to have increased at the expense of jurisdictions like Mauritius, which shares the same geographical client base. The FATF, FSF and the OECD themselves have not assessed the overall impact of their lists; nor do they appear to have examined carefully whether their approach to blacklisting (with the implicit intimidation and threat involved) violates established norms of international dialogue, negotiation and relations and whether their approach has resulted in tilted rather than level playing fields

Some IFC jurisdictions seem to have survived despite appearing on the NCCT list with little or no observable financial damage (e.g. the Cayman Islands 2000–2001), while others have been completely unplugged from international financial networks (e.g. Nauru after 2002). Respondents in Vanuatu, who of the three countries have the most first-hand experience of the effects of blacklisting, in particular emphasise the threats to correspondent banking relationships posed by blacklisting. Many major in-ternational banks now refuse to process transactions involving Vanuatu. The domestic National Bank of Vanuatu and remaining offshore banks have had to replace their correspondent banking relationships after being cut off by foreign institutions wary of being tainted by association.

With the advent of blacklisting as a tool for compelling IFC reform, through the effective but implicit exercise of extraterritoriality in a way that might itself be illegiti-mate under international law, multilateral standard setting organisations like the FATF have discovered a potent instrument to overcome small state opposition by effectively bludgeoning them into submission. Whether rightly or wrongly, a large majority of respondents in the three countries surveyed saw compliance, at almost any cost, as preferable to appearing on a blacklist. Despite the suspension of the FATF NCCT list and the declining salience of the OECD's 'unco-operative tax haven' list (which now includes only Andorra, Liberia, Liechtenstein, the Marshall Islands and Monaco), current moves by the International Organization of Securities Commissions (IOSCO) to pressure non-member IFCs to adopt its principles of information exchange or suffer blacklisting suggests that this issue remains relevant.

Lack of positive recognition

There is thus a strong feeling in the three countries studied that, for them at least, there are definite negative consequences involved with defying international initia-tives. Expensive compliance is widely seen as being preferable to non-compliance pre-cipitating inclusion on a blacklist. There is considerable frustration, however, that IFCs have not received much recognition for the sacrifices they have made since 2000 in meeting new international standards in the area of IFS regulation, either by the relevant international organisations or by OECD states.

Despite having standards that generally equal and, in important areas, actually exceed those of OECD states (e.g. immobilising bearer shares, establishing beneficial ownership of companies and licensing CSPs), Barbados is singled out for especially unfavourable treatment as a 'tax haven' under the laws of OECD members including France, Hungary, Italy, Mexico and Spain. Mauritius faces similar discrimination from these same countries, as well as Portugal, while Vanuatu is listed by Belgium in addition to all the preceding states.

An additional area in which meeting international AML/CFT standards might have been expected to bring benefits to small IFCs, but generally has not, is that of AML/CFT equivalence. Many OECD/FATF member states maintain 'white-lists' of countries adjudged to have equivalent AML/CFT standards thus relieving financial intermediaries in listed countries of the expensive and time-consuming task of replicating KYC/DD already performed in the specified foreign jurisdiction. Commonly, this white-list is simply the list of FATF members. This leaves small IFCs such as the three studied in this project at a distinct disadvantage, since FATF membership is explicitly barred to developing countries that are not considered to be 'strategically important' (i.e. large and significant extant or potential economic partners). Thus even though small IFCs may have made considerable sacrifices in meeting or surpassing the AML/CFT standards of onshore countries like Australia, Canada or the United States, they do not receive the same rewards in terms of market access for their IFS industries.

Finally, positive IMF assessments (under the Financial Sector Assessment Program, FSAP) of Barbados and Mauritius notwithstanding, bodies like the OECD, FSF and the FATF have made little provision for the positive recognition of IFCs meeting international standards, as distinct from simply not blacklisting them. The FSF three-tier list, characterising Barbados and (to a greater extent) Mauritius and Vanuatu as not meeting international standards, was withdrawn in 2005 as 'no longer serving its purpose'. The OECD has never formally removed 32 of the 35 countries listed in June 2000 as tax havens (the exceptions being Barbados, the Maldives and Tonga).

The case for compensation

A further question relates to whether the three states in question, and by extension small IFCs in general, have any case for compensation (independent of technical assistance) because of the negative effects of recent regulatory initiatives. There is no case for compensation relating to AML/CFT, because there is a fundamental presumption that countries should co-operate in combating serious crime without any expectation of gain. That presumption, however, ignores the reality that, in cases like Barbados, Mauritius and Vanuatu, the expense of adopting the new AML/CFT regime far outweighs any conceivable benefit the domestic economy might derive from doing so. If indeed the new regime did result in catching money launderers or terrorists (which almost every local practitioner doubts in the extreme) the main benefits derived from that outcome would still accrue elsewhere. The case of tax information exchange such as that specified as part of the OECD Harmful Tax Practices initiative, however, is different, and does present a strong case for OECD member states compensating small state IFCs.

Tax information exchange Double Tax Treaties are concluded on the grounds of mutual benefit for the two countries concerned. Less formal Tax Information Exchange Agreements (TIEAs) between OECD member state and small state IFCs do not provide mutual benefits, because these arrangements create a situation whereby small states bear all the expense of gathering and providing information and get nothing in return. In any given year, Barbados answers approximately 20–30 tax information requests from the US and Canada, with each case taking a Barbadian official between a day and two weeks to process. In an average year, Barbadian tax authorities would not make any information requests from US or Canadian tax authorities. However, because Barbados has formal tax treaties with both the US and Canada, the country receives substantial benefits (in terms of increased investment) that cancel out this pattern of 'one-way' information exchange. TIEAs conducted in the absence of such tax treaties or other specific benefits would provide OECD states with all the benefits (increased tax revenue) and leave small states with all the costs (collecting and providing information).

The need for tax information exchange to take place on a basis of mutual benefit is not an idea advanced in opposition to the OECD. Indeed, the OECD has explicitly endorsed this principle, most recently during the Global Forum meeting in Melbourne 15–16 November 2005. Yet the OECD model bilateral TIEA published in 2002 (which formed the basis of the Bermuda-Australia TIEA of November 2005) is poorly suited to delivering mutual benefits.

Tax information exchange between OECD and non-OECD states should be conducted on the same basis of mutual benefits as information exchange between OECD states. TIEAs by themselves do not compensate IFCs for the expense they must go to in bolstering OECD countries' tax revenues. One basis for this is for tax information exchange to take place as part of or alongside formal tax treaties with IFCs (as for example with the Austria-Belize treaty). Mauritius and Barbados have a strong interest in further expanding their tax treaty network. Where a formal treaty is not possible or appropriate (as is perhaps the case with Vanuatu) OECD countries should be willing to provide meaningful compensation to small state IFCs in return for tax information.

A good model of such is the TIEA signed between the Netherlands and the Isle of Man in 2005, providing the latter with compensatory concessions in the area of shipping and aircraft in return for providing tax information. The efforts of the International Trade and Investment Organisation (ITIO) to facilitate discussion between IFCs regarding tax treaty/TIEA negotiation strategies are also a welcome development.

13.4 Conclusions and future directions

This project has assessed the impact of recent multilateral initiatives to regulate IFS on the small state IFCs of Barbados, Mauritius and Vanuatu. The project is significant because the IFS sector is an important source of government revenue and general economic development for each country. It is timely, and perhaps even overdue, because up until now there has been no systematic and comparative effort to assess the costs and benefits of international tax and AML/CFT initiatives on IFCs. In aiming to come up with as broad and encompassing a view of the costs and benefits to the public and private sector as possible, the project has reflected the logic of a regulatory impact assessment (RIA).

The findings contained in this report mark the distillation of the three country studies. In turn, each of these studies reflects evidence in response to questionnaires and interviews, refined and confirmed in regional workshops. Though there are inherent limits on the ability to generalise from the present sample to the universe of IFCs, the pattern of costs and benefits revealed for the three countries studied are broadly suggestive of the experiences of other similarly situated small states. However, this report strongly endorses the need for further research to confirm this inference.

The overall conclusions reached by the project are summarised in schematic form below:

- At the broadest level, the costs of the recent multilateral regulatory initiatives in the area of international tax information exchange and AML/CFT have substantially exceeded the benefits for the three small state IFCs in question. This conclusion seems robust, even taking into account the measurement difficulties of assessing benefits compared with costs.

- The greatest direct cost to the public sector has been in hiring extra staff for newly-created or expanded regulatory agencies, and the associated costs of office space, training, IT and related expenses.

- Because the IFS sector provides 5-10 per cent of total government revenue, the downturn in the industry in the wake of the blacklists of 2000 flowed through to the governments' coffers. This decline in revenue from the IFS sector (either as licensing fees or tax revenue) has been reversed in Barbados and Mauritius, but has continued in Vanuatu.

- The greatest cost to the private sector has been setting up KYC/DD mechanisms, costs generally experienced through firms having to hire new staff, divert existing staff from core business activities, participate in training activities and seminars and invest in new IT. In Barbados and Mauritius, these costs have had a much more severe impact on CSPs compared with offshore banks, while in Vanuatu this distribution of costs was reversed. General concerns were expressed in Mauritius and Vanuatu that more onerous KYC/DD requirements had produced indirect costs, as clients have sought out other, less regulated onshore and offshore investment destinations.

- A high proportion of public and private sector questionnaire respondents identified the new regulatory initiatives as producing reputation benefits for their IFC, and this was generally considered the most significant positive consequence of the initiatives. However, both in questionnaire responses and in the workshops the same respondents were unable to identify any competitiveness or direct business benefits that might have resulted from this purported boost to reputation. The most likely explanation for this puzzling result seems to be that compliance avoided the severe or even fatal reputational damage associated with appearing on blacklists.

- The sacrifices made by the public and private sectors in all three countries to comply with the international tax and AML/CFT initiatives have largely gone unrecognised and unrewarded among multilateral standard-setting agencies (with the partial exception of the IMF) and OECD states. Despite introducing standards that are as strict as those applied onshore, and in important instances sometimes more so, onshore states have kept IFCs on national tax blacklists and have maintained barriers to market access. Although OECD states have been quick to request tax information from IFCs, they have generally been slow to match these requests with substantive compensation to ensure that an agreement along these lines adheres to the conventional principle of mutual benefits.

- Further research is required to ascertain the extent to which patterns found among these three IFCs relating to the developmental impact of recent international tax and AML/CFT initiatives generalise to the much larger number of IFCs worldwide.

Notes

1. Financial Stability Forum (2000).

References and Bibliography

Antoniou, A. (ed.) (2004) International Financial Services Sectors in Small Vulnerable Economies: Challenges and Prospects. *Economic Paper No. 60*. London, UK: the Commonwealth Secretariat.

Ballard, R. (2005) Coalitions of reciprocity and the maintenance of financial integrity within informal value transmission systems: the contemporary dynamics of *hawala* networks. *Journal of Banking Regulation*, Vol.6, No.4, pp.319–352.

Bank of Mauritius (2002, 2003, 2004) *Annual Reports*. Bank of Mauritius.

Bank of Mauritius (2003) Code for the Prevention of Money Laundering and Countering the Financing of Terrorism. Bank of Mauritius.

Barbados International Business Association (2004) Realising Barbados' Potential As An International Business Centre. Bridgetown, Barbados: BIBA.

Barbados International Business Association (undated) 'Working Together – Stronger Together'. Bridgetown, Barbados: BIBA.

Barbados Industrial Development Corporation (2005) Constraints to doing business in Barbados. Report No. BP 2002/56. Bridgetown, Barbados: BIDC.

Barrett, L. (2001) 'A Rational Response to an International Initiative'. Available (on password basis) at:
http://www.offshoreinvestment.com/magazine/issue?id=3D55=

Barrett, L. (2003) 'Big Brother' prevails and Vanuatu reluctantly succumbs. Available at:
http://www.offshoreinvestment.com [accessed 16 January 2008]

Basel Committee on Banking Supervision (BCBS), International Association of Insurance Supervisors (IAIS) and International Organisation of Securities Commissions (IOSCO) (2003) *Initiatives by the BCBS, IAIS and IOSCO to Combat Money-Laundering and the Financing of Terrorism*. Basel, Switzerland: The Joint Forum. Available at:
http://www.bis.org/publ/joint11.pdf [accessed 16 January 2008]

Bedi, R. (2006a) Cleaning Up the System. Singapore: *Asia Risk*, February 2006.

Bedi, R. (2006b) The Global Standard: Changes to the FATF Recommendations. Singapore: *Asia Risk*, February 2006.

Bedi, R. and Acharya, A. (2005) AML/CFT: New Policy Initiatives. Joint Report of Price Waterhouse Coopers (SNG) and the Institute of Defence & Strategic Studies (IDSS). PWC-IDSS Thought Leadership Series. PWC-IDSS: Singapore.

BIS (2001) Core Principles for Banking Supervision. Basle, Switzerland: BIS.

Blum, J.A. et al (1998) *Financial Havens, Banking Secrecy and Money Laundering*. Vienna, Austria: United Nations Office for Drug Control and Crime Prevention.

Bosworth-Davies, R. (2005) Weapons of Mass Coercion: The Influence of US Extraterritoriality. *Money Laundering Intelligence*, November 2005. NSW, Autralia: Delmonte Publishing.

Council on Foreign Relations (2004) Update on the Global Campaign Against Terrorist Financing. Washington D.C.: Council on Foreign Relations.

Cueller, Mariano-Florentino (2003) 'The Tenuous Relationship Between the Fight Against Money Laundering and the Disruption of Criminal Finance'. Stanford Law School Research Paper 64. Stanford, CA: Stanford Law School.

The Economist (2005) Special Report on Financing Terrorism. 22 October 2005.

Financial Action Task Force (FATF) (1990–2005) *Annual Reports*. Available at: http://www.fatf-gafi.org/findDocument/0,2350,en_32250379_32237235_1_32247548_1_1_1,00.html [accessed 16 January 2008]

Financial Action Task Force (FATF) (2000–2005) *Reports on Non-Co-operative Countries and Territories*. Paris, France: FATF.

Financial Action Task Force (2000) *Review to Identify Non-Co-operative Countries or Territories: Increasing the Effectiveness of Worldwide Anti-Money Laundering Measures*. Paris, France: FATF.

Financial Action Task Force (2001) *Review to Identify Non-Co-operative Countries or Territories: Increasing the Effectiveness of Worldwide Anti-Money Laundering Measures*. Paris, France: FATF.

Financial Intelligence Unit (Mauritius) (2005) *Annual Report*.

Financial Services Authority (UK) (2003) Reducing Money-Laundering Risk – Know Your Customer and Anti-Money Laundering Monitoring. Discussion Paper 22, August 2003.

Financial Services Commission (2003, 2004, 2005) *Annual Reports*. Available at: www.fscmauritius.org/ [accessed 16 January 2008]

Financial Services Commission (2003) Code for the Prevention of Money Laundering and Countering the Financing of Terrorism.

Financial Stability Forum (2000) Report of the Working Group on Offshore Financial Centres. Available at: http://www.fsforum.org/publications/publication_23_31.html [accessed 15 February 2008]

Gill, M. and G. Taylor (2002) Tackling Money-Laundering: The Experiences & Perspectives of the UK Financial Sector. A Report by the Scarman Centre, University of Leicester, sponsored by Andersen, Summer 2002.

Government of Mauritius/Ministry of Finance & Economic Development (2001) 'Report of the Steering Committee on Financial Services Sector reform in Mauritius. Port Louis, Mauritius.

Hampton, M. (1996) *The Offshore Interface: Tax Havens in the Global Economy*. New York: Houndmills & MacMillan Press & St. Martin's Press.

Harvey, J. (2004) Compliance and Reporting Issues Arising for Financial Institutions from Money Laundering Regulations: A Preliminary Cost-Benefit Study. *Journal of Money Laundering Control*, Vol.7, No.4, pp.333–346.

HM Treasury (2006) The EU's Third Money Laundering Directive: A Regulatory Impact Assessment. London: UK Government.

International Association of Insurance Supervisors (IAIS) (2005) *Insurance Principles, Standards and Guidance Papers*. Basel, Switzerland: IAIS.

International Tax and Investment Organisation (ITIO)/ Society of Trust and Estate Practitioners (STEP) (2002) Towards a Level Playing Field: Regulating Corporate Vehicles in Cross-Border Transactions. STEP and ITIO conducted by Stikeman Elliott: London.

International Monetary Fund (2003a) Barbados Financial System Stability Assessment (FSSA). Washington D.C.: IMF.

International Monetary Fund (2003b) Financial Sector Assessment Program (Barbados). Washington D.C.: IMF.

International Monetary Fund (2003c) Vanuatu Assessment of the Supervision and Regulation of the Financial Sector: Volume 1: Review of Financial Sector Regulation and Supervision. Washington D.C.: IMF.

International Monetary Fund (2005) Statistical Annexe on Vanuatu. Washington D.C.: IMF.

IMF and World Bank (2004) Twelve-Month Pilot Study, Anti-Money Laundering/Combating the Financing of Terrorism (AML/CFT) Assessments: Joint Report on the Review of the Assessment Program. Washington D.C.: IMF.

IMF and World Bank (2005) Anti-Money Laundering and Combating the Financing of Terrorism: Observations of the Work Program and Implications Going Forward [sic]. Washington D.C.: IMF.

KPMG (2003) Money Laundering: Review of the regime for handling Suspicious Activity Reports. London, UK: KPMG.

Mistry, P.S. (2004) 'Trends in International Financial System Regulation and Supervision' pp. 17–58 in Antoniou, A. (ed.) International Financial Services Sectors in Small Vulnerable Economies: Challenges and Prospects. Economic Paper No. 60. London, UK: the Commonwealth Secretariat.

Money Laundering Intelligence (2005) Industry Baulks at Costs of Compliance. Editorial in Money Laundering Intelligence, November 2005. NSW, Australia: Delmonte Publishing.

Organisation for Economic Co-operation and Development (1998) Harmful Tax Competition: An Emerging Global Issue. Paris, France: OECD.

Organisation for Economic Co-operation and Development (2000a) Towards Global Tax Co-operation. Paris, France: OECD.

Organisation for Economic Co-operation and Development (2000b) Improving Access to Bank Information for Tax Purposes. Paris, France: OECD.

Organisation for Economic Co-operation and Development (2001a) Harmful Tax Practices Progress Report. Paris, France: OECD.

Organisation for Economic Co-operation and Development (2001b) Behind the Corporate Veil: Using Corporate Entities for Illicit Purposes. Paris, France: OECD.

Organisation for Economic Co-operation and Development (2002a) Joint Ad Hoc Group on Accounts Model Tax Information Exchange Agreement. Paris, France: OECD.

Organisation for Economic Co-operation and Development (2002b) Access for Tax Authorities to Information Gathered by Anti-Money Laundering Authorities. Paris, France: OECD.

Organisation for Economic Co-operation and Development (2003a) Ottawa Report of the Global Forum on Harmful Tax Practices. Paris, France: OECD.

Organisation for Economic Co-operation and Development (2003b) Improving Access to Bank Information for Tax Purposes: Progress Report. Paris, France: OECD.

Organisation for Economic Co-operation and Development (2004a) 2004 Progress Report: The OECD's Project on Harmful Tax Practices. Paris, France: OECD.

Organisation for Economic Co-operation and Development (2004b) A Process for Achieving a Global Level Playing Field. Report by the OECD Global Forum, Berlin. Paris, France: OECD.

Organisation for Economic Co-operation and Development (2004c) Berlin Report of the Global Forum on Harmful Tax Practices. Paris, France: OECD.

Offshore Investment Company Formation Survey March 2006.

Price Waterhouse Coopers LLP (2003) Anti-Money Laundering Current Customer Review Cost-Benefit Analysis. Report prepared for Financial Services Authority (UK), May 2003.

Rawlings, G. (2004) Laws, Liquidity and Eurobonds: The Making of the Vanuatu Tax Haven. *The Journal of Pacific History*, Vol.39, No.3: pp.325–341.

Rawlings, G. (2005) Responsive Regulation, Multilateralism, Bilateral Tax Treaties and the Continuing Appeal of Offshore Finance Centres. Working Paper 74, Centre for Tax Integrity, Australian National University.

Reserve Bank of Vanuatu (2005) *Quarterly Review,* March 2005.

Report of Sub-Committee on Business Facilitation to the joint working committee of the Ministry of Industry and International Business, April 30, 2005. (Barbados)

Roberts, S. (1995) Small Place, Big Money: The Cayman Islands and the International Financial System. *Economic Geography* Vol.71, No.3: pp.237–256.

Sharman, J. (2004): 'The Effective Particiaption of Small States in International Financial Fora' pp. 59–76 in Antoniou, A. (ed.) International Financial Services Sectors in Small Vulnerable Economies: Challenges and Prospects. *Economic Paper No. 60*. London, UK: the Commonwealth Secretariat.

Sharman, J.C. (2005) 'The Offshore Sector in the South Pacific: Development Potential and Multilateral Pressures'. Pacific Island Political Studies Association (PIPSA).

Sharman, J.C. and G. Rawlings (2005) *Deconstructing National Tax Blacklists: Removing Barriers to the Cross-Border Trade in Financial Services*. Report for the Society of Trust and Estate Practitioners, London.

Suss, Esther, Oral Williams and Chandrima Mendis (2002) Caribbean Offshore Financial Centres: Past, Present and Possibilities for the Future. IMF Working Paper WP/02/88. Washington, D.C.: IMF.

Takats, E. (2005): A Theory of 'Crying Wolf': The Economics of AML Enforcement. Job Market Paper, Princeton University, Department of Economics, Princeton, New Jersey, 5 November 2005.

US Government Accounting Office (2006) Company Formation: Minimal Company Ownership is Collected and Available. Washington, D.C.

US Treasury (2005) Money Laundering Threat Assessment. Washington, D.C.

Van Fossen, Anthony B. (2002) Offshore Financial Centres and Internal Development in the Pacific Islands. *Pacific Economic Bulletin*, Vol.17, No.1: pp.38–62.

Weenink, B.G. (2004) Cost-Benefit Analysis of the Offshore Financial Sector in Vanuatu. Country Report, December 2004. Port Vila, Vanuatu.

World Bank (2003) Financial Sector Assessments Handbook. Washington, D.C.: World Bank.

World Bank and IMF (2003) AML/CFT Regional Videoconference South Asia region – Maldives, Pakistan and Sri Lanka. WB-IMF Global Dialogue Series. Washington D.C.

World Bank (2006) *World Bank Development Indicators*. Washington, D.C.: World Bank.

Yeandle, M. et al (2005) Anti-Money Laundering Requirements: Costs, Benefits and Perceptions, prepared by Z/Yen Ltd. Sponsored by the Institute of Chartered Accountants in England & Wales and the Corporation of London.

Internet sources

http://www.cia.gov/factbook, estimate of July 2005 [accessed 17 February 2006]

Offshoreon.com offshore news online (2006) 'Vanuatu', available at:

http://www.offshoreon.com/othertext/Vanuatu/Vanuatu.asp?juris=Vanuatu [last accessed 10 December 2005]

http://www.oecd.org/dataoecd/61/28/2634587.pdf [last accessed 16 January 2008]

The Division of Industry and International Business: bilateral investment treaties and double taxation agreements, available at:

http://www.barbadosbusiness.gov.bb/miib/legislation/treaties/bilateral.cfm [last accessed 18 December 2007]

International Monetary Fund: http://www.imf.org [last accessed 16 January 2008]

Summary Qualitative Responses on Impact of AML/CFT

	Private Companies	Regulators
	%	%
Strengthened Financial System Regulation		
Agree + Strongly Agree:	63.6	50.0
Disagree + Strongly Disagree:	36.4	0.0
Neither Agree nor Disagree:	0.0	50.0
Enhanced Reputation of Barbados as an IFC		
Agree + Strongly Agree:	63.6	50.0
Disagree + Strongly Disagree:	36.4	0.0
Neither Agree nor Disagree:	0.0	50.0
Increased Competitiveness of Barbados as an IFC		
Agree + Strongly Agree:	30.0	50.0
Disagree + Strongly Disagree:	44.0	50.0
Neither Agree nor Disagree:	30.0	0.0
Imposed Reasonable Extra Costs on Regulators		
Agree + Strongly Agree:	27.3	0.0
Disagree + Strongly Disagree:	27.3	0.0
Neither Agree nor Disagree:	45.4	100.0
Imposed Reasonable Costs for Reputation of Firm		
Agree + Strongly Agree:	18.2	0.0
Disagree + Strongly Disagree:	27.3	0.0
Neither Agree nor Disagree or NA:	63.6	100.0
Imposed Excessive Extra Costs on Regulators		
Agree + Strongly Agree:	27.2	0.0
Disagree + Strongly Disagree:	36.4	50.0
Neither Agree nor Disagree or NA:	36.4	50.0

Summary Qualitative Responses on Impact of AML/CFT

	Private Companies	Regulators
	%	%
Imposed Disproportionate Cost on Firm/Bank		
Agree + Strongly Agree:	18.2	0.0
Disagree + Strongly Disagree:	45.4	50.0
Neither Agree nor Disagree:	36.4	50.0
Imposed Prohibitive Costs: Considering Exit		
Agree + Strongly Agree:	27.3	0.0
Disagree + Strongly Disagree:	63.6	50.0
Neither Agree nor Disagree or NA:	9.1	50.0
Made Excessive Demands on Firm's HR capabilities		
Agree + Strongly Agree:	45.4	0.0
Disagree + Strongly Disagree:	18.2	50.0
Neither Agree nor Disagree:	36.4	50.0
Required Significant increase in Compliance Staff		
Agree + Strongly Agree:	44.4	0.0
Disagree + Strongly Disagree:	11.2	0.0
Neither Agree nor Disagree or NA:	44.4	100.0
Required Significant Re-Training of front-line HR		
Agree + Strongly Agree:	55.6	50.0
Disagree + Strongly Disagree:	0.0	0.0
Neither Agree nor Disagree or NA:	44.4	50.0
Required Significant retraining of back-office HR		
Agree + Strongly Agree:	77.8	50.0
Disagree + Strongly Disagree:	22.2	0.0
Neither Agree nor Disagree or NA:	0.0	50.0

Summary Qualitative Responses on Impact of AML/CFT

	Private Companies	Regulators
	%	%
Required Significant IT and IT-training investment		
Agree + Strongly Agree:	66.7	100.0
Disagree + Strongly Disagree:	11.1	0.0
Neither Agree nor Disagree:	22.2	0.0
Spent More on systems etc. than necessary for bus. growth		
Agree + Strongly Agree:	77.8	50.0
Disagree + Strongly Disagree:	11.1	0.0
Neither Agree nor Disagree or NA:	11.1	50.0
Diverted Attention from other Business Priorities		
Agree + Strongly Agree:	81.8	0.0
Disagree + Strongly Disagree:	18.2	0.0
Neither Agree nor Disagree:	0.0	100.0
Imposed very high and unnecessary admin. overheads		
Agree + Strongly Agree:	33.3	0.0
Disagree + Strongly Disagree:	22.2	0.0
Neither Agree nor Disagree:	44.4	100.0

Index

Considering the Consequences